National Matters

National Matters

MATERIALITY, CULTURE, AND NATIONALISM

Edited by Geneviève Zubrzycki

STANFORD UNIVERSITY PRESS
STANFORD, CALIFORNIA

Stanford University Press
Stanford, California

Printed in the United States of America on acid-free, archival-quality paper

Library of Congress Cataloging-in-Publication Data

Names: Zubrzycki, Geneviève, editor.
Title: National matters : materiality, culture, and nationalism / edited by Geneviève
    Zubrzycki.
Other titles: National matters (Stanford, Calif.)
Description: Stanford, California : Stanford University Press, 2017. | Includes
    bibliographical references and index.
Identifiers: LCCN 2016045538 (print) | LCCN 2016046511 (ebook) | ISBN 9781503601697
    (cloth : alk. paper) | ISBN 9781503602533 (pbk. : alk. paper) | ISBN 9781503602762 (ebook)
Subjects: LCSH: Nationalism. | Material culture—Political aspects. | Politics and culture.
Classification: LCC JC311 .N2917 2017 (print) | LCC JC311 (ebook) | DDC 320.54—dc23
LC record available at https://lccn.loc.gov/2016045538

Contents

Figures

National Matters

Matter and Meaning: A Cultural Sociology of Nationalism

Geneviève Zubrzycki

The essays in this volume address the role of materiality in composing national identity through everyday practices. They also consider the role of materials in concretizing states' control over definitions of the nation, and their ability to foment nationalist sentiments and collective actions. The contributors consider both the impact of materiality from the bottom up and from the top down, and the intersections at the meeting ground of mundane and monumental modes of materiality, so to say. From art objects, clay fragments, broken stones, clothing, food, and urban space, the contributors to *National Matters* show the importance of matter in making the nation appear real, close, and important to subjects. By giving attention to the agency of things and the capacities they afford or foreclose, the authors also challenge methodological orthodoxies of cultural sociology. These theoretically grounded and empirically rich case studies highlight how the "material turn" in the social sciences pushes our understanding of state- and nation-making processes in several new directions.

THEORETICAL CUES AND GAPS

Matter and Experience

The first gap filled by this volume is related to the notoriously problematic concern with "experience." The phenomenology of national identity has been grossly overlooked in the literature on nations and nationalism, in part because of the intrinsic difficulty of studying the subjective domain of experience, especially in historical research. The key work remains Benedict Anderson's *Imagined Communities*. That text mapped out the impact of perception, experience, and affect in causing the abstract idea of the nation to appear proximate, directly relevant, and salient to individuals.[1] Anderson stated in the first pages of his canonical work that it is ultimately feelings of filial love—fraternity—"that makes possible . . . for so many millions of people, not so much to kill, as willingly die for such limited imaginings [the nation]" (1991, 7). He returned to the issue of attachment and "self-sacrificing love" by arguing that while the affective bond to the nation is primarily achieved through linguistic means, we must look beyond the meaning of words themselves and consider the *experience* of simultaneity created through practices such as poetry reading and collective singing. These are key, he proposed, because their unisonance allows the physical realization of the imagined community, which in turn facilitates the emotional attachment to it (141–45).[2]

In a different but related vein, Michael Billig (1995) demonstrated that myriad daily practices constitute what he termed "banal nationalism." Banal nationalism is constituted by "ideological habits that enable established nations . . . to be reproduced," providing the mental "wiring" that can be "switched on" to ignite intense nationalist reactions, or "hot nationalism."[3] Billig was concerned with discursive habits that are constituted by, and constitutive of, a universe in which the existence of the nation is taken for granted, and in which national identity becomes so ingrained that one would be willing to die for one's nation at the flipping of that switch. While Billig was examining what he calls "established nations"—nation-states whose existence is recognized and unthreatened—the notion of banal nationalism can be usefully extended to "un-," "less-," or "dis-established" nations. In Poland, for example, banal nationalism played an important role in rendering the nation a self-evident fact, a fact that nevertheless needed to be inscribed and defended during long periods of statelessness (1795–1918) or occupation (1939–89) (Zubrzycki 2011). Everyday practices involving mundane objects can, however, also be used as a strategy to *de-* and *re-*construct national identity on new bases, as I show in my contribution to this volume (Chapter 9). And while Billig showed the importance of banal nationalism as a preexisting condition for hot nationalism, Alexandra Kowalski (Chapter 6) explores the process through which mundane objects and practices are incorporated into the national framework in the first place, providing a crucial missing piece to the overall puzzle.

If the "cultural turn" pressed scholars to consider national identities as partially shared ways of speaking and reading, recent scholarship on visuality and materiality suggest the importance of images, sounds, textures, smells, and even tastes.

Matter and Intertextual Affect

Sometimes referred to as the "iconic" or "pictorial turn," the attention to the visual has slowly left the confines of art history, cultural studies, and communications to enter the social sciences. In sociology it has made its strongest mark in historical and cultural subfields through the work of Victoria Bonnell (1997) on the power of visual means of Soviet citizens' political indoctrination, and of Robin Wagner-Pacifici (2005) on iconographic depictions of rituals of military surrender in legitimating transfers of political authority. Vision, like the set of techniques, groups, and institutions associated with it—glossed here as visual culture—is an irreducibly sociological phenomenon. Vision is not simply constituted through the physiology of sight, but is rather a learned and cultivated cultural process, which gains meaning through a social relationship between viewer and fellow viewers as well as among viewer(s) and the object of sight. It is that dialogical relationship—sometimes as social compact, sometimes as exerted control or authority—created by looking that poststructuralist theorists like Jacques Lacan and Michel Foucault called *le regard*, the gaze; qualified in its oppressive mode of political control as *le regard panoptique* (Foucault 1991).

Whether as a politics of control or as technique for forming community, the visual delineates the borders of imagined or desired communities. It provides a shared repertoire of images and objects that shape memory and identity (Morgan 1999, 8). Because images and objects act as concrete substitutes for, and embodiments of, abstract ideas, they are powerful agents of socialization, marketing, and propaganda (Barthes 2009; Bonnell 1997; Cushing and Tomkins 2007; Hall, Stimson, and Becker 2006). Deciphering the various components of what French historian Maurice Agulhon (1981) has called "pictorial discourses" set forth by institutions and social actors allows us to analyze the stories people tell about themselves. But precisely because visual symbols, complex pictorial discourses, and material things can be used as means of socialization or tools of propaganda in the hands of elites—what Chandra Mukerji (2012) calls "political pedagogy"—they can also become the objects of struggle between groups promoting different ideologies, identities, or political agendas. Such "iconoclash" (Latour 2002) in turn sometimes leads to iconoclasm, the discrediting and displacing of rivals through the destruction of their symbols (Morgan 2005). Tracking the making and unmaking of visual and material cultures affords insight into conflicts about, and changes in, political visions of the nation (Zubrzycki 2011, 2013a).

Analyzing images in relation to their various uses and contests about their meanings and deployments is likewise productive because such images hold a special capacity to mediate imaginary, linguistic, intellectual, and material domains (Nora 1997; Mitchell 1986, 1998; Rogoff 1998; Freedberg 1991). As W.J.T. Mitchell (1998) pointed out, attention to the visual in fact pushes us to attend to all the senses, since objects are perceived through multiple senses. The sight of a painting of Monet's water lilies, for example, cues tactile, olfactory, and possibly aural sensations. Studying images, pictorial discourses, and visual culture more broadly is thus necessarily an "intertextual" enterprise in which "images, sounds, and spatial delineations are read onto and through one another" (Rogoff 1998, 24).

The study of visual culture and visuality is therefore closely related to that of materiality, another interdisciplinary field that has expanded rapidly over the last decade, above all in anthropology and science and technology studies (e.g., Appadurai 1986; Keane 2003, 2006; Woodward 2007; Miller 2005, 1–50; Tilley et al. 2006; Auslander 2009; Fehérváry 2009, 2013).[4] Materiality studies is concerned with understanding objects, the ways individuals and groups interact with them, and the ways individuals and groups are constituted in and through the things they use. Such an approach sees the material world not only as an embodiment of values and ideational systems (e.g., Durkheim 1995, 2010), or a physical snapshot of social relationships (as a Marxist materialist approach would), but as lending shape and meaning, affordances and constraints, to social relationships. From this perspective, things even exert a form of agency as extensions of personhood that impinge on, and call forth responses from, social actors (Gell 1998). Works in materiality studies seek to transcend the dualism between subjects and objects to show how social relations are built in and through the consumption of material culture (rather than merely in its production, *pace* Marx). While these concerns have been taken up primarily by scholars in neighboring social sciences like history and anthropology, within sociology proper works by Mukerji (1994, 1997, 2012), Latour (2007a), Alexander (2008a,b, 2012), McDonnell (2010, 2016), Zubrzycki (2011, 2013a, 2016b), and Domínguez Rubio (2014; Forthcoming) have all demonstrated the value of this approach.

Within this body of scholarship, Chandra Mukerji's interventions deserve special notice. Mukerji has developed a sophisticated model of political pedagogy that takes into account the role of material culture in creating and shaping a shared consciousness and collective identity. She employs the model to explain, for example, why the gardens of Versailles—precisely because they were not discursive but rather "materially exemplary"—did not generate opposition to the political project they embodied, but instead shaped subjects' political allegiances through their experience of that specific material and social environment (2012, 5). In this volume (Chapter 1), Mukerji extends this argument to show how the extensive, classically inspired art world created by the Louvre's artisans made new political imaginaries and the grand political aspirations of the nobility at Versailles possible. In turn, those imaginaries and aspirations presaged and hailed the building of a strong state that could fulfill them.

Individuals experience historical narratives and national myths through their visual depictions and material embodiments, as well as in the built environment like architecture, monuments, and the landscape. This renders otherwise distant and abstract discourses close and concrete to them. It is through that "national sensorium" (Zubrzycki 2011) that social actors viscerally experience national narratives and myths. This in turn generates sentiments of national belonging and resonant emotional attachments to what is otherwise merely a distant imagined community. The more developed the sensorium, the more powerful it becomes. The multiplicity of sites, media, and sensory experiences is compounded to facilitate the convergence between multiple sensory sites of the nation, and multiple modes of their sensory perception. We know that nations have their soundtracks, sights, and tastes (Cerulo 1995; Biddle and Knights 2007; DeSoucey 2010; Hirsh 2013; Ichijo and Ranta 2015), to name only those three sensorial sites, but these can reinforce each other through multiple and densely layered synesthetic exchanges.[5] This is important because of the ways in which the national sensorium can link emotions harvested from various contexts. The point is that people learn to associate specific places, occasions, images, texts, and music. Scholars of nationalism must pay attention to the multiplicity of sensory "sites" in order to understand how they may overlap to durably nationalize subjects.

Matter and Meaning

In his theory of "iconic consciousness," Jeffrey Alexander (2008b) analyzed the intersection between aesthetics and materiality, a process by which an aesthetically shaped materiality comes to signify a social value. He defines icons as symbolic condensations that anchor social meanings in a particular material form. Meaning is thus made visible and tangible; it can be seen, felt, touched—in other words "experienced." As the signifier is made into a material thing, the content becomes form.[6] Maurice Agulhon was concerned by a similar process, namely that through which imagery (the visual representation, or form, such as the French revolutionary figure of "Marianne") comes to stand for the image (the concept which the imagery evokes, or the ideological content, here the French Republic). Both these interventions echo in certain respects the anthropologist Victor Turner's attention to the capacity of a given symbol—such as the milk tree for the Ndembu—to yoke ideological and affective forces together so that the material icon holds a charged meaning for members of a society (Turner 1967, 54).

What is key for our purpose is that these icons are not empty things; rather, they are "meaning" embodied. While this is partly consistent with Wendy Griswold's definition of "cultural objects," which are "shared significance embodied in form i.e. . . . . an expression of meanings that is tangible or can be put into words" (1987, 4–5), here meaning is necessarily material, not merely discursive.[7] Meaning is transmitted through sensual contact with the material object—the icon—which gathers and then imparts its power (e.g., Bartmański and Alexander 2012).

Within this interdisciplinary material turn, one aspect that needs further exploration is how the aesthetic and material form of an icon can in turn alter its "inner" content, its meaning. On this issue the works of Tia DeNora (2000) and the anthropologist Webb Keane (2003, 2006) provide useful leads. Inspired by the work of psychologist J. J. Gibsons, DeNora expands the concept of "affordance" to the sociological study of culture. The idea is that material objects have certain properties that can accommodate some uses more easily than others; they "afford" actors the possibility of interacting in certain ways with the object. The weight, size, and form of an artifact, for example, "affords" actors the possibility of carrying it, rolling it, or breaking it (or not). In a related but different vein, Keane's theory of "bundling" proposes that an object's very materiality, that is, the specific aspects of its form—its weight, color, the materials of its composition, relative malleability, permeability, mobility, and so on—endow the object with a life of its own and allow it to potentially acquire different significations than the abstract ones social actors initially "filled" it with. Material things, he argues, "always combine an indefinite number of physical properties and qualities, whose particular juxtapositions may be mere happenstance. In any given practical or interpretative context, only some of those properties are relevant and come into play. But other properties persist, available for promotion as circumstances change" (2006, 200). Every new deployment of an object, image, or word places it at risk, so to speak, of spinning out of one orbit or meaning into another. As William H. Sewell put it, "A given symbol—mother, red, polyester, liberty, wage labor, or dirt—is likely to show up not only in many different locations in a particular institutional domain (motherhood in millions of families) but in a variety of different institutional domains as well (welfare mothers as a potent political symbol, the mother tongue in linguistic quarrels, the Mother of God in the Catholic Church" (1999, 49). Any given flesh-and-blood "mother" is always only precariously signified; and this is equally true of any word, image, person, or thing. Controlling and stabilizing a given meaning requires cultural work.

The emphasis in this line of argument is on the semiotic *potential* of an object, as its manifold material properties can become socially significant at different moments. Nevertheless an object's potential semiotic range is never unlimited. This key point of the constraints of materiality cuts against the grain of certain sociological *doxa*. For example, while Durkheim understood the totem, idol, or icon as sacred and powerful because of its capacity to embody and materialize collective representations, he neglected any investigation into the materials that give shape to these abstract collective ideals, dismissing them as "nothing but a block of stone or a piece of wood, things which in themselves have no value."[8]

Robin Wagner-Pacifici (2010), by contrast, insists that "it is only by gaining access to the operations and logics of the inner workings of cultural objects that any cultural sociology can begin to track the meanings and resonance of these objects in the social contexts in which they appear," arguing further that "such knowledge of aesthetic objects actually provides insight into the ways that these objects *model* social reality in their own turn" (109; emphasis mine). Wagner-Pacifici refers primarily to art objects, but we can extend the argument to symbols and icons deployed in social action. This might be named "aesthetic revolt," the dual process whereby social actors contest and rework iconic symbols in the public sphere; those symbols acquiring, through those material manipulations, significations that push forward the articulation of new identities and provide momentum for institutional reforms (Zubrzycki 2013a). Material symbols and icons participate in the creation of the social, acting as *catalysts* for what Piotr Sztompka (1993) called moments of "social becoming."

MOVING FORWARD

Still, it will not be sufficient to simply claim that the context, content, and form of material objects or symbols and the performances orchestrated around them "all matter." The challenge is to show the specific ways in which these aspects are interrelated and interdependent, and to identify the fine chains of signification through which meanings are constituted, modulated, and disseminated—a chain that, once set in motion, turns the wheels of change. This daunting project is precisely what the authors of *National Matters* undertake in their respective contributions, and with wonderful results. Their success required taking semiotic, historical, and social dimensions of the relation between subject and object into account. The authors in this volume see pictorial discourses as not merely descriptive or reflective of national visions deployed by elites and consumed by the masses, but as inscriptive, ultimately *productive* of those very visions. Taken as a group, their projects understand icons as endowed with lives of their own (Mitchell 2005), and a material logic that potentially enables them to shape identities and transform society independent of the meanings initially attributed to them by actors; indeed, independent even of the stated intentions (or lack thereof) of the actors using them (Keane 2003, 2006). When "properly" recognized according to particular national cues, these images and artifacts cue paradigmatic stories and sentiments, *or their subversion* in iconoclastic acts. In fact, we argue that it is the relatively shared set of stories, images, and material symbols, and the disagreement as much as the consensus evoked in response to them, that generate "a nation"—however thinly coherent its culture may be, to borrow Sewell's apt formulation (Sewell 1999).

Scholars of nationalism have felicitously moved away from the study of identity as a constructed yet static thing to the study of identifications, the processes through which identities are formed and transformed (e.g., Brubaker 1996; Glaeser 1999; Brubaker and Cooper 2000). A recent body of scholarship has shown how national identifications are at once constructed in everyday life through personal interactions and institutional practices (Brubaker et al. 2006; Fox and Miller-Idriss 2008), but also through specific transformative events (Zubrzycki 2006). While we know from classical sociological texts, the anthropological literature, and cultural history that social solidarity is created through the manipulation of symbols during certain rituals and performances, and that these manipulations can sometimes generate new identifications (e.g., Durkheim 1995; Turner 1967; Hunt 1986; Ozouf 1988; Sewell 1996), we know much less about the role material objects and symbols *themselves* play in that process. Based on archival and ethnographic research, the chapters in *National Matters* begin to fill this gap.

Organization of the Volume

The chapters in *National Matters* show that the creation of national identity is not only located in political statements, legal texts, and official documents, but also embedded in images and objects, legitimized by institutions, and enacted in practices. These broad overlapping themes structure the volume.

In Part One, authors discuss the relationship between materiality—art objects, archaeological fragments, natural resources—and nationalizing institutions. In her chapter on French artisans and the Louvre's workshops, Chandra Mukerji puts forward a provocative argument: France became a strong state by creating an extensive art world. She shows that for political change to be possible—for France's hitherto weak state to be strengthened—new political imaginaries needed to be developed. Those new imaginaries, this new sense of political possibility, were fostered by an extensive program of arts and crafts by state-administered workshops at the Louvre, where artisans created art objects inspired by classical mythology and Rome, which in turn motivated political aspirations at Versailles that could only be fulfilled by a strong state. Inarticulate art objects like clocks, vases, and statues were more effective than political discourse precisely because they were inarticulate; it was through feelings, sensations, and the general elation inspired by the art world that the court at Versailles developed a desire for a grand France and strong state. Mukerji thus points to the crucial importance of (organized, administered) material pedagogy and to the power of objects to create affective states that act as motivators for political action. Mukerji's contribution reveals in dazzling detail the intricate links between materiality, experience, affect, political mobilization, and institution building.

While Roman-inspired, imposing art objects can foster grand political aspirations, Fiona Greenland (Chapter 2) analyzes why and how pedestrian and valueless ceramic fragments became the cornerstone of the Italian state's vision of Italianness. She argues that the state discursively turned the dirt that cradled those fragments into *Italian* soil. In so doing, the fragments become endowed with a sacred quality that further legitimizes national narratives promoted by the state, as well as the cultural policies it puts forth. Greenland points to the important dialectic between discourse and materiality, and between non-objects and state institutions. Even artistically insignificant pieces of objects can become sacred building blocks of the nation once discursively converted and protected by state organs.

Melissa Aronczyk moves back one step further, analyzing matter at its elemental level—geographic and geological properties—but turns her attention to institutions' technological ability of extracting raw resources and transforming them into "national" commodities. The process of the transformation of oil sands into oil is at once material, technological, and discursive. Aronczyk shows the work that Canada's national narrative on "abundant national resources" and on the Canadian people's "innate industriousness" is doing to validate environmentally suspect practices carried out by mostly foreign corporations. Her chapter presents an example of how institutions like state agencies, national corporations, and foreign businesses transform nature into (national) culture, which then recursively acts back on "nature" to become a very different matter than it was at the outset of the process.

Following these chapters on the political significance of the institutions promoting art-object making, discursively transforming fragments of objects into national treasures, and technologically turning grimy sand into precious national oil, Peggy Levitt brings us back to priceless objects by directing her analytical gaze onto a core national institution, the museum. She investigates Boston's Museum of Fine Arts's representations of diversity through the arrangement of its collection, and shows that the museum's pedagogical narrative is material at its very core, from the building itself—which acts as a durable, protective container—to the collection of artifacts it displays, to the collection's specific arrangement in space. While material artifacts taken alone may speak to the relevance of a given social group, their placement in the spatial economy of the museum betrays the ideological biases of the institution. Some objects, for instance, are segregated in space, or relinquished to less visible or rarely visited corners of the museum.

Unlike institutions and practices—the long-standing key social scientific categories and most-trafficked channels of empirical investigations—objects have been neglected both as an analytical lens and as the empirical focus of scholarly investigations. Authors in Part Two, "Things That Matter," shift their attention to mundane things in order to rectify this lacuna. They analyze the varied processes through which everyday, banal objects such as clothing, household items, or even foods shape a national ethos on the one hand, or normalize radical nationalist ideologies, on the other.

Claudio E. Benzecry (Chapter 5) shows that it is partly because the soccer player's body is metonymic for the nation that his jersey becomes significant. His effort, pain, and success stand for that of the nation. The jersey allows spectators—conationals—to *feel* the effort and pain of the players by *seeing* it, allowing them to share in the success or defeat of the team. Because the jersey's fabric, cotton, affords the visible display of bodily fluids like sweat, tears, and blood, it gives embodied form to abstract notions of solidarity, honor, and the love of country. Changing the jersey's fabric so as to make sweat disappear therefore suggests the denationalization or at least the trivialization of devotion to the nation, as the connection between player-as-nation and spectator-as-nation is weakened when the sweat stains are no longer part of the game. One of Benzecry's key points is that the jersey's specific textile and the "circuits" built through and around it constitute the jersey as a site of social relations and political allegiances, as well as capital flows.

While Benzecry analyzes a specific object and the implication of its constitutive fibers, Alexandra Kowalski (Chapter 6) focuses on the impact of visual depictions of objects and sites on a popular weekly television show and a monthly magazine in France in the 1960s and 1970s. She investigates the process through which mundane objects become objects of banal nationalism by retracing the emergence of the idiom "national heritage" in public discourse. Kowalski shows that it was specific technological and material conditions that made that emergence possible, namely the conversion and transfer of remote and singular "historic monuments" (via their televised reproduction) into objects of experience in people's everyday life. While "heritage" has been studied by historians through the paradigm of "representation" as a nostalgic discourse and ideology, she shows that this nostalgic discourse was only made possible by the colonization of everyday life and individual experience through and thanks to the circulating tropes carried by images of objects and ancient sites, and that these circulating images were increasingly (re)produced by audiences themselves.

Virág Molnár (Chapter 7) explores the intersections between material culture and new forms of nationalism in contemporary Hungary by looking at the manufacturing, sale, and consumption of radical nationalist commodities. She argues that the increasing right-wing radicalization of Hungarian politics and the growth of "uncivil" publics have been fueled by an expanding industry that effectively commodifies and banalizes these radical sentiments. By showing how consumer objects such as T-shirts give expression to new forms of radical nationalism, Molnár highlights an important dimension of everyday, banal nationalism. This analytical lens also helps to demonstrate that contemporary right-wing radicalism (much like other subcultures, as Dick Hebdige's *Subculture* [1979] pointed out for punk) is not a codified political ideology but a more fluid subculture in which expressive symbols, material objects, rituals, everyday consumption, and lifestyle patterns are essential carriers of political convictions and markers of group boundaries. These symbolic economies contribute to reconfiguring the boundaries between politics and the public sphere, allowing radical nationalist discourse to penetrate mainstream political discourse.

Finally, chapters in the last part of the volume gather around the theme "Places, Practices, and Performances." Kristin Surak (Chapter 8) examines how cultural practices can become sites for sensing, enacting, and even embodying the nation through experiences that tread a border between the ordinary and the extra-ordinary. She studies the Japanese tea ceremony as a site that facilitates a concentrated experience of Japaneseness within Japan. Hers is a meticulous analysis of how the spaces, objects, and practices of the tea ceremony are similar to, yet fundamentally distinguished from, mundane counterparts in everyday life. This disjuncture, as the tea ceremony transforms the ordinary into the extra-ordinary, demands a disciplined attentiveness that hails and sustains what many practitioners call a "Japanese experience." Like Benzecry's soccer players, the participants in the tea ceremony are metonyms for the nation, while also performing the nation in their craft and in their measured gestures. Moreover, Surak shows that the objects used in the ceremony have meaning and value only in relation to each other, during a specific ceremony. It is the practice, or the use of the object within a defined set of actions, that confers upon the object its specific meaning and value. Surak's analysis thus underlines the subtle yet powerful dialectical relationship between materiality and practice, as well as between objects and subjects. It is through that dialectic that national meanings and feelings emerge and are solidified.

My own contribution (Chapter 9) analyzes current initiatives by Polish memory activists as well as by many ordinary Poles to remember, commemorate, and even to resurrect Jewish culture in Poland, a country with very few Jews. By inscribing the Polish landscape with material markers of what was and is no longer—remnants of a former Jewish street, Jewish funerary stones used on a retaining wall, the site of the former Great Synagogue in Warsaw—a sense of void is created and Jewish absence can be felt by contemporary Poles. That void can be filled by visiting institutions like museums, which recreate the vanished Jewish world of pre-Holocaust Poland through material and phenomenological modes of storytelling; or by performing Jewish dances, learning Yiddish or Hebrew, or cooking and consuming Jewish foods. All these practices, these acts of salvage remembrance and performance, ultimately constitute, I argue, attempts by Polish social actors to expand and reshape the symbolic boundaries of the nation beyond the narrow confines of Polishness and Catholicism. Here material void and traces, as well as embodied practices and performances, converge to create a Jewish sensorium that challenges the dominant (and extensive) Polish-Catholic one and offers the potential to expand notions of national identity.

In the volume's final empirical case, Dominik Bartmański (Chapter 10) turns his attention to Berlin's Tempelhof Airport, which has been described as "an icon of an airport." Due to its material features, its eventful postwar history, and its recent closing and repurposing into a public park in 2008, Tempelhof's trajectory provides an analytical window into key changes in Berlin's urban culture and German identity more broadly. Bartmański shows that the social meanings of Tempelhof as a place emerged in the confluence of its material properties and affordances, its location within Berlin's urban context and current national narratives, and post-2008 cosmopolitan civil discourses. By disentangling this confluence, Bartmański not only sheds light on his empirical object of study; he also demonstrates the contributions of iconicity as a viable cultural approach to solving a social problem.

Contributions to Nationalism Studies

One key takeaway from the empirical cases presented in *National Matters* is that objects, institutions, and practices are not isolated pieces used in the construction of the nation and national identity. Rather they are tightly imbricated in the making and sustaining of the nation and national identifications and affiliations. The making of art objects at the Louvre's workshops in the seventeenth century was possible due to institutional support given to the Louvre's artisans, and thanks to their dissemination at grandiose events and performances at Versailles. Objects in a contemporary museum can socialize citizens into a given narrative because of the institution that arranges them in space. Fragments of objects, or raw natural resources, become meaningful via their discursive and technological transformation into "ancestral" objects or "national" resources. Because of that work, even non-objects can become emblematic of "the people," or heritage artifacts "of the nation."

While materials are densely woven with discourses and institutions, as well as practices and performances, they can also generate meaning independently of them. Objects can indeed tell different stories than the ones intended by the institutions controlling them: Peggy Levitt shows the unintended meanings and subtle hierarchies artifacts project toward their viewers or users depending on their arrangement in space, regardless of curators' intentions. Here one type of materiality (space, architecture) impacts another (objects) to suggest new meanings to visitors. Objects found in museums, displayed in sports arenas, or available for purchase in shopping malls take on different significations by virtue of the material environment in which they are marketed, exhibited, circulated, or discarded. The important point emerging from many chapters in this volume is that objects are hardly impotent. Able to convey meanings different than the ones initially intended by social actors and institutions, they retain their own autonomous capacities. In fact, their apparent muteness itself sometimes renders them able to speak with force, so to say. Objects can be powerful precisely because they are silent. As Chandra Mukerji argues in her chapter, it is the inarticulacy of art objects that not only made possible the imagination of a new form of political power, but also prevented opposition to that new idea. Virág Molnár demonstrates an analogous phenomenon in her analysis of nationalist commodities that are banalized to the extent that they become invisible; "mute," yet speaking volumes. The T-shirt and the touristic guidebook can be as impactful, if not more, than the political poster.

Another contribution of the volume can be found in its demonstration that the mundane, profane, and banal is no less significant than the extraordinary, sacred, and exceptional, and in its clear elucidation of *how* ordinary and prosaic things "act." Kowalski astutely demonstrates how banal material objects, regional foods, or architectural features and techniques become, through discursive practices and mediatic dissemination, sacred icons of the nation. Molnár shows how the commodification of radical nationalism tames that ideology, hybridizes it, and thus, perhaps counterintuitively, makes that ideology even more forceful because it now is diffuse and difficult to counter. It enters the mainstream in media purified of the taint of ideology, as simply part of the lived reality of a given society. The marketing and consumption of commodities from nationalist clothing and soccer jerseys to kosher vodka and klezmer music stimulate new national sensoria and catalyze expanded registers of tastes, desires, and sensitivities. Soccer jerseys become not only markers of a team and of the nation, but timekeepers of individuals' lifespans within the *longue durée* of national life. Objects can be both markers of time and of generations, as Benzecry shows. They may link expansive national genealogies, per Surak's close ethnographic analysis of the Japanese tea ceremony. The body, in fact, becomes an extension of the object, and via that material extension the individual—the Hungarian folk-rock fan, the Argentine soccer aficionado, the Japanese tea ceremony leader, or the Italian child visiting an archaeological museum—enters a lineage of other, unknown nationals to whom she becomes related: a *tradition.* Together the essays show how it is that through material objects and practices national genealogies are created and inhabited.

One final note: along with empirical rigor, the essays gathered here exemplify theoretical modesty. The reader will find here no claims to a silver bullet, no grandiose "New Theory of..." To the contrary, these essays assay to approach materiality in its complex engagement with other modes of meaning-making. We show that the attention to materials *together with discourses and practices about such materials* provides a more complete cultural sociology of identity formation and transformation, and a more accurate interpretation of specific political configurations, than interpretations attentive only to discourse, social movements, or to the media already marked *as* "political." That caution helped generate unusually subtle analyses of diverse national phenomena, analyses that contribute to our understanding of how national identity and nationalism emerge, are revised, or come undone. As a result this volume demonstrates the value, even the necessity, of expanding the methods and analytical approaches in sociology, especially those that give material culture and materiality their due in understanding, explaining, and teaching nationalism.

NOTES

1. George Mosse's work (1975) was also significant in showing the links between bodily practices, visions of the nation, and construction of the state,

but has had a more limited impact on the field than Anderson's *Imagined Communities*. On the literature on emotions and affect in nationalism studies, see Berezin (1994) and Suny (2006, 2009).

2. Here Anderson builds on and expands from Émile Durkheim's (1912) notion of "collective effervescence" through which individuals come to physically experience "society," reifying the abstract idea in the process.

3. Recent studies have pushed forward the idea of everyday nationalism by shifting the focus to practices of "ordinary people," which are not necessarily ideological but can nonetheless be significant (Edensor 2002; Brubaker et al 2006; Fox and Miller-Idriss 2008).

4. For a useful introduction to the key terms, theoretical approaches, and debates in studies of materiality and material culture, see Miller (2005, 1–50) and Woodward (2007). For key statements by specialists in the field on a variety of topical areas, see Tilley et al. (2006). On visuality, material culture, and religion more specifically, see McDannell (1995), Morgan (2005), and Promey (2014).

5. Synesthesia is the "transposition of sensory images or sensory attributes from one modality to another" (Marks 1978, 8) which "express . . . a relationship between features of experience that properly belong to different senses" (1). All sensory cues do not work the same way, however. In the hierarchy of senses, certain faculties of feeling the nation exert greater "ideological" force than others—in the sense of those perceptions becoming objects of conscious contemplation and the focus of debates as to their meaning. Heidegger, for example, noted how one is barely conscious of the street that "slides itself . . . along the soles of one's feet" (1962, 142). Even though the street against one's feet is much nearer empirically, and exerts more direct physical force than what the pedestrian *looks at* twenty paces hence, it is often the seen object that is affixed in thought. While some sensations may remain below everyday awareness, they may still serve as an important part of the national sensorium in the sense of generating habitual repertoires of action, and helping to create that which "goes without saying." These layered senses render the nation present, and endow it with emotional force.

6. Mabel Berezin, in her study of fascist theater in Italy (1994), has persuasively demonstrated that meaning could also be found in the mere artistic form, regardless of its actual narrative content.

7. Materiality studies scholars would reject that distinction, as a text is printed onto a page, bound into a book that one carries, opens, shelves or rips or burns; even oral tradition is embodied and material, as it is spoken, sung, or performed by bodies in specific material contexts.

8. Durkheim writes that "collective ideals can only be manifested and *become aware of themselves* by being concretely realized in material objects that can be seen by all, understood by all, and represented to all minds." Society therefore projects ideals of its own creation onto an object—a totem, an idol, an icon—thereby becoming conscious of those very ideals made materially explicit (2010, 49–50; my emphasis).

PART I

Materiality and Institutions

CHAPTER 1

Artisans and the Construction of the French State

The Political Role of the Louvre's Workshops

Chandra Mukerji

Accounts of state formation in the social sciences tend to focus on institutional transformations, such as military and legal reform, or the capture of the elites, treating what are functional outcomes of state formation as causes. They do not seek explanations of how institutional restructuring became possible when it had not been possible before. They assume that early states could only become institutionally effective by capturing or organizing known forms of power (Adams 2005; Beik 1997; Brewer 1989; Kettering 1986; Mettam 1988; Wallerstein 1974). Yet this is precisely what weak states could not do. Their empowerment depended instead on a shift in political logics that made entrenched political formations less compelling. It required a cultural change.

In the seventeenth century, the French state went from being particularly weak (Machiavelli and Donno 1966) to particularly strong—an absolutist state according to Perry Anderson (1974). The administration achieved this shift not by wresting control of the army from nobles or impoverishing those at court, but rather by constructing an art world (Becker 1982). Long after Louis XIV ascended the throne, nobles still supplied troops to the army even as the state trained them (Lynn 1997), and nobles in favor with the king at Versailles gained special economic opportunities (Cole 1964). It took an organized program of cultural production—an art world nestled in the administration—to advance state power. Political change required a change in political imaginaries, and the state's art world did the imagining.

The artists, artisans, and scholars who contributed to this program used classically inspired art and artifacts to craft images of imperial power for France. The sense of political possibility embedded in the art inspired political aspirations in elites that could only be fulfilled by a strong state—like that of Rome. Ambition lured high nobles into new relations of power.

The inarticulate objects of desire created in the art world were more effective than political discourse. Jean-Baptiste Colbert, Louis XIV's minister of the treasury and navy as well as director of the king's household, first tried to promote his patron's imperial ambitions through propaganda, but it failed. People laughed at the idea that a weak king could follow in the footsteps of Augustus and build an empire in the model of Rome (Burke 1992). But the program of classical revival in the arts made no claims; it simply made it plausible that France could revive Rome's heritage, including its political heritage.

The cultivation of political desire through the arts was part of a broader program of logistical governance instigated by Colbert (Mukerji 2009, 2010), and one with a particular goal. The classical revival at Versailles was addressed to France's high nobility, the great military elites necessary to the king's dreams for empire. The royal residence where these nobles were invited to live was turned into an immersive environment where classical revival echoed in the art, architecture, furniture, gardens, statuary, and multiday royal festivities known as *divertissements*. Nobles dressed up in costumes and enacted roles as classical gods and heroes, moving through elaborate sets representing Mount Olympus or other classical sites. The semiotic reverberations across statues, stage sets, murals, painted ceilings, costumes, furniture, and clocks built up the sense that France could achieve something more.

Norbert Elias (1983) has already drawn attention to culture—including material culture—as an important element in French state formation. But he ended up focusing on the expense of life at court, arguing that the nobility was impoverished by their cultural obligations at Versailles and so became dependent on the king. Elias underestimated the cultural power of

Roman revival at Versailles. He did not seem to recognize how art could shape thought, or how desire could have social effects—as sociologists do today (Benzecry 2011; Hennion 1993; Hennion, Maisonneuve, and Gomart 2000). He sensed that material life at court mattered, but missed that the pursuit of pleasure could be turned into a serious game (Ortner 2006).

Historians and cultural analysts of Louis XIV's court have been clear about the power of court festivities and the classicism of Versailles (Apostolidès 1981; Marin 1981; Néraudau 1986), but have argued that structures of meaning in the arts and rituals at court, not the inarticulacy of artworks, were the source of its political effects. But the nobles at Versailles were not well educated and were unlikely to recognize the "meaning" of particular classical myths, gods, heroes, or events in classical history. Walking among statues of Bacchus, Hercules, Diana, and Aurora, or acting out classical roles in plays and ballets, they surely *felt* more than understood the glory of the Roman Empire. Figures like Hercules and Diana conveyed warrior virtues even to those who could not name them: Hercules with his large frame, tight muscles, animal skin, and club, and Diana with her bow and arrow, helmet, and physical aggressiveness. The gods and heroes depicted at Versailles looked capable of building and destroying empires, and they were beautiful— something to desire. Nobles did not need a good education to be seduced by the passion in the art. And the inarticulacy of the cultural forms made them seem innocent. Nobles could become attached to dreams of Roman revival (Benzecry 2011; Hennion 1993) without being sure what it meant or what it implied politically.

The political seduction of nobles through classical culture at Versailles was delegated to the members of the academies given space in the Louvre, and to the artists and artisans housed in workshops and lodgings there (Ronfort and Museum 2009). They constituted an unusual set of administrative figures. Officials of the state were traditionally nobles who exercised personal powers through offices without clear jurisdiction. The members of the administration's art world—both scholars and artists— were overwhelmingly not noble and had only contingent authority, acting like modern bureaucrats in Max Weber's (Weber, Roth, and Wittich 1978) terms. They were servants of standing without independent voices, but still exercised enormous impersonal powers even over court nobles. They demonstrated what a state could do in imitation of Rome, and what an imperial France might be if the state could pursue that goal.

FIGURED WORLDS OF POWER

To make sense of how artists and artisans wielded their power, we need some understanding of material pedagogy. Figured world theory (hereafter FWT) provides a basis for it because it discusses cultural artifacts as cognitive tools (Holland et al. 1998; Mukerji 2010, 2012). FWT is an activity theory of learning from the psychology of education that explains how children learn to become members of their culture by building up repertoires of action around cultural imaginaries: enacting roles, organizing and inhabiting sets, using props, and putting on costumes that scaffold cultural imaginaries about who they could be and what they might do in the world. FWT argues that participants adopt roles they see in their social and cultural environment, and through their actions try to manifest the realities they assume to exist. In this way, they learn how to produce the figured worlds of their culture, both the activities and the imaginaries that make sense of and guide social action. The majority of the learning is performative, participatory, but it is scaffolded with material culture that makes it easier to enact some roles rather than others and conjure up some realities rather than others. The cultural program at Versailles was a means of constructing a new figured world, changing political imagination and action by material means. The artisans and scholars working for Colbert collaborated on the design of sets, costumes, and props that supported performances of Roman revival. The art world erected pedagogical scaffolding for a new political logic that foregrounded not patrimonial autonomy (Adams 2007; Mukerji 2012), but rather imperial power.

The figured world of France-as-Rome provided the French court with novel expectations about governance as a practice, suggesting new performances they could try. As Howard Becker (1963; Becker, Faulkner, and Kirshenblatt-Gimblett 2006) writes about art worlds and jazz communities, social worlds are brought into being and sustained through coordinated forms of improvised social action that are not scripted, but guided by expectations. Cultural imaginaries or figured worlds, I would argue, give form to expectations, providing guidelines for imagining what is expected and building social worlds to meet expectations.

Cultural imaginaries are experiential expressions of what people can do, how social life works, and how social action unfolds. They are forms of inarticulate knowledge, intuitive understandings of what exists. Social worlds embody those expectations in improvised actions and pursue those dreams. At Versailles, dreams of Rome provided the framework for making the French court seem an imperial center, turning play into novel performances of power (Ortner 2006) that encouraged courtiers to see their official powers as less wonderful than imperial glory.

Figured world theory is interesting not only because it describes inarticulate patterns of pedagogy, but also because it has a complex relationship to G. H. Mead's (1964) behaviorism in describing social constructions of reality. FWT attributes mental capacities to people (imagination), but supports Mead's anti-idealism by denying that *ideas* (articulate discourses) guide social life. It suggests that "behavior" rests on and builds on cultural forms of coordinated imagination: dreams, aspirations, and anticipations that are both vague and unspoken. In Mead's famous example of a baseball game (Mead and Morris 1962), the game is not a set of rules but a cultural imaginary about playing based on experience with games that people try to make real. To play, participants improvise and coordinate action as Mead describes, but they perform according to a sense of the game as they imagine it to be—building their imaginaries from multiple experiences or iterations of practice.

Figured world theorists generally focus on practices of cultural reproduction rather than change. Nonetheless, FWT is useful for analyzing the transformation of French political life at Versailles through art. It explains how inarticulate things could make new desires imaginable, and worth treating as real (Néraudau 1986).

As Elias (1983) has argued, the high nobles who came to Versailles had no reason to give up powers to the king. But the king needed to reduce the autonomy of nobles to have a stronger state (Beik 1944; Elias 1983; Kettering 1986). So the art world in the Louvre invented the Sun King, blurring the boundary between personal and impersonal rule, patrimonial authority and state power. Louis XIV as Sun King was simultaneously a king with the right to exercise personal will and a force of nature whose authority was impersonal and whose dominance over the earth was inevitable. The Sun King was not just any king, but one who ruled the earth because it was in his nature to do so, bringing fecundity and glory to his domain (Quintinie 1692). There were no limits to his power, and his destiny was assured. Louis XIV did not say, "*l'état, c'est moi*," but if he had, he would have been claiming not simply personal authority as king, but also impersonal powers as the natural inheritance of a Sun

King. This cultural figure, not Louis XIV, could assume new social powers without appearing to threaten patrimonial traditions. He was a figure from the classical past brought to life to lead the new empire.

THE WORKSHOP LOUVRE
AND CLASSICAL REVIVAL

The Louvre became the administrative center for the cultural program, and an art world filled with practitioners, critics, historians, and support personnel (Becker 1982). Louis XIV at first functionally and then formally moved his court to Versailles, and the noble officials that had traditionally inhabited the Louvre followed the king, leaving large parts of the old castle empty. Colbert tried repeatedly to remodel and expand the Louvre, enjoining the king to reestablish his court there, but to no avail. Finally, uncomfortable about leaving large parts of the palace vacant, Colbert allocated space to academicians, artists, and artisans. He gave meeting spaces to the academies, and workshops and lodgings to artists and artisans. In this way he made the Louvre (and nearby buildings in Paris) into an administrative center and art world (Goubert 1974; Le Roy Ladurie 1996; Soll 2009; Sonnino 1990; Becker 1963).

The artists and artisans of the Louvre inhabited a wing along the Seine—an area that had been redesigned by Louis Le Vau with large galleries for connecting the Louvre to the Tuileries Palace (Bordier 1998) and workshops and lodgings below. The Académie Française, the Académie de peinture et sculpture, and the *petite académie*, also known as the Académie des inscriptions et belle-lettres, were assigned space in older sections of the Louvre. Thus installed physically, both artisans and academicians contributed to the figured world of France as heir to Rome.

The academies were charged with deciding how the classical past would be used as a basis for French culture. Their members articulated connections between past and present, debating standards, codifying principles, and outlining the most appropriate ways to present Louis XIV as the Sun King and France as heir to Rome. The scholars understood that the classical heritage was a material legacy embodied in ruins, artworks, coins, and infrastructure, and they collected and curated ancient things, thereby designing a material legacy for Louis XIV that would link his reign to Rome and working with artists and artisans to make these objects into objects of desire.

The Académie Française worked not just on purifying the French language but on creating a dictionary, rooting the French language in Latin and embedding its authority in printed artifacts. The Académie de peinture et sculpture not only debated and taught aesthetic principles, but also curated juried exhibitions and awarded the prix de Rome to young artists to study at the French Academy in Rome, where they were expected to copy classical pieces. The antiquarians of Colbert's *petite académie* collected small artifacts like coins and small sculptures from the ancient world, using their inscriptions and imagery as models for glorifying Louis XIV in contemporary artifacts. In these ways, the academies in the Louvre took material objects seriously as key to ancient history and French destiny.

The artists and artisans, as members of the administration and bound to the state, were not members of Parisian guilds and bound by their constraints. In this sense, they undermined the guilds as autonomous institutions even as they used skills from artisanal traditions. Still, they took appointments in the administration or in the academies because those were badges of honor and respect. They became the equivalent of Weber's faceless bureaucrats (1968) in the sense that their work was treated as an effect of the Sun King, not their personal talents. But they ended up achieving what the king could not: engineer a historical transformation with an immersive environment of imperial desire.

The Royal Print Shop and Mint

The Louvre workshops where this dream world was brought to life included not just studios but also the royal printing house (Imprimerie royale) and the mint (Monnaies royales). The printing house and mint stayed at the Louvre because they required only relatively small spaces for producing artifacts like books, prints, coins, and medals. The large pieces like tapestries for the royal household were mainly made elsewhere in larger royal manufactures like the Gobelins. In addition, the printing house and mint were particularly important to the cultural program of the Louvre because they produced small artifacts that circulated broadly, and could disseminate public images of Louis XIV, his court, and classical revival. The Imprimerie royale had its own typefaces, including Greek and Roman type to further and foreground classical scholarship in France. The mint was originally intended to make new forms of currency, but centralizing money became politically difficult. Instead, the mint struck a series of medals celebrating great events in the reign of Louis XIV—following the Greek and Roman use of coins and medals for disseminating stories of glory (Bernard 1966; DeHaye 1970).

There were also artisans at the Louvre who designed prints and medals, including the famous engraver Israel Silvestre. He served as a visual documentarian of court life, engraving prints of important events, depicting royal houses and gardens, foregrounding the classical legacy in the art, and characterizing life at court by depicting its stages and performances. He provided a means of virtual-witnessing the dream world at Versailles, including the plays and ballets of the *divertissements* that brought the past to life (Delestre and Bouillon 1894).

The coin designers working with the mint at the Louvre included the director, V. Delaunay, a silver- and goldsmith who not only designed coins and medals, but in addition made objects such as glittering gold plates and silverware for the royal household out of precious metals. Jean Mauger was the engraver who designed the bulk of the historical coins, celebrating Louis XIV's reign. He created 250 of them, illustrating great victories, the opening of academies, the birth of a son, and the establishment of the observatory, among other things (DeHaye 1970). Medals and coins were the kinds of small artifacts used in the ancient world and collected by the *petite académie*, and were part of the classical revival improvised in the art world of the Louvre.

The Family Workshops

Most workshops at the Louvre were not royal manufactures, but were workspaces and lodgings for families and apprentices of important artists and artisans. The beneficiaries of the king's patronage included painters and sculptors, decorative artists, instrument makers, and those who produced court entertainments. Each contributed in a distinct way to the cultural imaginary of France-as-Rome, and Louis XIV as Sun King.

The painters and sculptors created the most obvious links both thematically and aesthetically between French art and classical culture. They were trained in classical methods, aesthetics, and mythology and defined what a Sun King was and could do by the way they depicted Apollo. Most of the painters and sculptors had spent significant time in Rome and learned the classical tradition by imitating works of ancient artists. They used this training to depict classical gods and heroes with appropriate attributes and poses, and to evoke events from ancient mythology or history for the requirements of the king's households.

One was Antoine Coypel, who specialized in painting historical scenes. He had a classical education and studied painting in Rome, and used classical aesthetics to paint scenes from the Bible, including the ceiling of the nave of the final chapel built for Louis XIV at Versailles. He eventually became Premier peintre du roi, and was ennobled finally for his service to the king. Guillaume Coustou the elder, a sculptor, won the prix de Rome, but refused to stay at the French Academy in Rome because of the rigid training there. Still, he returned to the king's service. He became a member of the Académie de peinture et sculpture and, in the eighteenth century, its director (Blunt 1980).

François Girardon, sculptor, was also among the French artists sent to Rome to study art, and one who later found favor with the head of the academy, Charles Le Brun. He made many statues for royal gardens, including the sculpture for the Bains d'Apollon that helped depict and define the Sun King. For his efforts, he was appointed Inspecteur générale des ouvrages de sculpture (Blunt 1980; Goldstein 2008; Mukerji 2012).

Decorative artists. The decorative artists living at the Louvre made the king's residences fit for a Sun King. They not only did the fine cabinetry for the interiors, but also produced furniture and other items of interior decoration. They made the royal residences glitter with polished brass and gilt on lead. They also provided the cabinetry for the walls of mirrors and windows that brought the sun into the world of the Sun King.

André Boulle, the best-known furniture and cabinetmaker of the period, known for his fine marquetry work, was delegated the most space of those at the Louvre—including some nearby workshops. He was called an *ébéniste* because he used rare woods as well as brass, pewter, and tortoise shell to make elaborately inlaid furniture for the Sun King (Ramond 2011; Ronfort and Museum 2009).

Jacques Bailly was another designer at the Louvre who was appointed keeper of the king's paintings. He worked on tapestry designs that celebrated the Sun King and also on illuminated books, including an elegant edition of Perrault's book on the labyrinth at Versailles. (Hyde, in Hunt, Conan, and Goldstein 2002, 18; Perrault and Bailly 1629). Finally, Jean-Baptiste Belin de Fontenay was a painter who specialized in flowers for interior design, including flowers for the queen's staircase.

Instrument makers. The instrument makers housed at the Louvre were "moderns" rather than antiquarians, but still helped promote the image of France as heir to imperial Rome by making tools of empire: instruments useful to territorial expansion and control. They were clock makers, gun makers, lens grinders, and others who served the navy and scientists in the royal academy as well as the king's household.

Clock makers were the most numerous and important instrument makers because pendulum clocks had been recently developed in France and were being designed to determine longitude at sea. Isaac II and Jacques III Thuret were pendulum clock makers, father and son, who were brought to France to work with Christian Huygens. Huygens developed a balance mechanism that he hoped would allow clocks to keep accurate time even in rocking ships at sea. The Thurets also created a large number of elaborate and sophisticated decorative clocks, working with cabinetmakers such as Boulle (Ramond 2011).

Balthazar Martinot—also at the Louvre—was probably the most respected clock maker of his period in France, and Premier valet de chambre for Louis XIV. In addition to clocks, he made precision instruments and scientific models that depended on elaborate and accurate clockworks (Da Vinha 2004; Plomb 1999; Ramond 2011; Lachièze-Rey and Luminet 2001, 111).

In addition to the clock makers, there was a gun maker, Bertrand Priaube, and a lens maker, Philippe Claude Lebas, who presumably could supply the military with guns and spyglasses, or build instruments of other sorts.

Producers of court entertainments. The artisans in charge of court entertainments were members of the Menus plaisirs du roi (the king's small pleasures) and the office of the king's household directed by the designer Jean Bérain. Members of this office were in charge of both the great *divertissements* in the royal gardens and daily diversions at Versailles. They built the sets for court performances, created the technology for special effects, designed the costumes for courtiers playing gods and heroes from the ancient world, and designed the props for these performances (La Gorce, Jugie, and Archives nationales 2010). They were the ones who dressed up nobles to act out stories of Rome and experience new kinds of power.

Vigaranis, father and son, created sets and special effects for Menus plaisirs and had both a workshop and lodgings in the Louvre (La Gorce, Jugie, and Archives nationales 2010). They were instrumental in drawing nobles into performances of imperial power, positioning them as gods and heroes in performances of glory. They were also being employed at this time in designing a theater for the Tuileries Palace that was attached to the galleries of artisans.

AN EMPIRE OF THINGS

To understand better the political work done by the art itself, I will focus on a few objects, illustrating the kinds of collaborations involved in producing the cultural imaginaries of the state: Girardon's statue of Apollo, a pedestal clock by Thuret, Boulle, and Bérain, and a costume by Jean Bérain. These pulled together in different ways fragments of the classical repertoire in art to improvise a vision of the Sun King's reign and the imperial glory it could replicate. The cases help to make the point that the inarticulate world of classical revival was the product of an art world that conjured up figured worlds in a social world.

Girardon's famous sculpture of Apollo in the Bains d'Apollon was the central figure in the grotto on the terrace at Versailles, and one of the most important pieces for defining the Sun King (Figure 1.1). According to classical mythology, Apollo carried the sun through the sky on his chariot during the day, bringing light and warmth to the earth and making it fertile and abundant. At night, he returned to his underworld home to bathe and rest. The sculpted Apollo was a god at rest, and equated with the monarch who rested nearby. The grotto itself echoed architectural forms of the château, and on front of the grotto above the doors there was a golden portrait of Louis XIV with radiating lines around the face like the sun. Nothing needed to be said to make the equation; no one had to argue that the two were the same; they were just associated within a cultural imaginary. This was what a Sun King might be.

The image of Apollo in the grotto was a product of the Louvre. Girardon collaborated on the design with the head the Académie du peinture

Figure 1.1. Girardon's sculpture of Apollo from the grotto, the Bains d'Apollon, representing the Sun King at rest. By Trizek. *Source*: Château de Versailles in partnership with Wikimedia France and Attribution-Share Alike 3.0

et sculpture, Charles Le Brun. Girardon's Apollo matched Le Brun's Apollos on ceilings and tapestries both at Versailles and at the Louvre. The reverberations among pieces helped to build the immersive environment in which this cultural imaginary became common sense.

This art world also produced a pedestal clock, now in the Metropolitan Museum of Art in New York, that celebrated the Sun King (Figure 1.2). The clock was made by a member of the Thuret family and the case was by Boulle, the marquetry furniture maker, based on a design by Bérain, the head of the Menus plaisirs du roi. Clocks with interesting mechanisms were entertaining as well as useful, and were often provided to the royal family by the Menus plaisirs with the help of artisans at the Louvre. This particular pedestal clock, by combining sophisticated clockwork with evocations of the ancient world, did even more. It advanced dreams by "moderns" about building on traditions of the ancients to create novelties of great value.

It is possible that the works of the pedestal clock were made by Jacques Thuret or his father, Isaac. Apparently both had worked on

Figure 1.2. Clock with pedestal attributed to André Boulle after a design by Jean Bérain with movement by Jacques III Thuret or Isaac II Thuret. *Source*: Metropolitan Museum of Art, Rogers Fund, 1958; www.metmuseum.org

the kind of balance mechanism with Huygens (Plomb 1999). Boulle's pedestal for the clock was classical in form and imagery; used a range of materials for the marquetry; and was centered aesthetically with a large brass face resembling the Sun King. This shining visage had above it radiating lines of pewter turning into forms like plants. It suggested Apollo's power to bring life to the earth with the heat of the sun. The marquetry, on the other hand, in suggestively integrating materials from around the world to create a beautiful whole, provided a vision of empire.

In the plays, ballets, and rituals at Versailles, nobles were immersed in a world designed by artisans. They were dressed up in costumes from the Menus plaisirs to become gods and heroes from the ancient world (Figure 1.3). And they were carried through fantasy worlds of classical revival using stage engineering by Vigaranis and Bérain. With artful special effects, members of the Menus plaisirs took nobles flying through the sky or sailing across the seas in stories of imperial power. The Vigaranis used pulleys and levers, ropes, pipes, fans, and wheels to create extraordinary worlds and special effects, fitting nobles into their scaffolding to revive the glory of the ancient world. The special effects helped to give the nobles who played gods and heroes special powers, and the sets provided the environments in which they exercised them. Nobles were literally put on scaffolding and were subordinated to narratives to make the performances work, experiencing the power of impersonal rule and the excitement of ruling the earth. They were learning new political logics by enacting them, and making them seem real on stage. Nobles taught themselves to want to belong in the world they were bringing to life.

CONCLUSION

When sociologists think of the growth of modern states, they normally do not think about art worlds or the role of artists and artisans in early administrations (Tilly 1975). They still believe in bureaucracy as the only important form of impersonal rule. Yet objects can also be wielded as impersonal tools of political pedagogy and objects of desire (Geertz 1985). When theorists think about the subordination of nobles to the state, they imagine nobles personally subordinating themselves to the king as a personal ruler, but Beik (1985) showed that to be false. Nobles subordinated themselves instead to a cultural imaginary conjured up by an art world built by the administration. The artists and artisans must have enjoyed the joke as they lured high nobles, their social betters, with seductive dreams of France as a new Rome. They were only servants of the state, working for the administration. But what they produced was a massive shift in relations of power. Their Sun King prevailed.

Figure 1.3. Costume by Jean Bérain representing mystery, with what appears to be a portrait of Apollo on the chest. *Source*: Wikimedia France from Gallica. bnf.fr/Bibliothèque nationale de France

Once France became a modern state, it was possible to reform the military and rationalize offices, but making the state powerful required something irrational and material, desirable but impersonal: a cultural imaginary and an administration to build it. Legal reform, subordination of the Church to the state, and the growth of state territoriality all were part of the transfer of power to the state (Carroll-Burke 2002), but they were legitimated with the cultural imaginary of France-as-Rome and the authority of Rome's logistical practices. Rome had great armies, developed legal archives to reduce noble autonomy, and built massive infrastructure to integrate its lands—all techniques of power cultivated by the French state. These were tools of power that Roman history made available, but they could only be exercised by the state once French elites set aside some of their traditional autonomy to seek glory—the dreams of glory built collaboratively at the Louvre (cf. Pasler 2009).

The inarticulacy of the cultural forms used to construct the New Rome and the Sun King at Versailles was crucial to their effectiveness (cf. Domínguez Rubio 2015; Forthcoming). Arguing that France could pick up the mantle of Rome was laughable when said out loud, and expressing the desire for empire was dangerous. To make any of this credible, it had to be *demonstrated*, not represented, felt rather than reasoned. France had to *become* more Roman as though by magic and to fulfill the will the king, and this required an art world constituted by objects created by artisans and used in performances at Versailles.

NOTES

I would like to thank the UCHRI for support of this work, and the members of the workshop on materiality funded by UCHRI. I would also like to thank CASBS for its support and the original working group on materiality that met at CASBS.

CHAPTER 2

In, On, and Of the Inviolable Soil

Pottery Fragments and the Materiality of Italian Nationhood

Fiona Greenland

Fragments of antiquity, from statue heads and column drums to coins and parchment scraps, have provided compelling substance to modern nation-states' claims to cultural continuity and political legitimacy. We saw, in the previous chapter, that the crafting of precious art objects inspired by Greco-Roman antiquity at the Louvre workshops made possible the imagination of a new form of political power that came to be instituted at Versailles. The discursive relationship between nationhood and historically significant cultural objects has been fruitfully analyzed and theorized by scholars of nationalism (Abu El-Haj 1998; Hamilakis 2007; Leoussi 1998, 2001; Zubrzycki 2011). The canonical works in this literature concentrate on the historical objects and images already heralded as integral to the collective identity of polities, including architectural ruins, artworks, and religious icons (Anderson 1991; Hobsbawm and Ranger 1983; A. Smith 1987, 1999; Mukerji, this volume). These works productively disentangle states' political aims from the symbolic and somatic aspects of the material circumstances of nationhood. They have, however, left us with two analytical blind spots. First, why do some old things become celebrated emblems of nationhood while others are ignored or destroyed? This question concerns the gap in our understanding of selectivity, especially concerning historical periods, past cultural practices, and past (perceived) ethnicities (Goody 2006). Second, how do mundane *fragments*—often aesthetically unpromising and monetarily worthless—factor into nationhood formation? This question speaks to our incomplete comprehension of partial objects, or material scraps that are parts of a previous whole and therefore are not easily recognized as commodities, totems, or icons. What these questions share is an inadequately theorized material base. Recent works have tackled this problem by identifying with better specificity the elements that make up cultural objects, including form, size, typology, text, image, color, origin, age, narrative freight, and materials, and conceptualizing the ways they interact and relate to convey meaning (Benzecry, this volume; Domínguez Rubio 2014; Féhérvary 2013; McDonnell 2010; Rose-Greenland 2016; Woodward 2007; Zubrzycki 2013a). What remains to explore is why and how we should pursue material specification in order to explain the institutional formation of nations and nationhood.

I present here a case study of ancient ceramic fragments and the role they play in contemporary Italian nationhood. Specifically, I focus on a pottery type known as *bucchero*, produced between the seventh and fourth centuries BCE in central Italy (Perkins 2016).[1] While Partha Chatterjee developed his own concept of fragmentary nationhood in *The Nation and Its Fragments*, my inquiry takes a different direction. Chatterjee was interested in the "fragmented resistances" of colonized Asian and African peoples in the face of the "normalizing project" of modular nationalism (1993, 13). For him, fragmentation refers to political disempowerment and local attempts to overcome it. By contrast, I look at material fragments and their potential to bring people together. Chatterjee does, however, offer an important caveat to any scholar of nationalism and materiality. Belonging to a national community is more complicated than possessing the right kind of material object. The ubiquity of potsherds should not be seen as an easy guarantor of national cohesion. Pottery fragments offer the *possibility* of imagined enchainment, a possibility that is brought to fruition through the active work of myths, civic rituals, knowledge formation, and curated displays.

In the first part of the chapter, I examine the existing sociological and anthropological literature for what it tells us about the place of material fragments within national cultures. I focus on theories from anthropologist

Tim Ingold (2007, 2012) to build a new conceptual framework for the sociological study of materials, materiality, and social relations. In the second section, I present the main empirical case: pottery fragments and their material and symbolic significance in later nineteenth-century Italian nationhood practices.[2] Using archival materials, I demonstrate how scientific treatments of ceramics facilitated bucchero fragments' intensified symbolic properties, as influential English and French scholars dismissed bucchero pottery as unsophisticated and derivative. Such fragments were so abundant that they were ground into mortar and piled up into retaining walls. After national unification, however, Italian archaeologists insisted that bucchero's humble texture and form were valuable as autochthonous markers of Italian ethnicity. Bucchero fragments were imbued with new meaning as ethnic markers, at precisely the moment in which inhabitants of the newly unified Italian state sought to find (and create) a stable, united group identity through imagined ancient genealogies. The final section places potsherds against the broader problem of explaining how and why materials matter for cultural sociology.

EMPIRICAL AND CONCEPTUAL ORIENTATIONS

There are many terms available to discuss the "national" frame of reference, including *nation, national identity, nationalism,* or something else entirely (cf. Connor 1994; Duara 1995; Guibernau 2007; A. Smith 2013). My interest, however, is in *nationhood,* which I understand with Rogers Brubaker as a political accomplishment rather than an ethnocultural fact (Brubaker 1992). This definition acknowledges the complicated and dynamic processes through which nation becomes and *is* fact, particularly for the people who inhabit its borders. These processes involve feelings and myths and memories, actual and projected (Anderson 1991; Mosse 1975; Zubrzycki 2011, 2013a). They involve, too, physical and visual attestations to the nation's realness (Quilley 2011; Rose-Greenland 2013a). Nationhood, then, is not a static entity but rather an ongoing process of imagining, performing, and contesting.

Empirically, the challenge for sociologists is to make a distinction between object and material, and (once we have done so) to determine how extensively we need to specify the properties and pathologies of materials in order to understand how material culture is mobilized for collective meaning. This sphere of scholarly activity has been strongly influenced by theorists of consumption, who with anthropologist Robert Foster regard consumption practices as having "the capacity to operate as powerful vehicles for materializing nationality" (Foster 2002, 117). But consumption framings do not account for the stuff—wood, paper, plastic, metal, cloth—of which objects are made. Further, the reduction of cultural objects to commodities severely constrains the "horizon of affect and meaning," to use Jeffrey Alexander's apt formulation (2003, 12) in which they are produced and received.

The phenomenon of reception, understood here as the response of viewers and users to material culture, involves more than consumption (Alexander 2008a). Zubrzycki's analysis of Polish national mythology shows that it is "not only located in texts or oral locutions, but is also embedded in visual images and material artifacts" (Zubrzycki 2011, 24). Humble objects, too, play a central role. Surak (this volume) demonstrates how the simple forms of tea ceremony equipment bridge materials and "nation-work" in Japan. The combination of materials and form gives the utensils their symbolic value in the ritual. One can hold a tea ceremony with plastic tea scoops and glass cups, but such a ceremony would fall outside the script of traditional Japaneseness. The fusion of macro historical myths and micro practices of ritualized taste, touch, and movement reproduce a shared understanding of what it means to be Japanese.

In every case, the cultural object presents two aspects: its "brute" materials (what it is made of) and its social materiality (the significance attached to it by humans). But as Tim Ingold reminds us, the relationship between materials and materiality is complicated: "Culture furnishes the forms, nature the materials; in the superimposition of the one upon the other, human beings create the material culture with which, to an ever-increasing extent, they surround themselves" (2012, 432). When our research agenda prioritizes materiality over materials, as when we focus on an object's iconographic symbolism and ignore its base matter, we are guilty of more than methodological bias. We are also participating in a fundamental distortion of the social world wherein "materials always trump materiality" (Ingold 2007, 12). Because objects' "material flows and formative processes" can never be fully halted, the constituent materials (the wood or steel or marble or paper that make up the object) will gradually alter the object's presentation. Through corrosion, desiccation, rot, expansion, and breakage, materials move through their life course—and the materiality imposed on them is along for the ride (Keane 2005). This is why a cultural object's meaning must always be understood as historically and socially situated.

Ingold advocates a particular form of object specificity in order to gain analytical purchase on the complex workings of materials and materiality. Sociologists are not petrologists or palaeoethnobotanists, scholars for whom scrupulous study of substance is vital to the epistemological commitments of their fields. But neither are the people we study fixated on material specificity in their daily lives. The sociology of materiality must therefore link materials with objects, objects with shared meanings and institutional processes. It is in *things* that shared meanings are crystallized, even as things are transformed by materials' unruliness (Domínguez Rubio 2014). When a metamorphic deposit of recrystallized carbonate minerals is carved by humans into the portrait of an emperor or queen, that lump of minerals has entered a new phase of its life as a marble sculpture. How long it remains in that phase depends on a range of factors, but when the statue is broken by iconoclasts or earthquake, or chopped up to fill a farmer's wall a few centuries later, the statue is long gone and yet the carbonate minerals carry on existing. This, too, is an example of materials trumping materiality. Every cultural object, Ingold reminds us, has two sides to its material character. On the one side is brute materiality, the simple fact of existing as a specific bundle of elements. On the other is social materiality, which is the outcome of raw material having been converted into a cultural object (see also Searle 1995 on brute and social facts). With this conceptual framework to hand, I turn now to the main case.

POTTERY AND NATIONAL CULTURE IN ITALY

Given two fragments of pottery (A and B), both found in Italy and made of the same soil composite, greater cultural value is assigned to the fragment identified with an ancient Italic people than to that with a more recent community. This is so even though all cultural objects found in and on the Italian soil and certifiably older than one hundred years are state heritage property. The distinction is constantly reinforced through cultural policy, museum display decisions, and archaeologists' classification practices. The older piece (fragment A) has the good fortune to be associated with a preferred period of Italian history. Italians have been prosecuted and tourists have been fined for collecting or damaging pieces like fragment A. We care about it because of its historical significance: "it" did this thing (transport olive oil to Caesar's Rome or set table at Etruscan feasts) with particular people at a particular time—events and scenes that we preconceive of as valuable. Fragment B, our forgotten shard, does not successfully make the transition from brute to social material. It is still just baked earth, separated from its once-intact vessel. But *classical* baked earth is social material, such that symbolic power transfers from the whole—whether an *amphora,* a *kylix,* or a cinerary urn—to the fragment. It is this aspect of material objects that presents itself forcefully in the study of Italian national culture. National culture, Surak (2013) reminds us, is an iterative process. A cultural sociological approach to materials and nationhood begins by sketching a relationship among (rather than causal arrows between) materials, objects, places, and people.

In June 1849, the city of Rome was under siege. Pro-republican fighters, under the command of Italian nationalism's guiding light, Giuseppe Garibaldi, were locked in battle with some thirty thousand French troops sent to defend Pope Pius IX's control of the Papal States. In response, Italians from across the peninsula flocked to Rome to support the republicans. Whatever enthusiasm for nationhood these men brought to the siege, however, after a month's trouncing by the French "their hearts beat high, but not with hope" (Trevelyan 1908, 203). Despite their valiant efforts, the Italian nationalists conceded defeat on 29 June. It would be another twenty-one years, with the withdrawal of the French garrison from the Vatican, before Italy could make complete its national capital at Rome.

As this episode reveals, the path to Italian nationhood was rocky in more ways than one. In histories of the Risorgimento, the siege is typically obscured by the marquee political events: the protonationalist insurrections of 1830; the declaration of the Republic in 1848; the first parliamentary meeting in Turin in 1860; the annexation of the Papal

States in 1870. Overlooked is the material relationship between the birth of the nation-state and the nation's mythical history. Garibaldi set up his right-flank gun battery atop the Monte Testaccio, a mound thirty-five meters high and one kilometer in circumference, constructed entirely of ancient ceramic fragments. To the uninitiated eye it was an unremarkable setting: a "strange mound, nothing more nor less than the rubbish heap where, in the days of the Caesars, the broken crockery of the world's capital used to be thrown away [now] surrounded by a few shabby houses" (Trevelyan 1908, 201). Yet whether knowingly or not, in fighting from the top of the heap of ancient potsherds, Garibaldi cued a key theme in nationalism discourse: the modern nation-state depends for its legitimacy on material proof of its past. From the Monte Testaccio, defenders of Italian nationalism drew physical and metaphorical support from the fragments of the Roman Empire, the epoch that gave the Risorgimento its mythical and ideological surge.

In the study of materiality and nationalism, as with the Monte Testaccio, there is more than meets the eye. Italy is a nation overflowing with monumental masterpieces in marble, bronze, and canvas. What place do humble objects, including pottery fragments, have in the production and sustainment of Italian nationhood? Why, in the specific contemporary space of repatriation and national patrimony, does the Italian state bother itself with broken bits of ceramic vases, lamps, and cooking pots?

One possible explanation is the law, which asserts the Italian state as the presumed owner of all objects of cultural and historic interest more than one hundred years old, found in or on the Italian soil. State policy considers heritage not a single entity but "broken down instead into component parts" (Pinna 2001, 62). The key concept is *beni culturali*, or cultural goods, a concept that allows for the possibility that any historical material object, irrespective of aesthetic qualities, has significance for the national community. As such, state officials are obliged to protect the state's cultural property, right down to the broken bits of *amphorae* that make up the Monte Testaccio or fill the errant tourist's carry-on bag. But this is a circular argument. Potsherds were inscribed in the law because they were already understood to be significant. The law did not invent significance for them. Another possible explanation is scientific. Archaeologists rely on potsherds to date stratigraphic layers and trace developments in technology, consumption, and economic organization. For this reason, the protection of pottery fragments abets knowledge production.

While potsherds do offer important diagnostic information to archae-ologists, conserving every one of them indefinitely is neither practicable nor vital to the discipline (Silberman 2015). Neither of these hypotheses, however, sufficiently explains the singular position of ancient potsherds in contemporary Italy. Instead, a third explanation must be considered. Potsherds are significant for their constitutive powers. Consider, for example, the 2016 museum exhibition in Sassari, Sardinia, sponsored by such major cultural agencies as the Ministry of Culture and the archae-ological superintendent of Sardinia (Figure 2.1). *Frammenti* ("Frag-ments") displayed fragments of ancient objects, highlighting the work of conservation techniques to piece back together ceramic vessels. The chief conservator, Daniela Rovina, explained to the press that the exhibition was "dedicated to a course of activity in which fragments become objects which help to reconstruct our history."[3] The publicity poster for the exhi-bition presented a fragmentary ancient face, in obverse and reverse, sug-gesting the potential of fragments to reveal new insights into history.

Outside the realm of official cultural power, in everyday speech pot-tery fragments sustain metaphors related to human conditions of sub-stance (*essere di còccio* is to be "old-school," literally to be made of ancient pottery) and well-being (*diventare un còccio* is to have one's health shat-tered). Such metaphors "objectify social relations, with different aspects symbolized at [various social] scales," argue archaeologists John Chap-man and Bisserka Gaydarska (2007, 5). Chapman and Gaydarska devel-oped a theory of purposeful rather than accidental breakage, insisting that deliberate fragmentation produced pieces that created and main-tained "lasting bonds between persons or groups—bonds predicated on material culture" (Chapman 2000, 226). The evidence from Etruscan sites does not point to deliberate fragmentation in antiquity, but it does elucidate material metaphors of intersubjective relations as refracted by national identity. Specifically, pottery fragments are associated with the sacralized national soil by being made from it and found within it, and their fragmentariness suggests a once-complete object that can be recon-stituted in the imagination. The fragment has intrinsic interest as a piece of ancient history (Renfrew 2001), or as a whole thing in and of itself, and it symbolically enchains the possessor to the (unseen, unknown) pos-sessors of the related shards.

Figure 2.1. Publicity poster for a museum exhibition on the restoration of pottery fragments. Entitled "Frammenti: Metodi e tecniche del restauro archeologico" (Fragments: methods and techniques of archaeological restoration), the show presented ancient ceramics pieced back together by archaeologists. *Source*: Center for Cultural Treasures Restoration, Sassari, Sardinia, February 2016

The Triumph of Fragments in Italian Nationhood

Contemporary defenders of the Italian nation do not fire guns from mountains made of pottery fragments. Instead, the fight for the nation's patrimony takes place in the realm of law enforcement and cultural policy. It is in the procedure of repatriation, a key space of state performance and ideology, where potsherds are symbolically inscribed into the project of restoring the nation's cultural patrimony to its imagined autochthonous land.

In Italy, as in many civil law countries, all antiquities belong to the state (with the understanding that local-level definitions of antiquities differ) (Gerstenblith 2008, 777). In common law countries the law prioritizes private property rights. A homeowner in the United States who discovers Native American artifacts in her backyard is, generally speaking, the legal owner of the artifacts because they were embedded in soil that she owns.[4] The situation is very different in Italy. First, the homeowner who discovers artifacts in her backyard is compelled by threat of fine and jail time to file a report (*denuncia*) with the police attesting to the discovery. Second, state actors including archaeological superintendents have the right to enter the property and inspect the findings. This very different scenario is explained by Italian cultural law, which considers objects of "artistic, historical and archaeological interest" as belonging to the inalienable heritage of the state. It does not matter whether those objects are discovered or as-yet embedded in the soil and thus functionally undiscovered (Pinna 2001).

When artifacts slip away from the Italian authorities, whether through coordinated theft or thoughtless tourism, the government pursues them. Repatriation is an ongoing process involving foreign governments, museums, archaeologists, and police officers. Some repatriation cases are made exemplary by being celebrated through press conferences and museum exhibitions. Two examples will suffice to illustrate what they entail and why they matter. In July 2013, three of Italy's highest-ranking members of the elite Art Squad presented the public with concrete evidence of the national government's latest victory in its war on crimes against culture. The setting was a press conference in Foggia's police headquarters. The officials announced that their latest sting operation, Operazione Tomb Raiders, had recovered some nine hundred archaeological artifacts from men described as looters. They presided over two long tables covered with archaeological objects, among them painted vases, bronze and silver coins, marble statuettes, and jewelry, most of them more than two thousand years old. Among them, too, was an assortment of broken ceramic pots. The logic linking jewelry with broken pottery was clear: artifacts found in the Italian soil are the rightful property of the national community and held in trust by the state.

The repatriation press conference and the museum exhibition sustain a discourse of nationhood in which ancient objects make Italy *Italy*, and its inhabitants Italians. The size, aesthetic polish, and monetary value of the objects, while noteworthy, are not the chief criteria for judging their merit as elements of nationhood. Instead, origin and age come first. This discourse belies a system of cultural accounting that emerged in the third quarter of the nineteenth century, through state bureaucracy as well as scientific archaeology, and has been streamlined and systematized through twentieth- and early twenty-first-century technologies and institutional processes (Kowalski 2012; Patriarca 2010; on cultural accounting via inventories, see Levi 2008).

This discourse is not unique to Italy. Many countries offer a strong narrative of national identity through antiquities (Abu El-Haj 2001; Colla 2007; Leoussi and Grosby 2007; A. Smith 2004). What is different about Italy's variant of this narrative is its emphasis on the scraps. In the realm of cultural rule, potsherds, along with cobblestones and bricks, are rhetorically constructed as integral to Italian national culture. Transforming rhetoric to practice is complicated, however. Etruscan and Roman potsherds are ubiquitous throughout Italy, so it is pointless and impossible to cherish each one. But they are also very old, which inscribes them in the state apparatus of *beni culturali*, and as such they are not readily disposable as are other everyday materials (such as drink cans and food wrappers). "Ubiquitous" and "everyday" overlap in meaning and scope, but whereas the nationalism scholarship assumes banality in the case of the latter, ubiquity is not interchangeable with banality (Billig 1995).

The broader point here is that reducing a cultural object to material properties, whether governed by nature or institutional expertise, gives an incomplete picture of the object's meaning (McDonnell 2010). As the concept of relative cultural autonomy reminds us, no single sphere of practices or beliefs governs the resonance of a given cultural object (Alexander 2008b). Ancient ceramic vessels and their fragments clearly illustrate this point. According to Italian law, ancient ceramics that were mass produced—for example, oil lamps and shipping containers—"do not have the merit of rarity [nor] testify to civilization."[5] A 1986 court case determined Roman oil lamps to be materially *autentico* in the sense of really and truly made of baked earth from Italy's substrate, but not culturally authentic in the sense of embodying national distinctiveness. This is the tension between brute and social materiality in action. What makes the Etruscan or Roman potsherd important to nationhood is its combination of material and historicity. A combination of archaeological and ethnological expertise, along with everyday reception practices, places ancient ceramics in relationship with modern nationalism.

Archaeologists, Pottery, and the Science of Ethnic Nationalism

"The national pottery of Etruria." That is how Henry Walters, a prominent nineteenth-century English antiquarian, described bucchero in his mammoth two-volume *History of Ancient Pottery* in 1905 (2:301). Bucchero, an unglazed, unpainted pottery normally black or grey in color, is found primarily in the regions of Tuscany, Umbria, Emilia-Romagna, and Lazio. Modern excavations date the oldest bucchero vases to the second quarter of the seventh-century BCE (Rasmussen 1979). Despite its far-reaching chronology, however, bucchero made for a dubious emblem of national identity. Walters wrote, "There are here [among bucchero vessels] no signs of inventive genius. The technique is purely native, but all is founded on foreign models. . . . In short, they reproduce for us what is wanting in our knowledge of early Greek metal ware" (2:303). Walters insisted that Etruscans would have made metal wares if they had the requisite technological knowledge and apparatus. But because they did not, they had to make do with baked clay. Bucchero was the "poor man's silver" (Brown 1968, xix)—or in this case the poor nation's silver. The plainness of bucchero, as exemplified by the pitcher in Figure 2.2, was its chief deficit. Walters was not alone in taking a dim view of bucchero. When George Dennis, the British consul in Rome, traveled to Vulci to see the excavations there, he reported seeing peasants deliberately crushing a "variety of small vases in black clay" (possibly bucchero wares) with their feet (Dennis 1848, 410). The heads of the excavation did nothing to stop the damage. Bucchero was seldom published, was snubbed by collectors, and was generally regarded as inferior to classical ceramics.

Figure 2.2. Bucchero pitcher, dated to the
sixth century BCE. *Source*: Chiusi. Museo
Archeologico Nazionale G.C.Mecenate—
MIBAC (Ministry of Culture)

From the point of view of Walters and others working in the *Kunstge-schichte* tradition, the problem with bucchero was that its iconographic embellishments were incised rather than painted, as is the case for Greek red- and black-figure vessels (Körner 2011, 139–42). Nineteenth-century scholars distinguished between ceramic fragments useful for "pictorial" study, and those better suited for "plastic" analysis (Birch 1873; Walters 1905). Pictorial study concentrated on figures painted onto the surfaces of ceramic objects, the classic example being fifth-century Greek vases with mythological scenes. Top scholars promoted themselves as experts in this subject, placing painted vases and other ceramics in a lineage of objets d'art along with marble sculptures (Marchand 1996, 58, on Eduard Gerhard's intervention; see also van Wijngaarden 1999). Plastic study focused on the shapes, wall thickness, and composite materials of ceramic wares, and it was given over to those engaged in the technical work of archaeological digs, a form of manual labor deemed second-rate by classical historians and art historians (Marchand 1996, 97; Trigger 2006).

The privileging of Greek masterpieces meant that native Italian ceramics were inherently inferior because they were later and apparently imitative.[6] Samuel Birch promulgated this view in his highly influential *History of Ancient Pottery*, the first comprehensive study of ancient ceramics (originally published in 1857). Birch summarized the issue as follows:

> In the application of form in art, the Greeks have excelled all nations, either past or present. The beauty and simplicity of the shapes of their vases have caused them to be taken as models for various kinds of earthenware [, but even] the cleverest imitations of nature, and the most elegant conceits of floral ornaments, whether exhibited in the efforts of Oriental or European potters, appear coarse and vulgar when contrasted with the chaste simplicity of the Greek forms. (5)

Birch's analysis was in line with the historical positivism of his generation of scholars. "Earthenware" offered a window onto the degree of civilization and intelligence of the "nations" of the past. The ancient Greeks were the exemplum of civilizational development because they had mastered *form*. Other ancient peoples were inferior, no matter the cleverness of their efforts to imitate the Greeks, because they never quite managed to match Greek object-forms. This meant that the Greek-influenced potters of southern Italy and Sicily, too, were mere imitators, their third-century BCE efforts representing "the last stage to which Greek painting could ever have reached" (Walters 1905, 1:491).

Already by Walters's time, however, archaeologists' appraisal of the usefulness and scientific function of pottery fragments had shifted. The legendary German archaeologist Alexander Conze, who rose to prominence in the 1870s through his digs at Samothrace, argued that proper excavation must take into account the "full study of the 'physiognomy' of each site, without regard to the artistic value of excavated fragments" (Marchand 1996, 97). Artistic adornment was deemed irrelevant to the technical work of scientific archaeology. With the creation of labels such as "Geometric," "Orientalizing," "bucchero," and "red-slip," pot

Figure 2.3. Bucchero fragments from San Basilio, province of Rovigo. The fragments are displayed in the town's cultural tourist center (Centro Turistico Culturale). Didactic materials explain to visitors that the fragments are from "the typical black pottery produced by the Etruscans, or what scholars call etrusco-padana." The latter term locates Etruscans in the Po valley, a space that is often invoked in discussions about distinct north Italian nationalism. *Source*: Sistema Museale Provinciale, photograph at www.smppolesine.it/ sbasilio/pagine/collezioni_img.php?img=6

fragments were fully enlisted in the scientific project of classifying artifacts as a means of accurately recording past events. This same system allowed pot fragments to be inscribed in the discursive work of nationhood (Figure 2.3).

While Birch, Walters, Conze, and other English, German, and French scholars were arguing over what they saw as significant about Italy's ancient ceramics, Italian thinkers were articulating their own alternative reckonings. Among excavators, Antonio Zannoni broke new ground by using pottery fragments to differentiate among Etruscan peoples and trace discrete lines of cultural development (Körner 2011). Zannoni explained how the fragments of cinerary urns traced the development of "extinct races" (*di razze estinte*) prior to the Roman occupation, placing Etruscans among the original nations of the peninsula (Zannoni 1871,

49).[7] The origins of the Etruscans have long been a contentious topic, and scholars still debate the evidentiary grounds for assigning them to one descent line or another. The obscurity of Etruscans' origins suffused them in mystery, such that Etruscans are indigenous to Italy or cosmopolitan foreigners depending on the broader social narrative in play. Zannoni, using the best archaeological material available to him, argued that the Etruscans had supplanted the Iron Age cultures known as the Pelasgians and the Umbrians. These groups were held to be Italy's autochthonous people, settled in Italian soil since time immemorial.[8]

Resurrecting the Etruscans in Practice and Material

Bucchero was aesthetically uninteresting to art historians and scholars of classical iconography, but in popular terms it became the star of the show. As a new generation of Italian archaeologists worked to match specific pottery forms with specific ethnic groups, Italian thinkers including Castellani embraced ancient fragments as affirmation of ethnic longevity and autochthonous validity (Körner 2009). Rescuing bucchero from the teleology of scientific archaeology, Zannoni, Castellani, and other Italian scholars, collectors, and nationalists transformed ancient ceramic fragments from rubbish to relics. Their theories traversed the boundaries of academia and were repeated and refracted through popular social discourse and practice (Ceserani 2012).

Italian nationalists based their political project on a platform of reviving Roman imperial unity. By the 1860s, however, Italians sought new sources of historical inspiration (Gentile 2009). The reasons for this shift are complicated; in brief, Italians' disenchantment with political unification spurred new creation myths about ethnic autochthony. As the influential classical historian Arnaldo Momigliano argued, "Italian scholars were looking for a new focus for their patriotic feelings and cultural interests. Deeply rooted in their regional traditions and suspicious of Rome for various reasons, they found what they wanted in the Etruscans, Pelasgians and other pre-Roman tribes. Local patriotism was gratified by the high antiquity of pre-Roman civilizations" (1966, 18–19). The Etruscans opened up Italy's "immense antiquity" and woke the *nazione* from its "epochal sleep" (Anderson 1991, 195). In north-central Italy, "Etruscomania" took hold through Etruscan pride parades, battle reenactments, costume revivals, and mass excavations of Etruscan tombs—a

Figure 2.4. "Entrance of the Etruscans into Bologna": scene from an Etruscan pride carnival, Bologna, 1874. Local citizens participate in a celebration of Etruscan history by dressing in period costume. The parade float features Etruscan objects, including bucchero wares. *Source*: Comune di Bologna; reprinted with permission

popular pastime for working- and middle-class families (Körner 2009) (Figure 2.4).

Materials were key to authenticating Etruscomania, ensuring that it was a *revival* rather than a *reinvention*. In this environment bucchero was the material ne plus ultra. In his wildly popular lecture tours, Zannoni emphasized this point. Pointing to his collection of Etruscan weapons, tools, jewelry, hair combs, and pottery, he told his audience members, "Not even Gods were dressed better than that. . . . Weapons, clothes, mores, everything expresses a sense of nationality, o Signori" (Körner 2009, citing Zannoni 1871). Etruscan artifacts thus served as vehicles for political and moralistic messages. Meanwhile, collectors and dealers rushed to Etruscan excavation sites to buy freshly excavated bucchero wares, and participants in Etruscan pride parades held aloft bucchero vases along with reproductions of Etruscan weapons and bronze helmets. Bucchero was the national pottery of Etruria, in Walters's theory and in ordinary Italians' practice.

Etruria was not technically a nation, of course, but Walters's poetic flourish points to the importance of imagining it as such. Napoleon reconstituted the region of Tuscany as the Kingdom of Etruria in 1801, and although the kingdom was short-lived it struck a chord with civic leaders and cognoscenti in Tuscany's cities. The Kingdom of Etruria stoked local belief in their cultural separateness from the rest of Italy, a belief intensified by widespread scholarly agreement that the Etruscans were of comparable cultural sophistication to the ancient Greeks without actually having *been* Greek (the corrupt historical profile of the Sicilians and southern Italians). The myth of cultural separateness is unsubstantiated. Archaeologists have demonstrated beyond doubt that the Etruscans were in contact with peoples throughout the Italian peninsula and were themselves not the first "civilization" on the peninsula. But the myth persists as social fact.

Pottery fragments and other humble objects "lent themselves more easily to positivistic sequencing and national typologizing" than did monuments and marble statues in nineteenth-century Europe (Marchand 1996, 112). Pottery fragments' infinite variations—in color, weight, thickness, ribbing, curvature, and wheel lines—offer many different plausible linkages to specific sites of consumption and manufacture. There are plenty of pottery types to go around in the game of ethnic claims making, whereas monuments and marble statues were restricted to a relative handful of metropolitan styles. Ancient pottery fragments are susceptible to contemporary national narratives, above all, because they cannot talk back through text or image.

CONCLUSION

Ceramic fragments are, at first glance, an unpromising empirical case for scholars of nationalism. They are too ubiquitous to be considered unique, too small to whip up a crowd, and too plain to receive singular veneration. The surprise, then, is that Italian cultural officials rally to the defense of potsherds, and archaeologists, museum directors, and ordinary citizens hail them as part of the lifeblood of Italians.[9] This is not explained by monetary value. Potsherds are monetarily worthless.

Nor is it explained by age. Although Italian cultural law is sweeping in its chronological jurisdiction, some ancient objects are in fact deemed culturally and historically *insignificant*. Ceramic fragments are essential to Italian nationhood because of what they are made of: clay, extracted from the soil in which the nation is discursively rooted. But where does all of this leave us, conceptually speaking?

On the one hand, I have emphasized materials. Specifically, I asserted that potsherds are symbolically important for their constitutive elements. Because they are made *of* the Italian soil, and found *in* the Italian soil, they belong *on* the Italian soil to the community that currently inhabits it. This dialectic between discourse and materiality reinforces the relationship between the two, and asserts the legitimacy of nationhood as an overarching institution represented as organically emerging from the soil. The natal properties of the soil are captured by archaeologists' preferred terminology for the physical space they dig into and record: it is the *matrix*, the Latin word for "womb." The soil gives birth to the artifacts that are then claimed as rightful components of the nation's cultural patrimony. From the entire class of artifacts, potsherds offer a symbolic double-hit: they are found in the soil, and they are made from the soil. On the other hand, I have stressed historicity. Baked earth is not intrinsically valuable. Historical context, including contemporary imaginings of past peoples and events, confers value on ceramics. State press conferences and museum shows about repatriation are key spaces in which state and academic authorities work out their narratives about what matters to the formation of the nation.

More broadly, I have suggested how sociologists might productively engage with close study of materials without losing sight of the broader social questions that drive our discipline. To do this, we must both specify the materials *and* establish our mode of engagement with the thing. It is not sufficient to assume one (abstract-cognitive) means of "knowing" an object since our study subjects' perception of the world is shaped by touching, smelling, tasting, wearing, and eating from materials (Zubrzycki 2011). This is why a formal program of material sociology must also clarify appropriate modes of analysis and data collection. How consistent or differentiated is the mode of engagement with the objects under study? Are we talking about a large range of things? Without sacrificing deep analysis of cultural objects on the altar of large-*n* statistical rule, we should ensure that our analytical framing is appropriate to the case.

This chapter has served in part as a reference exposition of these principles. It is also a test case of the limits of material specificity in sociology. Fragments of ancient ceramic vessels constitute and institutionalize nationhood along with powerful icons including the Roman Forum, the Coliseum, or the olive groves of Tuscany. They do so differently, however, largely because of what they are made of. Ceramic fragments provide a chthonic link with the motherland that affixes them with unimpeachable historical and ethnic legitimacy. This is the allure of fired earth, the object being at once *of* and *in* the national soil.

There is no single truth about ceramics. As a cultural category, ceramics are subject to contestation and carry contingent meanings across social lines and within social categories (Vincentelli 2000). But by situating them as material objects in the sociohistorical context of nation formation and institution building, we open a window onto how brute materials become some of the most potent social materials of all: the building blocks of modern nation-states.

NOTES

For their insightful comments and suggestions, I thank Geneviève Zubrzycki, Dario Gaggio, Fatma Müge Göçek, Tracey Heatherington, Terry McDonnell, and two anonymous referees. In 2014 I presented earlier versions of this paper at the annual conferences of the American Sociological Association and the Social Science History Association, and at the Culture, History, and Politics workshop at the University of Michigan. I am grateful for questions and ideas from audiences and discussants at each of these gatherings. All errors are mine. Research funding was generously provided by the Rackham School of Graduate Studies at the University of Michigan.

1. Many more pottery types than bucchero are associated with Italy's prehistorical and classical periods. A study of *terra sigillata*, Villanovan impasto, and Apulian red-figure wares, among others, would undoubtedly offer further clues (and possibly additional puzzles) concerning the place of pottery fragments in contemporary Italian nationhood. It is beyond the scope of this chapter to discuss them.

2. In this sense it is significant that the word "ceramics" is descended from the Greek word *keramos*, which means both "the clay of which something is made" and, more generally, "fired earth" (Oldfather 1920, 537).

3. "'Frammenti,' in mostra i tesori del restauro," *La Nuova Edizione Sassari*, 7 February 2016. http://lanuovasardegna.gelocal.it/sassari/cronaca/2016/02/07/

news/frammenti-in-mostra-i-tesori-del-restauro-1.12917576 (accessed 24 June 2016).

4. This is not the case with human remains or with artifacts specifically designated as "sacred objects," which are the legal property of registered Native American tribes, according to the Native American Graves Protection and Repatriation Act (NAGPRA) of 1990.

5. Pretura di Fermo, 25 June 1986. Parti: Cardarelli. Fonti: Foro Amm. 1987, II, 692.

6. For a more comprehensive discussion of how British archaeologists used Etruscans as a counterpoint to Greek cultural supremacy, see Izzet (2007).

7. In the parlance of Zannoni's time, "race" and "nation" were used interchangeably. See A. Smith (1987) for further discussion of this point.

8. The Etruscans were thus the next-best thing to the genuine indigenes, with the lingering question of foreign cross-pollination a useful device for associating them with desirable Hellenistic qualities. For a summary of the debate on Etruscan origins, see Perkins (2009).

9. On the idea of artifacts as "lifeblood" of the national community, see Rose-Greenland (2013b).

CHAPTER 3

Raw Materials

Natural Resources, Technological Discourse,
and the Making of Canadian Nationalism

Melissa Aronczyk

We frequently encounter national histories as histories of determined individuals, willful pioneers whose vision and tenacity carved the contours of territorial sovereignty. Inherent in these narratives are the romantic themes of progress, manifest destiny, and mastery over nature. Left out of these versions of national achievement, however, are the material affordances that make it possible to tell the stories in this way.

I am referring to three kinds of material: first, the material properties of the land itself—its geographic and geological properties—and the available technical means—equipment, machinery, tools, explosives—that make certain kinds of work imaginable and others not possible. Second, we might consider the ways that particular knowledges and logics are "materialized" in contractual and regulatory frameworks, professional organizations, military or other political institutions, and temporal arrangements (Foucault 1991; Davidson and Gismondi 2011, 23).[1] The third consideration is of material artifacts that work to embed these logics into the public consciousness—artifacts such as surveys, maps, letters, travelogues, archival collections, newspapers, advertisements, and other paraphernalia. All three modes of materialization, in concert or separately, enable and disable articulations of national identity at certain times and in certain places.

In Canada it is not possible to ignore the determining role of the first kind of material. Westward expansion through the Canadian Rocky Mountains prior to the Act of Constitution in 1867 would surely have been delayed if not for the prospecting by the Geological Survey of Canada and the building of a rail line by the Canadian Pacific Railway company. But to craft the tale of this technological expansion as a precursor to national feeling, and to extend this mythology into the twenty-first century, considerable work has to be done by the second and third kinds of materials.

This chapter charts the interplay of material and affective work in the making of Canadian nationalism through a close examination of the dominant national mythology known as the National Dream. The National Dream, a metaphor orienting identity and place around the material requirements of industry, has been used to characterize the building of the railway in the nineteenth century and the collective will to sovereignty in the twentieth. In the twenty-first century, this narrative has been deftly applied to Canada's most recent "national" industrial project: the extraction, development, and distribution of oil. Buried in the sand under the boreal forest across 142,200 square kilometers (over 88,000 square miles) in northern Alberta lie enormous deposits of a treacly black substance called bitumen, now recognized as the third-largest source of proven oil reserves in the world. Described as "the largest industrial project in history" (Davidson and Gismondi 2011, 1), the assemblage of mining operations, refinery plants, storage and waste facilities, and pipelines, both actual and planned, promises to draw the contours of a new global empire.[2]

I conduct a genealogy of the origins of this myth, providing historical and social context for the periods in which the myth became visible and material as well as actively productive of the national imagination. I chart two distinct lineages in the articulation of Canada's National Dream. In the first section, I look at the promotion of the railroad by the Canadian Pacific Railway Company and its sympathizers in the second half of the nineteenth century, drawing on archival sources and historical treatments of Canada and the railway in the period, as well as speeches, maps, and advertisements. I then examine the myth's "rebirth" and popularization in the late 1960s via the publication and promotion of a romantic history of the railway. In the second section, I describe the present-day promotion of oil sands infrastructure and industry, making use of ethnographic fieldwork conducted in 2014 in Fort McMurray, Alberta. The guiding thread connecting these historical moments is the ongoing effort in each instance by state and corporate actors to present the foundations of national unity as both emerging from material infrastructure and also sustaining it.[3]

Beyond the case at hand, I aim at revealing aspects of continuity and change in the discursive structure of nationalism itself. If "the task for scholars of nationalism," as Geneviève Zubrzycki argues (2011, 22), "is to identify when, why, how and to what extent national mythology 'works' in concrete cases," the question is how the material and discursive interact to produce similar affective investments across a range of concrete cases. As William H. Sewell (2005) has described, "The relationship between language and built environment should be understood as dialectical" (365), whereby semiotic practices give rise to material matrices that in turn enable and constrain possibilities for further meaning making.

THE PROMOTION OF TRADITION

Scholars of nationalism working in the "constructivist episteme" (Apter 1999, 214) have demonstrated that the nation is the product of both remembering and forgetting; that its seemingly primordial traditions can be invented for diverse purposes and to serve various interests; and that its past is always subject to the contexts and content, form and performance, of its elaboration in the present (e.g., Zubrzycki 2013a). Yet in our haste to point to the constructed nature of our national selves, we sometimes overlook ways that past patterns repeat themselves in modern contexts.

One of these repeated patterns in the making of Canadian identity is the particular style and form—the genre—of historical narration. In his historiography of early Canada, M. Brook Taylor (1989) notes a particular tendency for writers to indulge in a "National interpretation" of Canadian history. Similar to, but distinct from, Whig history, which is devoted to a partisan notion of progress, the National interpretation "promoted the concept of Canada as a nation housing a common people who sought common goals and inhabited a common land. . . . Advocates of the National position used history to confirm their predispositions and were unapologetically anachronistic in their reading of the past" (166).

The reason for this National interpretation, Taylor finds, is that it is mainly the product of *promoters*, individuals who stood to profit in some way from the account they provided. In the eighteenth and nineteenth centuries, chronicles of North America written for European audiences were largely devoted to attracting these populations to their shores:

> Among the many men on the spot upon whom European governments, potential investors and settlers, and the simply curious relied for information, promoters were those who had tied their personal fortunes to the fate of the colony observed. In most cases this was why they were where they were . . . contemporary Europeans were to a disturbing extent dependent upon promoters for information about the New World during those crucial early years of acquisition and settlement. (Taylor 1989, 11)

To account for the National interpretation of history is to attend first and foremost to the context-specific claims and interests of these interpreters and the way in which these figures earned the authority to interpret. By whom, via what means, and for what reasons did the origin myth of Canada's history as a technological nation, as the product of a National Dream, get told; and how were the many alternative versions of the historical record left out?

In what follows I argue that the motivating force propelling Canada's dominant national mythology, the way in which this national mythology "works" over time, is through what Andrew Apter (1999) calls "the subvention of tradition": the sponsorship and promotion, by state and commercial actors, of a particular set of beliefs and behaviors that advance these actors' own strategic interests and values. The point of the subvention of tradition is to foster a "culture effect"—the notion that a national culture is "visible and autonomous" from the state and private capital, even as it is underwritten by them (215). Neither Canada's national railway, nor its national pipelines, was ever the product of a solely domestic, or solely political, will. Rather, they are the complex and contingent outcome of domestic political struggles, personal vendettas, commercial competition, injections of foreign capital, transient and displaced populations, and most importantly, the interests of a (then British, now global) empire. That such massive and variously motivated projects could become symbols of a singular national consciousness is a symptom of the "culture effect" at its strongest.

FOUNDATIONS OF THE NATIONAL DREAM

Building the Canadian Pacific Railway, 1867–1935

The Canadian Pacific Railway (CPR) was never intended solely as a nation-building enterprise. In order for a project of such massive scale and requiring such massive injections of funds to be built, its proponents had to convince the "mother country" of the railway's relevance to the empire. CPR officials promoted the project in Britain as a thoroughfare between Europe and Asia. The CPR understood its mission not as a national endeavor but as a global purveyance of transcontinental traffic. The company arranged for mail subsidies with England for Pacific service; developed the Pacific harbor and negotiated for steamship lines, eventually building its own ships; established a telegraph system; created first-class coaches and dining and sleeping cars on its trains; and built a network of hotels along the railway lines (Gibbon 1937, 300–307). The CPR carried passengers and freight, focusing especially on building up trade with Asia. Canada's rail infrastructure was thus abetted by other physical infrastructure projects that would have a major effect on not just national but also international spatial arrangements.

In order to obtain the necessary favors and funds of the government officials on site, however, an essential cause was to help Canadian political figures and their publics visualize the nation. The "visionaries" of the CPR were not only the capitalists and politicians but also the geological surveyors, mapmakers, engineers, and chroniclers whose representations of the land made tangible the idea of a Canada from "ocean to ocean" (Grant 1873). One example of such a chronicle is indeed George Grant's *Ocean to Ocean*, written in 1872 and published the following year. A Presbyterian minister, the Reverend George Monro Grant accompanied a member of his congregation, the CPR's chief engineer Sandford Fleming, on a surveying trip from Halifax (Nova Scotia) to Victoria (British Columbia) along the planned route of the railway. His account of the 5,314-mile, three-and-a-half-month expedition, "so popular that it went into several editions and was serialized in the newspapers" (Berton 2001a, 42), functioned as a sort of advance public relations tract for the company's project. "What we see in Grant's work is not so much a vision of the west as it was in 1872 but of the west as Canada of the post-Confederation period wanted it to be" (Jackel 1979, 7). This idealized West was free of American competition (for either rail lines or settlers) and deeply beholden to the superiority of British institutions:

> I shall not parade statistics to show the material progress that we
> are making, for material progress is only one—and not the most
> important—element in the history of a people. The growth of national
> sentiment throughout every part of the great Dominion, unattended
> possibly with the noisy ebullitions that more excitable peoples delight
> in, more than corresponds to our material progress. And insight into
> our stock and fibre, combined with that true imagination that realizes
> manifest destiny—imagination which is the vision of the people more
> than of the most gifted individual of the people—entitles Canadians,
> while legitimately cherishing pride in the past and present, to look for-
> ward with confidence to the future of their country. (Grant 1873, 394)

Such a "National interpretation" is clearly anachronistic, as Taylor (1989) has argued. By coloring in the history of a voyage along a not-yet-built route with "purple" national prose, Grant sought to draw a portrait of Canadian identity. The pedagogical function of the portrait was clear: "Canadians, in their quest for political order, social stability, and national identity, used history as a source of examples with which to implant in the minds of younger generations (and even mature politicians) an established pattern of acceptable conduct, to secure conformity by habit, not law" (166).

Of course, in projecting a strong image of national unity, this portrait also excluded populations and practices whose presence might detract from it. Some of these exclusions were deliberate—Grant's patriotic loyalty to the Crown meant that the "noisy ebullitions" of "excitable peoples" likely refers to Americans—and some the product of well-entrenched habit. Local indigenous peoples, for instance, while acknowledged in the cast of characters listed at the outset of the book as "Guides, Voyageurs, Packers, etc." and described in various passages, were no more part of Grant's collective dream in this period than were the flora or fauna.

The dominance of these "sponsored" images is a major factor in historical writing about nineteenth-century Canada. Chronicles of the company's efforts written in this period are often presented, at least implicitly, as histories of the Canadian nation. Three tropes dominate this literature: (1) the material benefits of the country in terms of geography, natural resources, and fertile soil, made possible—or at least accessible—by the CPR; (2) the genius and foresight of the political and commercial elites of the day; and (3) the possibility of a properly Canadian identity midwifed by the railway. This latter trope was both heavily anti-American (so as to stem competition from U.S. railway companies trying to build lines in Canada) and loyal to the British Crown (to maintain the financial and symbolic support of the mother country). The contradiction between anti-American sentiment as a strong motivation for the railway and the influx of American capital and capitalists involved in the railroad enterprise is testament to the multiple inconsistencies that can nevertheless constitute a national discourse.

When the railway was completed, in 1885, the population of Canada was four and a half million residents, nowhere near enough to make the railway a profitable enterprise. A central preoccupation of the railway's stakeholders and Conservative politicians was therefore to promote and populate the newly joined territory. Through the CPR's Department of Colonization and Development, an incredible range of visual artifacts was created to represent the Canadian nation to the European public. Pamphlets, advertisements, posters, maps, photographs, slide shows, and traveling exhibitions were dispatched to Europe to encourage potential immigrants to settle in Canada (Francis 1997; Peel's Prairie Provinces, n.d.). Government representatives, such as Governor-General Lord Lorne, were also sent abroad to deliver public lectures and hobnob with British journalists in an effort to acquire favorable press (Berton 2001b, 35). These massive promotional efforts made the CPR the prime exponent of a united nation with a collective sense of itself. As Francis writes, "The CPR 'created' Canada not by binding it together with steel rails, but by inventing images of it that people then began to recognize as uniquely Canadian" (1997, 28).

A second but no less important reason to encourage settlement around the railway was the system of land grants enforced by the contract signed between the CPR and the Canadian government. In addition to a government subsidy of twenty-five million dollars; duty-free imports of rail equipment; free (and permanently duty-free) land for railway yards, stations, and other buildings for operation; and the ownership of the lines, the contract awarded the CPR twenty-five million acres of public land, against which it could issue land-grant mortgage bonds (Berton 2001a, 355; Canadian Pacific Railway Company 1881). Since the value of the land was correlated to its cultivation, it was strongly in the CPR's interest to bring people there as quickly as possible.

A singular champion of this promotional vernacular was John Murray Gibbon. A Scotsman, Gibbon was hired by the CPR in 1907 as European Publicity Agent, "responsible for presenting Canada and the CPR effectively to the European public" via his home in London (Neilson 2011, 129). Gibbon organized press junkets and exhibitions, designed posters, pamphlets and advertisements, and fed newspapers content (some true, some entirely contrived) designed to educate British journalists as well as potential immigrants and tourists of the benefits of the newly joined Canada. By 1913 he had become General Publicity Agent and moved from London to Montreal. In this capacity he continued to publicize Canada as a destination and the CPR as its intermediary.

For the next thirty years Gibbon engaged wholeheartedly in the subvention of tradition in the form of literature, music, and folk arts festivals. Sixteen arts festivals were organized and run by Gibbon for the CPR in the late 1920s. The festivals employed artists, provided content for the radio broadcasting networks, and commissioned new Canadian compositions, in addition to promoting hotels, museums, and other institutions which stood to benefit from the events (Neilson 2011). The connection many made between the CPR and Canadian culture through the festivals was evident in the press coverage the festivals received: "All this remarkable fostering [of Canadian culture] would be of wonderful assistance to a railroad. It is culture first and last that makes a race great, it is culture that brings the proper immigrants and settles them—and thus adds immeasureably to a railroad's earning power" (Glynn, quoted in Neilson 2011, 133).

Nationalizing the Dream, 1964–1974

Despite the best efforts of the CPR's many boosters, sponsors, and underwriters, it was not until a century after Canadian confederation that the railway entered the popular imaginary as the vertebrae of the Canadian nation.

Even by the late 1950s, it was clear to many that the rail line serviced some populations far better than others; and political infighting undermined the notion of the railway as a cause of national unity. Before history could be framed as geography, a narrator was needed to spin this tale.

With the publication of his book *The National Dream* in 1970, the Canadian author Pierre Berton, his publisher, and his publicist sought to reenvision Canadian culture as a culture of confidence, determination, and obstinacy, in which notions of progress and manifest destiny nourish the formation of a collective will to sovereignty and independence. With the Canadian Pacific Railway as his muse, Berton and his entourage set out to craft a new national consciousness, one which suited not only the "new nationalism" of the time but also the desire to cement Berton's own personal legacy.

In his lifetime Berton wrote some seventy books, more than a hundred magazine articles, and over a thousand newspaper columns. He lent his name to radio plays, film scripts, skits, and songs. He was also a television personality, hosting local and international figures on *The Pierre Berton Show*, which ran for eleven years from 1962 to 1973. He was deeply involved with cultural policy and participated in a number of commissions and helped author their reports. Each of these media served as promotional devices for one another; and all of them promoted the celebrity of Berton himself.

In inventing the metaphor of the National Dream, Berton sought to recreate the railroad as the literal and figurative backbone of Canada, a discourse that Maurice Charland (1986) calls technological nationalism. The discourse of technological nationalism gains its power by "creat[ing] the conditions of its own reproduction" (197): it enables and perpetuates a powerful myth of the state as both the engine and the product of space-binding technologies, and presents national consciousness as mediated by the state. Technological infrastructure thus appears as "the material condition of possibility" for the Canadian polity and its people.[4]

The project of the National Dream was not Berton's alone but was rather conceived with his longtime publisher, Jack McClelland. It was McClelland who first wrote to the Public Relations and Advertising department of the CPR to gauge interest in the "total public relations potential" of a book about the company that would be published in the context of Canada's centennial celebrations in 1967 (McKillop 2011, 410). The project was part of a broader strategy adopted by the McClelland &

Stewart publishing house to best competition by "corner[ing] the market" (415) on books about the centennial: a dramatic example of the subvention of tradition at work. CPR president N. R. Crump's archivists and
press services staff provided Berton with company materials, and made
the company superintendent's business cars as well as hotels along the
railway available to him and his assistant so that they could experience
the CPR holdings for themselves (484–85).

As Berton's biographer explains, the project's scope came to exceed
the history of the railway for a number of reasons. Central among these
appears to be that Berton sought to write a book that would cement his
legacy as a historian of Canadian culture. "In the months when Berton
assembled the Canadian nation in his mind and put the story of one of
its greatest ventures on paper, he was aware of the culture of fear in the
Canada of his own day, and set out to do something about the problems
that fuelled it" (McKillop 2011, 493). More than a historical chronicle of
nineteenth-century events, then, *The National Dream* was a promotional
device for a particular self-serving version of Canadian unity: one which
articulated Canadian sovereignty as the product of private and public
enterprise; celebrated the pragmatic nationalism born of technological
achievement; and marginalized populations and practices that appeared
anathema to it. A passage toward the end of the book's first volume
encapsulates these themes:

> The contract [between the CPR and the Canadian government to
> build the railway line] was the most important Canadian document
> since the British North America Act. . . . It represented a continuation
> of the traditional partnership between the private and public sectors,
> which always had been and would continue to be a fact of Canadian
> life whenever transportation and communication were involved. The
> geography of the nation dictated that the government be in the trans-
> portation business. . . . The express and telegraph systems, the future
> transcontinental railways, the airlines and the pipelines, the broadcast-
> ing networks and communications satellites—all the devices by which
> the nation is stitched together are examples of this loose association
> between the political and business worlds. Like the original CPR they
> are not the products of any real social or political philosophy but simply
> pragmatic solutions to Canadian problems. (Berton 2001a, 354)

A second, perhaps equally important reason for Berton's "National interpretation" of history was that Jack McClelland believed the book would

sell more copies if it explicitly tied the history of the railway to the history of Canadian identity. Canadian nationalism, of the sort that married political will to a national spirit, was more effective than the history of workers and the physical work required to build a railway in the nineteenth century. That McClelland also used Canadian nationalism to promote his own company's agenda was clear: the company's profit margins would increase with a book promoting national identity, particularly in the context of the late 1960s. The "new nationalism" of this time was rooted in fear; fear of both American encroachment and Quebec's growing enlightenment and resultant separatism. The National Dream was therefore not only about celebrating national unity as the product of material progress but also about articulating a narrative that would foreclose on threats from within (Quebec) and without (the United States).[5]

To ensure that profit was forthcoming, a massive PR effort was mobilized to promote The National Dream. A book launch for the press was followed by a series of appearances by Berton at various events and a tour of Western Canada (McKillop 2011, 499–502). The book was a best seller, reprinted (in a single volume) for the United States market as well as in an illustrated version. It was selected for the U.S. Book-of-the-Month Club, the first Canadian book ever to have been so honored. Another launch party and round of publicity was held for the 1971 publication of the second volume, entitled The Last Spike. The books editor of the Calgary Herald newspaper labeled Berton "perhaps Canada's best salesman of nationalism" (McKillop 2011, 513). This interpretation was helped along, no doubt, by the television miniseries based on the book, also called The National Dream, which aired in eight one-hour episodes on the Canadian Broadcasting Corporation network in 1974. The TV scriptwriters were supplied with reference material and images by the CPR's librarians.

It is in the reception of the book that we see how Berton's promotional story came to foretell the future. Editorials and reviews used the book's narrative to speculate on the current political situation, issuing commentary on the Trudeau administration and on the apparent encroachment of American influence (McKillop 2011, 504–6).[6] Even Berton's biographer was caught up in the rhetoric, suggesting:

> The National Dream resonated with Canadians far beyond its explication of their history, significant as that was. In a time of confusion,

uncertainty, and fear for the future, Berton gave them hope. Canadians had tackled impossible tasks before, and had prevailed. They had repelled American influence, and built a railway with little American or British financial support. They did so when their political system was in as much turmoil, and was even more corrupt, than in their own day. . . . All that was needed was national will. (McKillop 2011, 506)[7]

The effectiveness of Berton and McClelland's National interpretation is evident in its codification in state policy, due at least in part to Berton's participation on federalist committees and delegations which promoted government support of Canadian cultural industries (McKillop 2011, 495). The narrative of the National Dream is now part of the standard history, replicated in museums, textbooks, state archives (Library and Archives Canada), and in the study guide for Canadian citizenship applications.

If, as Charland has written, the effect of technological nationalism is a "disembodied" culture, the ostensible purpose of the National Dream was to restore body and soul to the Canadian persona. Berton's book and its publicity offer a prime example of the interplay of material and ideational factors in the ongoing process of Canadian nationness. Print capitalism (Anderson 1991) established a market for the National Dream as an affective trope of pan-Canadian goodwill. At the same time, the book activated and extended a discourse of state power that could be drawn upon for diverse purposes: the politically expedient vision of Canada as a unified, federated state, independent from its colonial parent and its southern influences; a retrospective rationalization of national destiny, linking steel rails and territorial obstacles to cultural pride and justice; and an economic justification for ongoing construction of large-scale infrastructural networks of exchange.

In the next section I extend these observations to the present context. My aim is to show how this discourse was mobilized in the service of the oil industry, functioning both ideologically and phenomenologically to yoke national identification to industrial development. State and commercial interests tout the oil sands as the new "National Dream," evoking Berton's now-famous phrase. The metaphor of the National Dream lends moral value to the rationalized project of industrial oil production. It allows the construction of a network of pipelines across the continent to be promoted by the federal government not only as "an extraordinary catalyst for economic growth" but also as a "powerful symbol of

Canadian unity" (McKenna 2012). Selectively interpreting the features of the Laurentian thesis (Berger 1976; Creighton 1937; Innis 1962), which described the colonial exploitation of staple resources, state and corporate stakeholders assert the spatial fix of the tar sands both as evidence of a collective national obligation and as a source of collective national pride. In the hands of oil sands advocates, Canada's "national dream" of the present reflects the unifying properties of its materially instantiated past.

THE NATIONAL DREAM IN THE TWENTY-FIRST CENTURY

History : Geology :: Future : Technology

Museums have long been recognized as institutions that not only reflect but actively shape national identity (Hinsley 1981; Kaplan 1994). The curating, cataloguing, and placement of museum objects construct a vision of the national self and its role in the world. This vision typically reflects national ambitions for the future as well as homage to the past. Museums also reflect the values of their donors and visitors—sometimes to the detriment of more complex representations of their home population, as Peggy Levitt observes in Chapter 4 in this volume.

At the Oil Sands Discovery Centre in Fort McMurray, Alberta, the role of its state and commercial sponsors is front and center. The objects on display celebrate a nation whose core identity comes from the land—not merely from the work upon its patriotic soil but deep below the surface of the earth. If its history is literally buried in geological sediment, the country's future is presented as a matter of technological and industrial innovation to unbury its riches, sanctioned and supported by the benevolence of its government sponsors. Here the material and the national are inextricably joined (Figure 3.1).

At the front desk, next to pamphlets advertising helicopter tours and fact sheets prepared by the Canadian Association of Petroleum Producers, sits a small cardboard box labeled "Oil Sand Sample Kit—$9.99" (Figure 3.2). Inside are two small Ziploc bags and a vial. One bag is marked "Oil Sand," the other "Tailings Sand." The vial reads "Bitumen." Despite the quasi-scientific package and labels, the substances in the sample kit

Figure 3.1. Wall hangings in the auditorium of the Oil Sands Discovery Centre in Fort McMurray, Alberta, summarize the mantra espoused by the tar sands industry. *Source*: Author, July 2014

appear prehistoric: black, treacly ooze leaks out of the oil-sand bag. The juxtaposition of scientific clinicity and natural, raw deposits, joined in a display of technical mastery over the environment, is the primary element of "discovery" promoted by the center—and an apt demonstration of the transformation of brute materials into social ones (see Chapter 2).

In addition to the sample kit there are many other opportunities for visitors to engage with the materiality of the oil substance. An interactive exhibit near the entrance encourages visitors to "Dig and Sniff" the oil sands through a plastic dome. Center staff perform live demonstrations of the process by which the oil is separated from its chemical bond with

Figure 3.2. Sample sand kit for sale at Oil Sands Discovery Centre. Samples are also available on eBay. *Source*: Author, July 2014

the sand. Two films, *Quest for Energy* and *Pay Dirt*, are screened on a continuous basis, summarizing the narrative espoused by the Discovery Centre's sponsors, the Alberta government and the major oil extraction and distribution companies in the region, as well as more recently by the Canadian government.

Essentially, the story proceeds as follows: millions of years of geological processes saw the development of vast natural deposits of bitumen in the sandy floor underneath the taiga of what would become northern Alberta. Generations of explorers marveled at the possibilities, but none could unlock the central mystery of how to get the oil out of the sand. Throughout the late nineteenth and early twentieth centuries, undaunted and intrepid individuals, "entrepreneurs, engineers and visionaries," pursued their singular obsession. The government played a nurturing role, sponsoring research and the construction of an experimental plant and permitting private companies to test the plant's commercial viability.

Figure 3.3. "Experience the Energy" tour guide photographing tourists. *Source*: Author, July 2014

In 1967, following years of complex deal brokering between the government and potential investors over royalties for the lease of the land and the purchase price for the oil produced, the Great Canadian Oil Sands (GCOS) project, established and supported by Sunoco (Sun Oil Company, later renamed Suncor Corporation, Canada's largest energy company) and its president, John Howard Pew, came "on stream." The GCOS project produced 30,000 barrels of oil per day. In 1974, construction began for a second major oil sands operation, Syncrude, which would by 1978 produce 125,000 barrels of oil a day. As technical mastery of operations increased, supplies of conventional oil dwindled, raising interest and investment in the oil sands as a reliable and secure source of oil over decades to follow.

This narrative is repeated in the tour of present-day facilities. The "Experience the Energy" tour bus departs from the center, driving up Highway 63 past the new $180 million Suncor Community Leisure Center to reach the Suncor mining site. Armed with statistics and technical details, the tour guide's script is crafted to prepare visitors for the visual experience of technological utopia (Figures 3.3, 3.4).

Figure 3.4. A bucketwheel reclaimer at the Giants of Mining outdoor exhibit, part of the "Experience the Energy" tour. These machines were retired because they were too expensive to maintain. This one was put up for sale. *Source:* Author, July 2014

Two features are apparent during the tour. In order to "see like a state," to borrow James Scott's metaphor (1998), one must inscribe legibility into, and project legitimacy onto, processes and policies that are not necessarily certain or defensible by all actors involved. Thus the tour guide may recount the number of workers at Suncor's massive facilities and offer the fact that the plant never closes, without showing the visitor what these conditions require: the import of thousands of temporary foreign workers, flown in and housed in on-site barracks (but not counted in official censuses). She may describe the company's pioneering efforts at land reclamation, while giving short shrift to the effects of tailings ponds (wastewater that remains after the oil extraction process is completed) or the overuse of freshwater. She will explain that the operators like Suncor do not own the land; they lease it from the state government and are "provided the opportunity to recover the resource on behalf of the people of Alberta"; but absent from this script is the explanation of the lasting effects of mining on the quality of the land or the patterns of its inhabitants (Figure 3.5).

Figure 3.5. Company as place. The main highway through Fort McMurray leads to Fort MacKay or to the Syncrude Oil plant. *Source*: Author, July 2014

A second notable feature of the tour is the absence of the National Dream narrative. There are several reasons for this absence. First, as Davidson and Gismondi (2011) explain, the nation-state is the wrong unit of contemplation for the development of the oil sands. "The Province of Alberta, rather than the Canadian federal government, has historically been not just the most active political body associated with tar sands development, but also officially has the greatest level of authority to do so" (10). This history, mired in regional battles over resource distribution and various failed schemes to implement a national energy program, precludes the embedding of a national discourse in this part of Canada.

A second, related reason has to do with various properties of the commodity itself. The oil sands are not a national resource, if by "national" we are referring to their distribution across a nationally bounded territory. They are buried in the earth under the forest floor in a remote region of northwestern Canada. As Fiona Greenland observes, the "brute materiality" of a thing is as relevant as its social materiality (see Chapter 2). The oil commodity is not only physically fixed in space but also chemically bound to another material, from which it must be separated if it is to become a commodity in the first place.

Neither are the oil sands a national resource if by this appellation we mean they are meant for the use of the national population. Canada is less a user than it is a major exporter of unconventional oil. Oil is Canada's largest commodity export, and approximately two-thirds of all crude oil production in Canada is exported to the United States.[8] Though the Canadian government does not have reliable statistics on foreign ownership in the Canadian energy sector, 2015 estimates suggest that 40–50 percent of the sector is foreign owned.[9]

Finally, they are not a national resource if by "national" we mean that they express the common commitments, interests, or character of a national people, either to themselves or to a global community of interlocutors. Considerable contestation exists from nongovernmental organizations, aboriginal groups, activists, and the international community. Yet this latter point has been deemed a priority for the federal government. If the oil sands cannot be made national by practical means, the focus would be rather on the nationalization of oil in the collective imaginary.

The "New" National Dream: Canada as Petro-Nation

On 14 July 2006, the then-recently elected prime minister of Canada, Stephen Harper, addressed a crowd of business and government elites at the Canada-UK Chamber of Commerce in London. Held up against the context of nineteenth-century exhortations for the building of the Canadian Pacific Railway discussed above, the speech offers a fascinating parallel, as well as a blueprint for the next eight years of Conservative Party rule.

Harper began by expressing his country's gratitude toward the "benign" and "brilliant" actions of the motherland in Canada's formative years, retrospectively casting the empire's rule as the root cause of the former colony's current strengths in industry and security. Britain's influence stemmed not only from the Confederation era but centuries prior, when "much of Canada was effectively owned, operated and governed" by the Hudson's Bay Company. Thanks to Britain's long-standing "genius for governance," Canadian sovereignty and heritage were emblems of pride and beacons of international reputation. The historic bonds forged between the gentle empire and its loyal New World subjects made of Canadians "eternal allies."

As an ally, Canada now stood to return the many favors bestowed upon it by Britain, in the form of energy. Canada is becoming "a global energy powerhouse," the result of enormous technical and capital investments in the "ocean of oil-soaked sand under the muskeg of northern Alberta." Moreover, Canada was "a stable, reliable producer in a volatile, unpredictable world," a nation whose people "believe in the free exchange of energy products based on competitive market principles, not self-serving monopolistic political strategies." For this reason, he intoned, "policymakers in Washington—not to mention investors in Houston and New York—now talk about Canada and continental energy security in the same breath."[10]

In its themes of security, attractiveness to foreign investment, and commitment to the commodification of resources, Harper's speech echoed a chorus of voices from political and commercial spheres dating back to the early twentieth-century attempts to commercialize the oil sands. In his appeal to Britain as benevolent parent, however, Harper sought to yoke the oil sands to the sentiment contained in the promotional documents of the nineteenth-century boosters: that nation building is predicated on the building of infrastructure, even as this infrastructure is designed to serve purposes beyond those of the nation itself.

Representatives and proponents of the Harper administration lost no time in repeating these missives, positioning the oil sands as a transformative nation-building endeavor in both the material and the symbolic sense. Many made explicit reference to the National Dream, evoking "the sepia photo of men in stovepipe hats driving in the last spike of the transcontinental railway" (Prentice 2011) or the "indomitable will of our early railroad pioneers against the rugged Canadian terrain" (McKenna 2012). In op-eds, government-sponsored reports, chamber of commerce speeches, and industry ads, oil sands promoters insisted on the national boon afforded by energy development: jobs, economic growth, public revenues, and technological innovation.[11]

It was arguably oil company representatives who fostered the initial connection between the railroad and the pipelines. In a speech at the Empire Club of Canada on 8 December 1994, then-CEO of Syncrude Canada, Eric Newell, rhapsodized:

> One hundred and ten years ago, Sir John A. Macdonald had a vision of holding this country together. The Canadian Pacific Railway became a symbol of pride and a focus of business growth in the last century. And with prosperity came a unity of purpose that kept this country together for a long time. . . . I think it's appropriate that today, in a railroad hotel, I tell you about a new national dream. We want to rekindle the spirit of 1884, when optimism reigned as the last spike was hammered in.[12]

Optimism and unity of purpose remain a motivating influence behind contemporary publicity efforts, such as oil company Cenovus's advertising campaign, "More than Fuel," in which the iconic representation of the "last spike" is featured. "Conviction, tenacity and determination are traits that have long been associated with Canada," indicates the Cenovus website. "We're a nation with a will to succeed. We're a nation that can make the impossible possible. That same sense of conviction, tenacity and determination that built our country helped unlock the oil sands—one of Canada's great natural resources—when no one thought it was possible."[13]

Commentators in Canada decried the "petromania" (Karl 1997) of the Harper administration and argued for delays in regulation and environmental legislation that could stem the development of oil infrastructure (e.g., Hoberg 2014; Linnitt 2013). Meanwhile, lobbyists for government and industry were retained to promote Canadian oil as "ethical" and "conflict-free," attempting to insert moral relativism into considerations of oil consumption and to tie social values to economic interests.[14] Government partnerships with private industry increased under Harper's watch, not only in technological and economic realms but also in cultural ones. In November 2013, the Canadian Museum of History announced a new sponsor through 2018, the Canadian Association of Petroleum Producers.

CONCLUSION

Every version of the National Dream as a form of Canadian cultural autonomy—from its "original" vision in the mid-nineteenth century via the transcontinental railway to its memorialization in popular media one hundred years later, and on to its current elaboration in the debate over Canada's oil sands—has been sponsored, underwritten, and promoted by transnational state and market forces. These forces yoke material property to moral progress, providing a salient account of how state and market actors have historically participated in constituting both the symbolic and material parameters of the nation-state. I have argued that these state/market parameters are not dichotomous but are rather mutually constitutive in the articulation of national consciousness.

Like all myths of national consciousness, the National Dream is both a prospective and a retrospective narrative. To elaborate the National Dream in the present, in any present, is to conjure a particular role for past moral and material structures and to advocate for a particular version of their future. Its power derives from the articulation and repetition of its form, even as its content changes over time. Tellingly, it is studying the absences or elisions of content that may yield the greatest insights. The theme of materiality in the constitution of national consciousness should also be accompanied by an awareness of immateriality: that is, what is elided or excluded from the national record. Networks of exchange are made powerful by what is not allowed to circulate or what is made to disappear. As we have seen above, the National Dream renders invisible multiple forms of contestation against such a unifying narrative of progress. These invisible forms include both social and material factors: precarious labor conditions; French-speaking and other minority populations; environmental hazards; regional disputes; and international production chains.

Barney (2017) writes that technological nationalism transforms global economic interests into the collective ideal of the nation, harnessing industrial development to collective well-being. To link national identification to the notion of technological prowess is also to promote a culturally and politically "neutral" narrative, in which all forms of resistance become unnecessary obstacles to technology's progressive march. To promote a narrative of progress, destiny, innovation, and efficiency, and to use this narrative to promote national attachment, is a cunning strategy. It is not just a means of making raw materials like steel or oil into a source of national identification; it is a way of transforming national identity itself into a natural resource in the collective imagination.

The subvention of tradition requires technological nationalism; it allows the state and corporate actors to present the foundations of national unity as both emerging from the infrastructure project and also sustaining it. Thus national consciousness is harnessed as a "raw material" in its own right. And like all raw materials that need to be brought to market, the work of promotion is paramount. By turning culture into nature, the grounds of possibility for a truly "material" national culture can be achieved.

ON 1 May 2016, a massive wildfire leapt out of the forest and into the streets of Fort McMurray. Hundreds of thousands of hectares of land smoldered and buildings burned to the ground as nearly ninety thousand residents left their homes. News footage of the oil sands mecca captured desperate ironies: a snaking line of cars and trucks, out of gas and abandoned along Highway 63 as owners tried to evacuate; black carbon, char, and ash falling through the sky like sparks as houses burned to the ground. No one would dare dream such a scene; and so no metaphors have been applied. But stark evidence of the conjoining of materiality and nationality is found in the political contests now being waged over how to rebuild the ravaged town, where to build new pipelines, and at whose feet to lay the blame. In moments of crisis, the link between our material existence and our national narratives is revealed to be even stronger.

Following Timothy Mitchell's (2011) analysis of "carbon democracy" as the production, institutionalization, and nationalization of "petroknowledge" (139), the Canadian context today allows us to observe the merger of national interests with the national oil sands industry and its attendant technologies. Rather than seeing this as a new development, the genealogy I have traced in this chapter reveals the long-standing interplay of material and affective features in the national infrastructure. The building of a nation is at once a material, technological, discursive, economic, and institutional project. By combining and overlaying these paradigms, we observe how the nation is made to matter across time and space.

NOTES

I am grateful to the Rutgers University Research Council for funding to support the research for this chapter.

1. By "temporal arrangements" I am thinking of the invention of "railroad time," or international standard time, adopted in 1884.

2. In 2015, three major pipeline distribution projects were the TransCanada Corporation's Keystone XL to transport oil to the United States (rejected in

November 2015 by U.S. president Barack Obama); the TransCanada Energy East project (which would extend across Canada toward the Atlantic Ocean); and the Enbridge Northern Gateway project to take oil to British Columbia, for ocean transport across the Pacific to Asian markets.

3. A similar argument has been made in regard to other places and other times. See Weber (1976) on nineteenth-century France; Bouzarovski and Bassin (2011) on contemporary Russia; and Guldi (2012) on nineteenth-century Britain.

4. As Charland demonstrates, this material condition is not merely attributed to the past; it is also a rhetoric of the future. The introduction of subsequent networks—radio and television broadcasting, air, road, and water travel, postal service, telephones—was given legitimacy in Canada via the articulation of a technonational necessity.

5. Tellingly, for specific populations in Canada, notably Québécois, Acadian, and aboriginal groups, the National Dream is not a recognized cultural trope. The execution of Métis leader Louis Riel in 1885 and subsequent limitations to French-language instruction in certain provinces foreclosed on the applicability of the National Dream to French-speaking Canada; though one does find evidence of a *"rêve national"* in federal state-funded institutions such as museums. See, e.g., "Sur les rails du rêve national" at www.mccord-museum.qc.ca/fr/clefs/circuits/GE_P2_4_FR

6. During his candidacy for prime minister in 1967–68, Pierre Trudeau campaigned on the platform of a "Just Society": a vision of equal opportunity for diverse populations in Canada and a federated state independent from Britain and the United States. Media commentators treated his personal charisma, along with his economic and political nationalism, as a dramatic illustration of the National Dream realized.

7. It is perhaps important to note here that McKillop's biography was published by no other than McClelland & Stewart.

8. This is a 2010 Government of Canada statistic. See www.nrcan.gc.ca/publications/statistics-facts/1239#sec2

9. Andy Blatchford, "Level of Foreign Ownership Unclear in Energy Sector as PM Seeks More Cash." www.ottawacitizen.com/business/Level+foreign+ownership+unclear+energy+sector+seeks+more+cash+memo/11670502/story.html

10. Canadian prime minister Stephen Harper also invoked the National Dream metaphor to characterize such infrastructural development in the Arctic. See "PM Harper Announces the John G. Diefenbaker Icebreaker Project," 28 August 2008. Transcript: http://pm.gc.ca/eng/news/2008/08/28/prime-minister-harper-announces-john-g-diefenbaker-icebreaker-project

11. See, e.g., the American consulting firm IHS's "Special Report: Oil Sands Economic Benefits," January 2014 (www.ihs.com/oilsandsdialogue); Alan Arcand, Michael Burt, and Todd A. Crawford, "Fuel for Thought: The Economic Benefits of Oil Sands Investment for Canada's Regions," Conference

Board of Canada, 24 October 2012; and publications generated by the Institute for Oil Sands Innovation at the University of Alberta.

12. Eric Newell, "Canada's Oil Sands: It's Time to Awaken the Sleeping Giant." http://speeches.empireclub.org/61089/data?n=31. Newell is currently a special advisor to the provost of the University of Alberta.

13. See www.cenovus.com/news/canadian-ideas-at-work.html

14. See, e.g., activities of the Canadian Association of Petroleum Producers in the Energy Framework Initiative; TransCanada press releases (www.transcanada.com/news-releases-article.html?id=1499651); and the Ethical Oil Institute (ethicaloil.org).

CHAPTER 4

Simultaneously Worlds Apart

Placing National Diversity on Display at Boston's Museum of Fine Arts

Peggy Levitt

Many readers may remember visiting museums when they studied history at school. We descended, half-dazed, from the overheated school bus and were quickly ushered into hushed galleries where an earnest guide described iconic national works of art. We learned what it meant to be part of the nation, not just by reading textbooks or by memorizing speeches, but by engaging with materials that embodied its ideology, values, and spirit.

Today we live in a world on the move. In 2013, 232 million people, or 3.2 percent of the world's population, were international migrants (United Nations Information Service 2014). When you combine that with the growing numbers of internal migrants, particularly in places like India and China, it becomes clear that mobile lives are increasingly common, although not by choice for the vast majority. Creating successful multicultural societies and a global community that can respond to global problems is the challenge of the day. So if museums in the past helped create national citizens, do they now help create global citizens too? How is the nation displayed in relation to the globe and what is it about the countries and cities where museums are located that helps explain their curatorial choices?

To answer these questions, I visited museums in Europe, the United States, Asia, and the Middle East. I talked with museum directors, curators, and policymakers about the paintings, iconic objects, and benefactors that define their collections. No museum I visited told an entirely national or global story. Instead, the nation always reared its head in depictions of the cosmopolitan, and cosmopolitanism always came with something of the national (Zubrzycki 2006; Daugbjerg 2013; Macdonald 2013). Rather than seeing these as competing, I think of cultural institutions as falling along a continuum of cosmopolitan-nationalism whose two constantly changing parts mutually inform and transform each other (Levitt 2015). In fact, in some cases it is by recognizing and representing the nation's internal diversity, and thereby redefining the national, that some institutions connect to the cosmopolitan. Where a museum is located along this spectrum arises from the intersection between national and urban cultural politics and the globalization of culture, an encounter that not only transforms museums but to which they are important contributors.

In this chapter, I explore these questions by focusing on the Museum of Fine Arts (MFA) in Boston. The MFA opened its new Art of the Americas Wing in November 2010 with great fanfare. The addition, which cost approximately $504 million and took nearly ten years to complete, includes four floors with fifty-three new galleries (Shea 2010). The wing is laid out so that visitors can grasp the storyline whether they enter on what the museum calls the foundation level (and others call the basement) or on the ground floor—that American art was never made just in the U.S.A. But the nation-state still plays the starring role in the MFA's story. The resulting display is more diverse, but that diversity is spread across the exhibition, never adding up to what feels like a critical mass. Work by Native American, women, Latino, and African American artists is salt-and-peppered throughout—subtly there but spatially segregated. Visitors learn what constitutes America more clearly, a more nuanced and differentiated view looking inward, but they don't learn much about how that changes things when they look out—how international influences have shaped the country's understanding of its position in the world. The MFA, therefore, falls closer to the national side of the cosmopolitan-nationalism continuum.

The museum's collections, funding, history, and curatorial expertise as well as its role in the national museological distribution of labor go a long way in helping to explain these choices. But how the MFA puts the nation and the world on display also reflects Boston's cultural armature— its social and cultural policies, demography, history, and institutions. Long-standing ideas about community, equality, and the collective good continuously echo in the ways things get done at the museum. Particularly important is the urban and national diversity management regime or how racial, ethnic, or religious difference gets talked about, measured, regulated, and ameliorated and whether it is seen as a problem or an opportunity. Finally, the MFA's choices also reflect how the United States sees itself on the global stage and what its future aspirations are—where the nation is in the arc of its nation-building and global claims-staking projects and the kinds of citizens it believes it needs to get there (Levitt 2015).

MUSEUMS AND NATION BUILDING

Ever since the leaders of the new French Republic opened the doors of the Louvre to the French people, museums have played an important role in imagining and creating nations. To grow strong, new nations needed to perform themselves well enough so that complete strangers would claim the knowledge and rituals on display as their own. What got included in the collection and who created it sent clear messages about what groups belonged and what the nation stood for. But connection and belonging generally stopped at the national border. Because the nation was defined in opposition to other nations and ethnic groups, people who were out of place—such as immigrants or religious minorities—were not likely to see themselves represented or, if they were, not without serious biases (Duncan and Wallach 2004; Hooper-Greenhill 2000; T. Bennett 1995; Macdonald 2011).

What's more, not everything on display was "of the nation." By displaying artifacts from other lands, countries showed that they were powerful enough to collect and control the world beyond their borders (McClellan 2003). While early on these materials were displayed taxonomically, they were later grouped into evolutionary sequences with the nation generally occupying the highest rung. Visitors learned that other cultures made clothing, tools, and artwork, but that theirs were better. Museums, therefore, not only created nations but justified their imperialist projects. They exposed visitors to a certain kind of knowledge based on a certain set of values. The ordering and reordering of objects, or their spatial positioning, and their contiguity, or position in relation to each other, legitimized particular social and political hierarchies, privileging some ways of knowing while excluding others. Culture and identity could be represented as simple, factual, and real. The museum's content (or its collection) and form (or how these objects are arranged in space) worked dialectically to socialize visitors into "official" and unofficial narratives. The trained visitor arrived ready to exercise a particular kind of gaze and to internalize a specific kind of "truth" and Western-centric cultural ranking (Sherman 2008; McClellan 2003), often uncritically imbibing the official storyline without recognizing its alternative.

These hierarchies stubbornly persist. They are reflected today in the distribution of what museum curators jokingly refer to as "real estate." How the square footage in a museum gets carved up sends clear signals about what its priorities are. Even museum architecture reflects these assumptions. Think of the grand staircases we ascend to enter some of the world's great museums. The polished stone makes visitors feel they are entering a temple of wisdom where sacred, unquestionable truths are safeguarded for posterity. Think of museums' elegant, high-ceilinged entrance halls. The symbolic messages of Western superiority and triumphant progress are embedded in the blueprints.

Great changes, however, are underway throughout the museum world driven, in part, by widespread migration and by the heightened cultural contact between diverse groups it brings about. How should museums respond to the increasing diversity of their nations? In countries where museums depend on private donors and visitor numbers to survive, how will they attract future generations of visitors and benefactors? How will museums balance the competing imperatives of nationalism and cosmopolitanism?

My research treats cosmopolitanism as an empirical question. Did the museum professionals I spoke with think their work contributed to creating cosmopolitans and, if so, in what ways? As Saito (2011) proposes, our conversations revealed three broad components that do not necessarily come together. For some people, cosmopolitanism was an idea or ethos. For others, it was a set of skills and practices that we need to engage with different people and experiences. For others, it was a political project—what would a cosmopolitan world look like, and what would we have to do to create it? Cosmopolitan values and skills generally included such things as curiosity, tolerance, empathy, listening, critical thinking, and being open to interact with different people and experiences. Human rights, democracy, and gender equality were also mentioned, but by no means by everyone.

Many people are unwilling or unable to sign on to creating a more cosmopolitan world. Citizenship status, class, and gender are just some of the factors that make cosmopolitanism more accessible and appealing to some than to others. Nor is the idea to agree on a standardized shopping list of "universal" values. In fact, rejecting understandings of cosmopolitanism that don't match our own is a distinctly uncosmopolitan stance. Rather, my work revealed that cosmopolitanism might be best understood as recognizing the importance of having a respectful, constructive conversation about what our common ground might be, having the openness and skills to participate in that dialogue, and then, based on that conversation, taking steps forward to create a more cosmopolitan world.

The cultural and heritage sectors are frequently sites where the tensions between cosmopolitanism and nationalism get negotiated. UNESCO World Heritage sites, international music compositions, and world literary festivals are just some of the places where these struggles play out (Levitt and Nyiri 2014). Daniel Levy and Natan Sznaider (2006) argue that we are witnessing a transition from national to cosmopolitan memory cultures. Institutions such as Holocaust memorials and museums take us beyond collective memories framed as belonging to particular national or ethnic experiences to those framed as "the global" or "of humanity," where the central message is "Never forget."

But Sharon Macdonald (2013) and Mads Daugbjerg (2013) write that cosmopolitan and nationalistic portrayals are often deeply intertwined. The reinvention of the Danish battlefield Dybbøl as a site of peacekeeping rather than a site of conflict, argues Daugbjerg (2009), relied on Danes' perceptions of themselves as a nation of tolerance and humanitarianism. He uses the term *cosmopolitan nationalism* to remind those who celebrate the cosmopolitan ideology of contemporary museums and heritage that are often framed from a nationalist perspective. Geneviève Zubrzycki (2001) also uses the term *cosmopolitan nationalism* to describe how intellectuals and activists promoted a new version of the Polish nation. They were not just cosmopolitans, because they embraced "Polishness" as a meaningful category constructed at "home" and in the diaspora but that also had broad, worldly horizons. As a result, the nation "is still important because of its affective weight and is important as a frame of action, although it is difficult to 'do nation-ness' in quite the same ways in which it was formerly done. . . . It is not so much the nation being displaced or 'cracked' by cosmopolitan memory as the nation presenting itself as cosmopolitan through harnessing shared pasts as part of its own" (Macdonald 2013, 215).

These writers open the door to a more relational review that sees cosmopolitanism and nationalism as mutually interdependent and constantly in conversation with each other. They also drive home how greater worldliness sometimes arises from the recognition and embrace of the diversity within—the redefining of the nation itself as more diverse—which then connects to the diversity without.

Where many of these discussions fall short, however, is that they do not tell us enough about how cosmopolitans are "made"—what Will Kymlicka and Wayne Norman (2000) refer to as the little-understood ways in which we actually do multiculturalism, or what Ulrich Beck and Edgar Grande (2007) recognize as the frequent mismatch between cosmopolitanization and the production of cosmopolitan sentiments. As a result, warns Craig Calhoun (2008, 110), "cosmopolitan theories need to be supplemented by an emphasis on the material conditions and social institutions that make this sort of cosmopolitan inhabitation of the world possible—and much more likely for some than others." We need to shift away from the cosmopolitan to cosmopolitics (Latour 2004): not simply dreaming of a time when people recognize that they inhabit the same world, but actually taking on the daunting task of seeing how that "same world" can be created.

How then did the MFA, in creating its new Art of the Americas Wing, contribute to these efforts? How is the nation materialized in the objects that were put on display, in their position within the gallery, and in their placement in relation to each other, and what is the subsequent position of the United States on the cosmopolitan-nationalism continuum?

ART OF THE AMERICAS

According to Elliot Bostwick Davis, the John Moors Cabot Chair, Art of the Americas, curators' aspirations for the visitor's experience are materialized in the physical layout of the Art of the Americas Wing. Each floor has a central core of galleries, where the main storyline is told, and the surrounding galleries are jam-packed with additional materials where visitors can dig deeper and learn more if they choose. "All told," said Bostwick Davis, "the Art of the Americas Wing represents three millennia of artistic production across four levels of architecture that is intended to tell a story of both/and, through central spine galleries and galleries that surround those, opening up windows, much as one would on a computer screen, to reflect greater breadth, depth, and nuance to the overview represented in the center of each of the four floors." On two floors, there are even "behind-the-scenes" galleries where visitors learn the backstories about curatorial choices, important donors, and controversies over different conservation techniques.

Each level of the new wing opens with an iconic object or visual aid, placed in and outside the gallery doors, which serves as a sort of shorthand for the chronological period to come. These also symbolically communicate the central message of the exhibition—that American art was always influenced externally, whether by indigenous artists from other parts of the Americas or by art produced in Europe and Asia.

Outside the door, on the "foundation" or basement level, there is a map of the Americas, indicating transitions in power and control (e.g., in what is present-day Peru, the labels "*Tahuantinsuyo*," "Viceroyalty of Peru," and "Peru" capture the change from Incan to Spanish to independent rule). A stunning display of elegantly lit, not-to-be-missed, waist-high ceramic funeral urns greets visitors once they step inside the gallery. The first thing you see, said Bostwick Davis, "are five spectacular K'iché burial urns, produced by the Maya in the southern highlands of Guatemala in about 750 AD." "These were produced," she went on, "by a highly sophisticated culture, with its own court rituals and portraiture. We wanted people to see ancient American art and Native American art on their own terms." The museum also wants people to see that American art never took shape in a vacuum. From the very outset, cultural connections to other parts of the world influenced what the nation created. American art, visitors learn, did not start with John Singleton Copley, or with New England furniture and paintings (Bostwick Davis 2009). Indigenous American materials are its foundation, literally and figuratively in this display, but you must go down a flight of stairs to get to the "beginning."

In fact, the layout of this foundation level is characterized by a kind of "segregated diversity" that is replicated throughout the wing. Visitors see masterpieces from Central and South America in the core galleries. Scrimshaw, ship models, colonial furniture and paintings, and the foundation from a seventeenth-century Massachusetts home surround these in the adjacent side galleries. We grasp that these objects were produced at the same time, but because they are displayed in separate spaces they seem to have little to do with each other. They are, in essence, simultaneously in worlds apart. The official narrative, as expressed through the choice of objects and how they are interpreted, is that these colonial experiences were intimately connected, but the unofficial narrative, as expressed by their placement in space, suggests that they evolved in parallel universes. The ancient American materials are, as Mukerji suggests elsewhere in this volume, rendered inarticulate or mute because they are displayed on the lowest rung of the spatial hierarchy.

Perhaps the most spatially separate group of objects is the Native American materials from the United States. They are in a gallery at the back of the floor that is easy to miss if you are not looking carefully. A showcase filled with older and contemporary pottery greets visitors— this mixing of space and time is repeated throughout the gallery. Curators wanted visitors to understand that these cultures and traditions are still very much alive today. "Unlike most galleries at the MFA," the wall text reads, "this one mixes old and new. Many of today's Native artists feel close kinship to the past and often discuss their works' connections to traditional art. Much of this recent work addresses the questions of identity and the challenge of finding a balance between continuity and change—of seeking freedom *within* tradition as well as freedom from tradition." But it is difficult for the untrained eye to distinguish between older and more contemporary objects. Obvious contemporary works are placed at the rear of the gallery, including *Greasy Grass Premonition #2* by David Paul Bradley, which depicts Custer, in Andy Warhol-type repeated stamps, imagining what would become his last stand, and Mateo Romero's *Tewa Buffalo Dancer.*

The MFA started collecting pre-Columbian art in the late 1800s. The first pieces came into the collection in 1879—the result of a trade between Harvard University archaeologists working in Peru and an MFA team working in Egypt. Still, said Dorie Reents-Budet, curator of the art of the ancient Americas, the collection is weak compared to the museum's other holdings. Until the new wing became a reality there was no permanent curator because "it's little-brown-people stuff, you know, it's not art. . . . There are still many museums in the United States that have the pre-Colombian collections in the 'Hall of Man,'" reflecting "the nineteenth-century attitude about non-Western cultures as being objects of study, of scientific inquiry into the science of human development rather than art."

A reflection in one of the behind-the-scenes galleries acknowledges this history. "In terms of collecting Native American art," Gerald W.R. Ward, Katharine Lane Weems Senior Curator of Decorative Arts and Sculpture, tells visitors, "this institution was interested in those materials from the time of our founding in 1870 until about 1900 or 1905 in which we amassed a collection, particularly of ceramics but also of other things as well. . . . Then we lapsed into the hiatus of well over fifty years in which there was relatively little interest in Native American or Indian materials. And, really, for the better part of fifty years, the emphasis was on Colonial American art, European art from France, Britain, Italy, and that was the way the museum tried to acculturate its visitors over the years, [until] there began to be an expansion of the canon of what is 'beautiful.' Beginning in 1985, or '84, we began to be much more interested, pursued objects with much more vigor since, and now five different curatorial departments collect Native American materials." But while the MFA is clearly trying, at this point it is very difficult to catch up.

The internationalization of the American art story, or the idea that iconic national objects are in fact quite cosmopolitan, continues on the next level. Visitors are sometimes told this directly, when they read the wall text, but more often they must engage with an additional source, such as an audio guide or the exhibition catalogue, to get the full picture. Paul Revere's iconic *Sons of Liberty Bowl* from 1768 greets them when they enter the gallery. Revere created this silver masterpiece to honor the ninety-two members of the Massachusetts House of Representatives who protested the Townshend Acts, an important precursor to the American Revolution. Along with the Declaration of Independence and the Constitution, the Liberty Bowl is one of the country's most important treasures. What few people know is that the Liberty Bowl is modeled after a Chinese punch bowl. In the second half of the eighteenth century, as North American colonists grew rich from international trade, they also acquired art and artifacts from the East, including Chinese silks, porcelains, and wallpapers. In fact, said Dennis Carr, assistant curator of decorative arts and sculpture, almost any piece of silver in the last half of the eighteenth century would have been Chinese inspired: "There are very few objects that are purely American or purely Chinese. We are trying to tell a complex story. Great nationalistic objects actually tell a very global story." The nation is a window for understanding the global, but not the other way around.

A row of chairs, which graced eighteenth-century homes from Boston to Venezuela, also drives the same story forward. "During the 1700s," the wall text reads, "artistic styles crossed political borders and jumped oceans like never before." This gallery, the viewer is told, puts these places and styles side by side. "Can you tell the difference between Boston and Philadelphia, New York and Barbados?" the wall text asks. "The point is," said Carr, "that all of the Americas was going through a colonial experience at this time. It could be Dutch, Spanish, Portuguese, French, German. . . . Their governments might differ radically, their cultures might be different, but there were also lots of similarities; they were all participating in a new kind of globalized market for goods for the first time . . . I think there is a lot more connection throughout the Americas than the average person realizes or fully understands." In this case, difference is showcased side by side to drive home that colonial aesthetics and consumer aspirations were similar throughout the region.

Another radical change for the museum is the Spanish colonial gallery. Since many of the museum's most important donors were from New England, the paintings and living room furniture they donated overwhelmingly reflect the New England experience. So how to expand that portrait to include Spanish colonial America? The curatorial term "adjacencies" is key to the answer. Objects are placed near each other so visitors can grasp the connections between them. After Revere's Liberty Bowl come exquisite, intricately decorated silver chalices and liturgical objects, made in sixteenth-century Bolivia and Peru. Just as the Pennsylvania legislator Timothy Matlack stares out powerfully and majestically from the canvas, so does Don Manuel José Rubio y Salinas, the archbishop of Mexico, painted by the mestizo Miguel Cabrera in 1754. Displays of colonial power and authority, whether captured in crucifixes and communion wafers, or legislation and legal briefs, have a lot in common. By placing silver made in New England in the gallery next to silver made in Peru, the museum shows that Paul Revere was not the only one making amazing silver masterpieces.

"What is interesting to me," said Erica Hirshler, senior curator of American paintings, who has worked at the museum for nearly thirty years, "is to see what kinds of real estate is being given to different kinds of art. When I first came here in the 1980s, when we talked about colonial art, we were talking about New England and Anglo culture. We were talking about Copley and his relationship with England. . . . In the new wing, for the first time, we have a Spanish colonial gallery and that is a huge change for us. It sounds like it shouldn't be, but it is for Boston—a kind of bastion of Anglo culture—to acknowledge that there was a huge colonial presence somewhere else."

The story of American art's porous boundaries continues on the third floor where visitors are greeted by John Singer Sargent's *The Daughters of Edward Boit*. But Sargent, they soon learn, while born to American expatriates in Florence in 1856, spent his childhood traveling throughout Europe. He did not visit the United States until 1876. Sargent's teacher Carolus-Duran admonished his students to study the Spanish painter Diego Velázquez and Sargent did just that. He made the requisite pilgrimage to Madrid's Museo del Prado, copying Velázquez's *Las Meninas* which, Hirshler believes, served as a model for his portrait of the Boit daughters (Hirshler 2009).

Even the way the next main gallery is laid out, in a salon style, hints at America's connections to the outside world. It tips its hat at the mode of hanging paintings from floor to ceiling that was popular in elegant European homes and at public art exhibitions. All of the works are by painters who were, in some way, influenced by European art. "It is a very outward-looking space," said Hirshler. "It is about America at that time having almost as much of a cosmopolitan culture as we think we do now." It's not that the omnipresent Hudson River School is not represented. It's just not center stage like it would have been in American galleries of the past. "This is huge," she said. "We are looking for connections with other places and more and more willing to acknowledge them. We are more willing to see how American art fits within the context of European art instead of only talking about what is American about it."

"One of the messages of the new Art of the Americas Wing," summed up Bostwick Davis, "is that the art of the United States and the colonies of New England are intimately connected to the art of the Western

Hemisphere. This wing is very different from every other wing of American art—and there I am referring to the art of the United States—because it displays the art of the ancient cultures of the indigenous Americans (ancient and Native American art) extending back to 900 BC and the prehistoric period for the Native American collections. From there, we situate the art of the United States, which reflects our major strengths in the art of seventeenth-, eighteenth-, and nineteenth-century New England, within a far more global context. It is a case of both the art of our region, colonial Boston at the core, and that of the broader nation and the Americas."

But when it comes to showcasing Boston's diversity or the diversity of the nation at large, one curator admits that "the museum is still behind the curve." You still have to look hard to find it. How much progress is made, and for whom, can depend on how vocal a particular community is, how much money it has, and whether its immigrant members arrived with traditions of art collecting and museum going.

Newly acquired and long-held objects created by artists of color are sprinkled throughout the galleries, sometimes in the "core" areas and other times in spaces that are prominent and marginal at the same time. Recent acquisitions include a 1965 painting by Argentine avant-gardist Cesar Paternosto entitled *Staccato*, and a 1943 painting, *Untitled*, by the Cuban artist Wilfredo Lam. One gallery features paintings by the Mexican painter Jose Clemente Orozco and the Chilean Roberto Sebastián Matta Echaurren, but they are exhibited in the context of a discussion about the historical influences of internationalism, as the wall text explains: "Many artists from Europe and the Americas, uprooted by war and revolution, gathered in New York City, where they shared ideas, techniques and innovations. The works in this gallery reveal the international nature of modernism in this period, demonstrating the Mexican, Chilean, French, and German influences on the origins of American Abstract Expressionism."

Segregated diversity also characterizes the treatment of materials by or about African Americans. The central folk art galleries contain little produced by African American artists. Outside them, however, in a bridge leading from one part of the building to another, three ceramic works created by and about the black or immigrant experience in the Americas are featured prominently. Visitors must pass them when walking from one set of galleries to another, but they feel as if the works are in a hallway—highlighted but marginalized at the same time. There is a portrait pitcher of Toussaint Louverture, the former slave who led the Haitian Revolution (1791–1804), which was the first successful slave revolt in the Americas; a Face Vessel made by African Americans in South Carolina; and a pitcher by Karl Muller dating back to about 1876, which according to the text, "embodies several nineteenth century American themes: immigration, western expansion, gambling, and beer drinking." One side illustrates a scene from the "The Heathen Chinee," an 1870 poem by Bret Harte in which a California miner confronts a Chinese immigrant over cheating at cards.

Curators purposefully decided not to "ghettoize" minority artists. "There is no gallery of African American art or of women artists," said Hirshler. "We wanted to put the paintings where they would naturally go. Women artists should be in the same gallery as male artists. It's not helpful to set them apart in a different room. You cannot change the canon unless you integrate the canon." The result, however, is that in many cases visitors do not realize these artifacts are there—they must actively read the exhibition for diversity because it is not clearly signaled in the wall texts or the spatial arrangements.

In November 2011, the MFA took an important step toward filling one of the most conspicuous gaps in its collection. It acquired sixty-seven works by African American and Afro-Brazilian artists. A small number are displayed near one another in the contemporary galleries, and the museum recently published *Common Wealth: Art by African Americans in the Museum of Fine Arts, Boston* (Sims 2015) to hightlight this work. According to Bostwick Davis, such works "greatly enhance the MFA's Art of the Americas holdings, allowing us to tell the broader story of American art."

So where does the MFA fall on the cosmopolitan-nationalism continuum? According to curator of education Barbara Martin, the museum is changing and, taken together, these changes add up over time. "If we effectively communicate the human dimension of the art from each culture and that then cumulatively leads you to those clicks—'Oh, that's what I do,' or, 'That's what my grandfather used to say'—that leads you to a resonance across cultures." In other words, she believes the museum is slowly moving toward the cosmopolitan end of the spectrum.

In essence, summed up Bostwick Davis, the museum is trying. "We are of course limited by the collections, those we care for and the many we acquired to begin to express the art of the Americas in the wing, about 3,500 in all," she said. "But the wing is really a statement of our ambitions, as we all realized it would not be possible within the decade we worked steadily on the project to represent the full breadth of the rich artistic expression of the Americas. That said, the galleries reflect a greater range of artists, from those who were indigenous Americans to those unknown to us today, a greater representation of women artists, both young and old, so-called folk artists or who were self-taught, Latin American artists, and artists of color to name a few."

WHY HERE, WHY NOW?

The new Art of the Americas Wing tells a story about how the nation changed in response to its connections to the world. It is not a story about what Americans need to do in response. The wing is pitched high and elegantly; you have to look and listen hard to see and hear the stories of people of color, which are few and far between and, in the case of Native Americans, stand alone in a separate gallery in the basement. What explains these choices?

Part of the idea of telling an "Art of the Americas" story grew out of an institutional restructuring orchestrated by Ann and Graham Gund Director Malcolm Rogers when he arrived at the MFA in 1994 (Mr. Rogers declined my request for an interview). To promote communication across mediums and between the people in charge of them, Rogers combined American Paintings and Decorative Arts and incorporated some of the Latin American materials previously "included" in Europe. He also folded in a collection of ancient American materials, including the K'iché burial urns I have described, which never had a home of their own. Staff slowly came to see these holdings as the basis for their retelling of the American art story because they come from the place where the narratives they wanted to tell begin. These shifts also resonated with the changing demographics of the museum's visitors. It behooved the MFA to showcase minorities, and Latinos in particular, given their growing numbers in the city and the country at large.

The United States, in fact, is well on its way to becoming a majority-minority country. In 2008, the American Association of Museums launched its Center for the Future of Museums. Its first report, *Museums and Society 2034: Trends and Potential Futures*, illustrated the widening gap between American and museum visitor demographics (CFM 2008). Before 1970, minorities made up 10 to 13 percent of the U.S. population, but by 2008 the figure had risen to 34 percent and was predicted to reach 46 percent by 2033. Yet only 9 percent of museums' core visitors were minorities. The report, according to founding director Elizabeth E. Merritt, "went viral." It "painted a troubling picture of the 'probable future'—a future in which, if trends continue in the current grooves, museum audiences are radically less diverse than the American public and museums serve an ever-shrinking fragment of society" (Farrell and Medvedeva, 2010, 5).

The changing face of Boston mirrors the changing face of the nation, but the MFA's visitor profile had not kept pace. The museum's traditional donor base is white, upper class, and aging. Because it is largely privately funded, the MFA urgently needed to recruit a new generation of visitors and donors. This was certainly on the minds of some of the Art of the Americas staff when they thought about their reinstallation. They wanted Bostonians, future board of trustee members, and tourists of color to see themselves on the walls. They wanted to tell stories that appealed to more diverse audiences. One such narrative is that what got made in America is strongly influenced by forces outside the U.S.A.

Boston also plays a very particular role in the national museological landscape in the United States, just as the MFA plays a unique role in Boston's organizational field. Many tourists come to Boston to learn about colonial American history, and the public expects the museum to tell that piece of the national story. The museum's reliance on visitor fees and benefactors' donations limits how much the tales it tells can change. "European art," said Erica Hirshler, "is not being asked to tell a story about European history in this context in the same way that these objects are asked to tell our national story."

Like the city where it is located, the MFA also plays a particular role in the urban museological ecology, with a unique function in the organizational distribution of labor. While few institutions could preempt it as the key places to learn about regional colonial art, few visitors expect the MFA to be on the cutting edge of contemporary American art. In contrast, the Peabody Essex Museum, for example, located just north in Salem, Massachusetts, can use its colonial holdings to tell a more global story because visitors do not look to it as the "go to" place to learn about colonial America. "The MFA," said Hao Sheng, Wu Tung Curator of

Chinese Art, "is as global as a museum in New England can be. It still has to meet the expectations of Euro-American visitors."

Urban cultural policy also affects museum practice. Until 2014, Boston had no office dedicated to cultural affairs or a clear cultural policy. Former mayor Thomas Menino, who was in office for over twenty years, did not make arts a priority. While he supported affordable housing for artists, promoted open studios, and organized art fairs in the early 1980s, the fiscal crisis later that decade, and its 2007 iteration, decimated much of what little municipal support there was. In 2014, the Boston Cultural Council (BCC), one of the few sources of support for arts and culture, distributed $144,419 to fifty-five grantees (BCC 2014). In stark contrast, in 2015 the budget for New York City's Department of Cultural Affairs was $148 million, including $108.5 million for the Cultural Institutions Groups and $28.5 million for cultural programs.

Since the MFA receives so little direct funding from the city and state, it is all the more beholden to visitors and donors. According to Brooklyn's Terry Carbone, Andrew W. Mellon Curator of American Art at the Brooklyn Museum, one of the many reasons the American story gets told differently in Boston and New York is because "you have different masters. You have different funders. The people who funded Boston's galleries funded something very important. There is a level of tradition embedded in those galleries that was important to those funders, and to the director, I'm sure. I think because we weren't doing something so grand and public, we had a little more flexibility. I think there are a lot of funders that wouldn't be interested in underwriting what we did [referring to Brooklyn's reinstallation of its American collection in 2001]."

The kind of national story the MFA tells and how that narrative is linked to the rest of the world also reflects Boston's cultural armature. The city's economic and political genealogy and its early position in the geopolitical hierarchy shaped the kinds of cultural institutions it created. Boston's founders believed they were creating a city that would serve as a model to the rest of the world. Their "city upon a hill" would inspire all of mankind, a shining beacon that would attract "the eyes of all people" upon them (Winthrop 1838). Boston would never be just any city but a place distinguished by its accomplishments, achieved in God's name, which benefited mankind—a "hub" of the universe, which is still its nickname today.

As the port towns of Boston and Salem grew, so did the visibility of different cultures and, more importantly, different *ideas.* But by the nineteenth century, many of the former sea captains who were the region's wealthiest individuals had turned to manufacturing. By the late 1820s, a strikingly interconnected, self-referential group of about forty Boston families, known as the Boston Associates, emerged and slowly assumed control of the quickly modernizing city. Like their Puritan forefathers, this group stressed public service. They would go on to create institutions like the Museum of Fine Arts, not as individuals but as a cohesive community that shared economic interests as well as last names. These reflected the conflicting legacies at the city's core: a faith in elitism and the power of high culture alongside an impulse to elevate the masses by introducing them to that culture; an interest in and begrudging respect for cosmopolitanism combined with a sense that America needed to chart its own way and that the city and the nation would be a model to other nations; and a suspicion that people who spent too much time abroad were possibly disloyal (Rennella 2008).

That is why, says Dorie Reents-Budet, the ancient American materials are still "in the basement. In another city, like Los Angeles, this stuff would have been on the top floor, but Boston is a Northern European city, not a Latin American one." This is, on the one hand, about "the browning of America, but it's also about getting the white folks to recognize that this is okay. That these folks who are coming from Latin America are coming from these countries with this incredible historical heritage."

Finally, the lack of global focus that characterizes the Art of the Americas Wing says something about how the United States sees itself in the world. The United States, writes Michael Ignatieff (2005) and John Ruggie (2005), suffers from American "schizophrenism": no other country spends so much time promoting human rights and democracy while also supporting rights-abusing regimes, opting out of treaties, and insisting that domestic law always trumps international agreements. The nation's destiny is to spread democracy and to be a role model to other nations. Boston's self-image as the "hub of the universe" that would inspire mankind has the same genealogy. "It is something more than the ordinary narcissism and nationalism that all powerful states display," writes Ignatieff (2005, 5). "It is rooted in the particular achievements of a successful history of liberty that U.S. leaders have believed is of universal significance, even the work of Providential design. For most Americans, human rights are American values writ large, the export version of its own Bill of Rights," and America is "the last imperial ideology left standing in the world, the sole survivor of imperial claims to universal significance." It is no wonder that the MFA falls closer to the "nationalism" side of the cosmopolitan-nationalism continuum. To this day, many Americans still equate globalization with Americanization and simply believe that the rest of the world should come here.

CONCLUSION

More and more people choose to or are pushed into living lives that cross borders—earning livelihoods, raising their political voices, caring for family members, and saving for retirement in more than one nation-state. They will call many places home: the scattered sites where their dispersed family members live, where they work or study, the places they remember and dream of, and the homes they long to return to and rebuild. Their movements, bringing languages, faiths, traditions, and histories into daily contact, even diversify societies that still insist they are not diverse. And all this unfolds in a world plagued by economic crisis, heightened ethnic and religious strife, and declining social protection.

A world on the move produces opportunities and anxieties, more wealth, and much more inequality, a decentering of power into more loci where power gets concentrated anew. It is no surprise that countries across the world are grappling with how to create citizens who can live successfully in diverse neighborhoods and who actively engage with the world at the same time. To be sure, what happens inside museums alone is not going to solve the problems of integration and immigration. And institutions are constrained by their histories and their collections—they must work within the parameters of what their funding, their origins, and their curatorial expertise and interests will allow. But museums are an underutilized tool in our many struggles for social justice. They can provide a space for finding common ground and for starting some of those conversations that are so difficult to have but are so desperately needed. They have to if they are to remain vital and viable in the twenty-first century.

Despite firm commitments by curators to diversify and internationalize the American art story, the new Art of the Americas Wing at the

Museum of Fine Arts in Boston is still overwhelmingly a celebration of the nation. Visitors expect this from the institution—it has long been its role in the urban and national cultural landscape. Because it is privately funded, it must continue to please its most loyal visitors and benefactors.

Moreover, Boston's cultural armature, and the deeply held values from which it grows, also limits the extent to which the museum can change course. Boston's founders flirted with cosmopolitanism while strongly asserting their position as a role model to the rest of the world. They felt responsible for "civilizing" the teeming masses but strictly forbade them from entering their clubs.

Finally, the MFA's decisions about what objects it puts on display and how they are positioned in relation to each other also reflect how the United States sees itself in the world: as a global leader that is so large and powerful it does not really have to engage with anyone else and, when it does, only on its own terms. Because it believes it lies at the center of the geopolitical universe, its citizens do not need to be particularly globally oriented because, for many, being global means being American. Even when the MFA internationalized the American story, it was a new story about what constitutes the nation rather than a repositioning of its place in the world. Museums are not the only places where this uncosmopolitan stance and narcissism come through.

Reading museums through the lens of materiality, space, and institutions brings into focus several things that have long been hiding in plain sight. As Mukerji and Greenland have also discovered, it reveals the tension between the official, articulated discourse of the museum and the mute, unarticulated parallel story that is expressed in the spatial arrangements of the objects. The reflexive visitor holds these two narratives in tandem and decides for herself how to make sense of the disjuncture between them. Yet I fear that many visitors take what they see at face value and do not notice the alternative, conflicting plots.

NOTES

1. Gerald Ward, Behind the Scenes Galleries, audio text.

PART II

Things That Matter

CHAPTER 5

A Brief History of Sweat

Inscribing "National Feeling" On and Through a Football Jersey

Claudio E. Benzecry

Take a look at the photographs below and see if you can identify when they were taken. Of course, some of the people on the top left seem ancient in comparison to those in the picture on the bottom right, but the two extreme images work as a bridge in time, underscoring the continuity of what a soccer team looked like for an extended period of time. We can notice in the pictures how the team's jersey has not changed; no add-ons are inscribed on it, no advertisements, no sponsors, and the colors have been largely stable and constant (a muted blue and gold). Moreover, the jersey fabric choice of cotton and the maintenance of the original colors were unaltered until 1981 (Figure 5.1).

The jersey for Boca Juniors, one of the leading teams in the world and, more importantly for our argument here, one of the top two teams in Argentina,[1] went almost unchanged from 1926 to 1980. The lack of branding meant an absence of concerns about whether the jersey was an original or a copy, as the only elements needed to identify it were the blue and yellow colors. If you were a fan of the team, you knew how to recognize it, how to appropriate the team's colors by purchasing a replica that only needed to resemble the team's official equipment, and how to

Figure 5.1. Boca Juniors' teams from 1940, 1954, 1969, and 1977. *Source:*
Archivo General de la Nacion, Buenos Aires, Argentina; www.mininterior.gov.
ar/agn/documentos-fotograficos.php

demonstrate your love for the team by stamping its colors on any rag,
flag, or shirt. The traditional continuity of the jersey guaranteed the recognition of the team, its colors, and what it stood for. It articulated a
logic of difference with respect to other teams, in which Boca was both
part of Argentinean soccer at large and stood distinctively as the most
popular team in the country, and it closely associated itself with masculine values such as courage and grit. The continuity of the jersey in time
also made for a longer chain that connected different (even nonsucces-
sive) generations of players and of fans. The jersey is part of a genealogy that links team members to each other, fans to each other, and fans
and team members. What became disrupted once the jersey was altered,
then, was not only the totem but what it stands for (the team) and its
genealogy (ancestors).

The question then is what happens when the jersey changes? What
happens when what used to be a "cemented" chain of associations
between the colors and the materials of the jersey, and the meanings

linked to it, are abruptly destabilized? What happens to the lineage of the team, its genealogy, and the bonds formed between and among team members and their fans? In telling the story of how the jersey for Boca Juniors changed thanks to the intervention of brands by transnational corporations (both as makers of the jersey and as sponsors for the team), this chapter aims to answer the following questions: What happens when a totemic object becomes disfigured? What is it that becomes disfigured from it and with it? What are the efforts to denounce the transformation and to restabilize it? The chapter has a subsidiary objective as well to explain not only what gets lost with the new jersey, but also the new lines of action afforded by the object in its new configuration.

1981: THE YEAR OF LIVING DANGEROUSLY

Most Argentinean aficionados point to San Lorenzo club as the catalyst for the destabilization of football jerseys as they used to be, as that was the first team to include an advertisement on its jersey, in 1981. With the team sunken in an economic and sport crisis that resulted in it being relegated to the second division of Argentinean football, the idea of selling the front of the jersey to a local candy brand was derided as a desperate measure and was closely attached to the wane in powers of the team. Diatribes against the advertising flourished and were later followed by jeremiads against the intrusion of sponsors and new designs for the jersey. Most fans had related to the jersey as a totem, a noncirculatory symbol that stabilized both the object and its meaning, as well as the selves attached to it.

Boca's jersey went unchanged from 1926 to 1982, even though there were some minor details added: in 1949–50, the player's number was placed on the back of the jersey; in 1955, the jersey incorporated the team badge of the Argentinean Football Association; and in 1981, the club added four stars (representing the number of South American and World Club Cup Championships won) on the left side of the jersey, over the player's heart. Later, in 1993, the club's team badge was placed directly over the heart as well. By 1984, marketing was still so underdeveloped that when Boca had to play against Atlanta, a team with similar colors on its jersey (although striped), it did not have an alternate official jersey to wear. Instead the equipment team improvised with the white training gear, writing the number of the player, on both the jersey and the shorts, with a marker.

Boca had toyed with the idea of having sponsors on its equipment for a while. For instance, in 1967, Crush, a soft drink company, paid for the stadium rights for five years, which included dressing the players before the game in orange sweaters bearing the logo of the brand. During the late 1970s, the star goalie, Hugo Gatti, sold advertising on his individual goalkeeper jersey. Nevertheless it was not until 1981 that the brand providing the clothing to the team became noticeable (with the Adidas logo over the heart of the players and its three stripes on the arms and shorts), and it was not until 1982 that sponsorship appeared on the jersey. The brand was Vinos Maravilla, a cheap wine sold in Tetra Brik.

Tradition was presented as the guarantor of identification. Complaints about changes were usually presented in the form of a "we look like [another team]" comment. For instance, the 2003 jersey (which lacked the yellow stripe on the back) was received with complaints such as, "We look like Brazil's Cruzeiro," or "We look like Italy's national team, but with yellow numbers. This is treason to the club's main symbol. It is like River in the '80s when they did not have the stripe on the back and looked like Huracan."[2] Being misidentified or misrepresented dilutes the power and prowess of the jersey in the eyes of all involved—players, coaches, and aficionados. Material continuity (which includes the jersey's colors), on the other hand, is associated with the enduring power of the jersey. To wit, a common phrase that could be heard at La Bombonera stadium or in coffeeshop conversations is *"Les ganamos con la camiseta"* (We beat them with the jersey). But where does this association between the jersey, its colors, the team, and its supporters come from? To understand this, we need to consider how the totem became configured in the first place, and unravel the genealogy and process woven into the very fabric of the jersey.

WHAT'S IN A JERSEY?

Argentina imported two competing models of bodily and moral care: the Germanic, based on gymnastics, and the English, based on games and team sport (on the distinction, see Mosse 1996). Professional football developed in Argentina in a double movement of popularization and nationalization, by which recent Italian and Spaniard immigrants quickly adopted the practice, "making it Argentinean" and becoming creole in the process (Archetti 1999, 2001). The national style consti- tuted itself in opposition to the British style—as teams from the United Kingdom came to the country on tour—emphasizing how the Argen- tinean male was less disciplined and mechanistic but more skillful, individualistic, and agile; using street smarts versus the machine-like collective character of the Brits. Later on, Argentinean teams came to reflect upon themselves and what would make them stand out against their counterparts in friendly matches in Europe (Frydenberg 2011), building and validating their style after how the press presented them in those trips. Thus the European gaze has accelerated Argentinean self-recognition in a distinctive way of playing. Continual matches against Uruguayan teams (including the Olympic game finals in 1928 and the first World Cup final in 1930) also contributed to the process. Masculinity was also associated with virility, courage, and strength, so the ideal national football team was composed of both individual ability and grit.

As teams transitioned from amateurism to professionalism, they became closely associated with their neighborhoods of origin (Fryden- berg 2011). They established their identity via an agonistic relationship with a local other. Boca Juniors originated in the early 1900s and distin- guished itself from the then-nearby River Plate.[3] The two teams represent two very distinctive poles in the local imaginary: River is the team of skill, while Boca has historically been associated with grit. They consoli- dated as the two most popular teams in the country in the 1940s. River did so thanks to a series of very elegant and offensively skilled teams; Boca, on the other hand, became the team known for its effort, cour- age, and tenacity. This representation consolidated on the idea of "*garra*" (grit) thanks to the many defensive teams in the mid-1950s and 1960s through which the club won five championships. Sweat became the met- aphor through which grit was (re)presented, and it makes visible the link between masculinity, virtue, and football. The effort of the players is also validated by the effort of fans in the stands, who actively engage in jump- ing and singing throughout the whole game. Jerseys on and off the field get soaked with sweat, become saggy, and stay wet for most of the game, finally getting stuck to the body and signaling to the stands that the play- ers on the field are giving their all.

The jersey is the centerpiece of a larger set of goods,[4] which includes caps, headbands, body painting, and flags—called *trapos* or rags—made and inscribed by the supporters with their names and the neighborhood where they reside.[5] In the "war" between teams' supporters, flags and jerseys become special trophies that help to forge bonds within, and enmity between, groups of supporters. They are also the central goods in political alliances between the enemies of an immediate rival team or the teams' worst enemy. Argentinean fans have a special way of referring to these political alliances: "*hacer la amistad*" (to do the friendship). Alliances are signaled by exchanging flags or jerseys, and nonritualized forms of violence usually include stealing jerseys and flags from the rival team only to then put them on display as a way of stealing the rival team's own turf and symbolic power.[6] The supporters of big clubs like Boca usually sing that they do not "do the friendship," implying a relationship between their colors and its totemic or noncirculatory character.

The football shirt is of iconic significance, defining a club's visual identity through its role as sporting uniform and fan identifier. The uniqueness of the team colors is usually established via an origin story. In Boca's case the colors of the club would be those of the flag of the first boat that passed by the nearby dock. The first ship was a Swedish tanker, so the first jersey had a diagonal yellow stripe over a blue background. In 1910 the club started using the jersey it still wears today: blue with a wide horizontal yellow stripe. Such origin stories abound in Argentinean football. Rather than the discovery of the true cultural roots of the football jerseys, the origin story's place inside the team narrative can be understood as a process whereby authenticity was invented and cultivated. It is an example of what Eric Hobsbawm and Terrence Ranger (1983) and Richard Peterson (1997) have respectively called "the invention of tradition" and the "fabrication of authenticity."

ENTER THE SWOOSH: WHAT CAN YOU DO IF YOUR JERSEY STAYS DRY?

If 1981 was a key year, as the first time a brand visibly materialized on the team colors, 1996 was a hinge year when it comes to Boca's equipment, since it is then that Nike became the provider of sporting equipment for the team in a relationship that is still—as of 2016—ongoing. It is thanks to Nike that Boca has three designs per year: one for local games, one for when it plays as a visitor, and a third, alternate one, mostly used when a rival team has the same colors (and even if not, since the team is contractually obligated to wear it regardless, in friendly games or sometimes in international matches). What was until then a relatively stable (and continuous) object became systematically reinvented. While there had been some changes—mostly involving the change of brand or sponsors from 1981 until 1995—the arrival of Nike resulted in the imposition of a commercial logic of novelty, superimposed on that of continuity over time.

Nike's involvement in the garment market also fueled the technological transformation of the jersey material. Nike has greatly advertised the dry-fit concept for the Argentinean market. The system is based on a polyester micro fiber used to control moisture. It eliminates perspiration in two layers: the first one is in direct contact with the skin and absorbs the moisture, which then gets transported to the second layer where it spreads itself and immediately evaporates.[7] The jersey also protects the players from ultraviolet sun rays, since it has a powerful SPF 30 sunscreen.[8] Yet the jerseys sold on the general market are 100 percent polyester, a great difference from the cotton that governed the jerseys during the pre-Nike era (Adidas used a formula composed of 50% cotton, 50% polyester until Nike's competition forced it to go with a polyester formula as well).[9] This material change underscores a process that had started in 1981: the separation between the jersey used by team members and those available to fans for their everyday use. If the 1981 jersey had broken the identity between the two by marking the outside of the jerseys with sponsors and advertisements, Nike transformed the inner part and with that the feeling of having a shared armor (or second skin) that bonded fans and players.

Scholars of branding have focused on Nike (Lury 2004; Lash and Lury 2007) to call attention to how it promotes a dematerialized version of objects, in which marketing is more important than the production process itself. They have also called attention to how brands like Nike produce singularization—the personalized attribution of value beyond what it costs to produce something—instead of the homogeneity that one would expect from the production of commodities, thereby introducing quality into the means of exchange and showing how product definition is accomplished within market relations as well as with objects of consumption. Lee and LiPuma (2002) have pointed to how circulation constitutes meaning and aims to produce intelligibility, providing a set of directions for what the product should stand for (Nakassis 2013). Branding is a process that works toward producing a semiotic monopoly and instilling a logic of difference. But given that Boca was already a distinctive marker of difference, what happens when the logic of branding aims to impose itself where there already was a landscape of meaning and valuation?

The arrival of Nike destabilized what was a very stable field of objects and meaning. The generic product that existed before precluded the problem of whether something was a copy or an original. The introduction of branding, on the other hand, meant the introduction of the possibility for surfeits to exist, as well as for the original object to proliferate; now the original colors would matter less than the brand as an anchor to guarantee the authenticity of the jersey. The commercialization of the new Boca jersey by Nike exploited—as Mazzarella (2003, 20) writes—the gap at the heart of the commodity form, allowing for the separation of its material and immaterial elements (on this, see Luvaas 2013, 129). So Boca became destabilized both as an object (given that now a jersey has to have dry-fit technology to be authentic) and as a sign (so products with the Nike signature are now perceived as original, regardless of whether the colors are Boca's). This first destabilization challenged both the work of Boca presenting itself as the same over time (since the link between sweat and masculine virtues now appeared as vulnerable) and what distinguished Boca from other teams (since the colors could change from one season to the next). As I'll show in the next few pages, complaints about the arrival of Nike were divided into two camps, with some focusing on the materials of the jersey while others—indeed most—instead focused on the design. In the latter, the opposition is as much about the tension between national values and transnational corporations as it is about the team becoming unrecognizable. The object goes from being a totem to becoming a site of contention among different stakeholders (Zubrzycki, 2013a).

In 1998, after Nike incorporated dry-fit technology into the jersey, Senator Cafiero (a former governor of the state of Buenos Aires, the most important of the country) wrote a fiery opinion column in *Clarín*, Argentina's main newspaper, called "Let's Sweat the Jersey!" (Cafiero 1998). In it, the senator wondered about the paradox of a team whose fame was built on effort, stamina, and dedication having an anti-sweat jersey:

> We want to see the players soaked in sweat. Can you imagine Tano Per-
> nia or "Little Lion" Pescia [two players best remembered for their effort
> and rough game] leaving the field with an immaculate jersey after 90
> minutes of coming and going? By these means, all the solidarity and
> the effort spilled over by Cagna and Fabbri [two of the players dur-
> ing 1998] will be in vain, or better said, in an anti-perspiration jersey!
> . . . How can we demand or implore our players to give everything on
> the field and soak their jersey with sweat if the jersey itself precisely
> prevents them from doing so? What will be next? Jerseys with auto-
> matic wash and dry or suede shoes for night games? . . . No Sir, I do not
> want for my team this kind of "light," dispassionate, postmodern and
> anti-perspiration costume. I want a shirt that leaves a puddle on the
> locker room floor. That shows, with no shame, the result of honest work
> and being worn out. By these means, if we do not like our team we can
> always start chanting: *la camiseta de Boca se tiene que transpirar* [Boca's
> jersey must be perspired!].

In Cafiero's words, sweat is what inscribes effort on the jersey. Much like tides make their own measure, sweat is here its own mark, what mea-sures grit and effort. And sweat is also what unites the bodies on the pitch in communion with the bodies chanting in the stands. The para-doxical relationship here is that what makes the Nike jersey distinctive and authentic (the lack of moisture) is at odds with what makes Boca unique. If we can poetically say here that some of the masculine virtues of the nation are woven into the jersey, even beyond the textile itself, we will see in the following testimony a more explicit version of the materi-ality of the nation, beyond its official symbols (Billig 1995).

In 1996, while preparing its first jersey for the Argentinean market, Nike had scared the fans by adding two small white lines (each one-inch wide) to separate the yellow stripe from the blue background. Diego Maradona, the most important player in Argentinean history and a sym-bol of Boca, complained—and campaigned—against the jersey, saying, "It looks like the University of Michigan's shirt not Boquita's jersey." In 1998, the opposition became even stronger as people seemed to challenge the new jersey with regard to two basic features it represented, nation-hood and effort, signified in the first case by the fluctuations in design since the transnational company took over, and in the second by the technologically enhanced fabric. About the first new jersey, Maradona complained:

> This is unbelievable. How can they make a different jersey! Today they include the white stripe, then they widen it, tomorrow they put red and black and it becomes Chacarita's [another Argentinean football team] jersey! If Americans come and give us $200 million we are not going to change the national flag. In today's world everything is money, but there are some things we should defend. And Boca's jersey colors is one of those things.

Maradona's allocution intertwines the complaint regarding the transformation of the design with a second (and more serious) lament: that in defacing the jersey as a totem, Nike was also aiming to direct the meaning of the jersey to a milieu outside the logic of national and territorial inscription and toward a declassified, deritualized, individualized version of soccer.

Far from these being the only protests over the yearly changes in the jersey, objections to the design continued over time: in some cases protesters referred to the lack of identity with Boca; in others they made allusions to issues of masculinity; and in yet-other cases to the loss of the team's power if it associated with the new jersey. In 2009 protesters campaigned against the inclusion of the logo of LG Corp, the South Korean electronics company, under the premise that red and white were the colors of River and that the president of the team was allowing the colors of the archrival, printed at the center of the golden stripe, to be next to the heart of the players. In a newspaper article protesters complained that they shouldn't sell their colors for market reasons.[10] LG was paying two million dollars a year for the advertisement, while protesters had a Facebook page with five thousand members and went into the team's training facilities, attired with jerseys from past seasons, to protest the new model.

In late 2012 the team premiered a violet jersey to be used in the summer friendly tournaments, at odds with the historical colors of the team. Salient in this case was that Nike challenged the protesters on its own Facebook page with a violet-colored post: "Boca does not win with just its colors" (*Boca no gana sólo con los colores*),[11] going against the one-on-one homology between team, colors, and power.

But the protests over the violet jersey were little in comparison to the fury awoken later, in 2013, by the unveiling of a pink jersey to commemorate the 105th anniversary of the club.[12] Martín Palermo, one of the contemporary idols of the club, who had then just retired, complained that the pink shirt felt like a "marketing ploy" and restated the conviction that the team jersey should be blue and gold. Veteran coach Alfio Basile (who coached both Boca and the national team) stated that the jersey was an affront to masculinity, highlighting that "when he was a player, it would have been impossible to have that on a soccer pitch, rivals would immediately have considered you gay." But he later reflected that "things have changed, and *now the team has to sell jerseys*" (my emphasis). He wasn't wrong. Despite the fact that fans protested on social media (with the hashtag #noalacamisetarosa), newspaper articles reported that the pink jersey was one of the team's best sellers (50,000 in 2013 versus 14,000 for the violet shirt).[13] Worried about the divisive character of some designs, the team president declared later in the year that he would consult with Nike to make sure they never do jerseys without yellow or blue, and to communicate that he did not want any more shirts that divide Boca's fans.

CAN A TOTEM BE RESTORED?

Despite the many complaints about the changing colors of the team, diatribes stopped over time about the place of advertising on the jersey itself. How did advertisement go from being an unwanted appendix to an integral part of the jersey? In fact, the naturalization process by which advertisement became an integral part of the jersey caused one more change. If we examine a late 1980s Boca jersey, the texture of the sponsor's logo is different from that of the jersey fabric, the result of a patch being ironed onto the jersey. By 2003, Boca's Nike jersey instead had the sponsor's logo printed directly on the jersey. Moreover, the kind of brand and advertising that was attracted became over time a marker of the team's power. The coming of advertisement as a big part of the fiscal stability of a football team has changed the dynamics of how the power of the team is represented—the amount of the contract is on display, not only on the jersey but in a longer series of jersey presentations, from fashion models to wall-to-wall advertisements at the stadium. As an example, when Racing Club went into bankruptcy, one of the key issues was that it could not find a sponsor for its jersey (Brazilian firm Topper did not want to have its name attached to the jersey of a team in distress, nor be an advertiser on the front of the jersey). As a result, Racing started the 1998 season with a self-designed jersey that had no advertisement and with no training equipment (which sponsors normally provide). Its jerseys bore the inscription of the internal club political line of the newly elected president: "*Frente Grande Racing.*"[14] On a similar note, Huracán went into 1998 with two sponsors for the jersey, one on the back and one on the front, which was perceived as a fair representation of the dwindling power of the football team.[15] On the opposite side of the spectrum, Boca's contract attracted Nike, a big fish in the sports industry. Nike paid $30 million in 1996 to provide Boca jerseys for six years. It still pays the team $5.62 million a year.

Having now explained at large what happened to branding and sponsorship and how they became naturalized in use by soccer teams, our next question should be how fans perceive this phenomenon, and how much the logic of symbolization present in the jersey-cum-totem opposes itself to branding, or how much they may actually complement each other.

Fans have used the new styled jerseys as a way to be able to mark the passing of time. As much as a status marker, the brand serves as a temporal landmark, which precisely indicates when the jersey dates from, and to which incarnation of the team it belonged. The commercial sponsor, once seen to degrade authenticity, has over time been folded into the very notion of the object's authenticity. One interviewee, when asked which Boca jersey he had, answered: "I have a Parmalat, circa 1992. The one used by Manteca Martinez and Márcico" (Figure 5.2). He referred to the players who marked that era, but also identified the object according to its advertisement. It was easier than referring to the maker of the time, Adidas, since there have been Adidas jerseys with other advertisements. It was visually more compelling and obvious to refer to the advertisement since the brand appears in every TV and print image, but also because it stays in our memory. As a River Plate supporter told me, "I have the glorious [jersey], the Fate one." Fate sponsored the team when it won its first and only Club World Championship in 1986.

But it is not only these supporters who frame their references to jerseys and points in history by means of a vocabulary that refers to, and reduces them to, the name of the sponsor. A quick look at the e-commerce site Mercado Libre (Argentina's poor man's eBay) supports our hypothesis.

Figure 5.2. The Parmalat jersey, sold on an e-commerce site, next to an article of *El Gráfico* magazine, with Beto Marcico celebrating the 1992 championship. *Source*: Courtesy of mercadolibre.com

"La de Sanyo. Auténtica" is the header for the link to Adidas's 1994 River Plate design. The advertiser for that season was the Japanese appliance brand Sanyo. In this context, the usual way of phrasing the product is to list the team, designer, and advertiser in that order. The year of the jersey is optional, and is usually used to refer to minor variations. When the past needs to be symbolized, sellers do so either by including the name of a player of that era or by a reference to an advertiser that lasted a short period of time (like Sanyo for River Plate).[16]

Given the previous resistance, it is perplexing then that by the 2000s one of the largest spikes in sales for the team was not brought about by a particular championship, or by the arrival of a new design. To both the purist's and the designer's eyes, the 2002 Boca Juniors jersey looks the same: the colors are the traditional blue and yellow; the neckline is the same; the fabric is still dry-fit; the stripes are the same thickness; the insignia is in the same place; and there is no new team inscription. The only element that changed was the team sponsor.

The reference to advertisers has become such an important way of guaranteeing the authenticity of the product that facsimile producers

Figure 5.3. Counterfeit jerseys for Boca Juniors on the team's 2012 tour to Mendoza. Notice Martín Palermo's number 9 jersey with different advertising. *Source*: Author

have incorporated advertisements into their jerseys. If what had previously distinguished originals from copies was the incorporation of an advertiser into the jersey, then one of the few ways of trying to maintain the privilege of dictating the codes of use of a particular product and its availability was shattered. In the image above, taken outside of a stadium in Mendoza for the 2012 tour of Boca Juniors, we see how the changing of sponsors reflects what is on display: jerseys with old sponsor LG signal idolized striker Martín Palermo, who retired the previous season (Figure 5.3),[17] while jersey's sponsored by BBVA are for Juan Román Riquelme, still with the team at the time.

The designs, which were at first resisted, have over the long run been reappropriated by consumers, generating a new configuration. The new object afforded something that the previous one could not: how to make temporal sense of the different iterations of jerseys and teams, thanks to new designs and sponsors. Also, particular jerseys get closely aligned with the fate of the team, so if the team wins the championship, cup, or league, the brand and advertiser become both temporal and status markers for the fans; and all this while still affording fans the ability to give an account of themselves in which they love their team, as expressed in their love for the team's "authentic" jerseys. Moreover, the changes in design allow fans to further "express" their love for their team in shopping for as many design variations as possible (every time there is a change in sponsor, or a new alternate design, for instance).[18] For those who still insist on interpreting the authenticity of the jersey under the preexisting frame in which authenticity meant noncirculation of the original jersey design, there is one design option: attaching themselves to a "retro" design, investing with cathexis a simile that valorizes a "pastoral past" and negates the current state of affairs. Nike puts on display the product of an imagined pastoral past that it has, in fact, helped to destroy—a past of amateurism, of skill, loyalty, and dedication; an invented past when certain goods were not allowed to circulate; a past with no sponsorship of the jersey.

These are some of the available resources[19] present to still sustain the attachment to the football jersey-object as it was, pointing not toward the new established configuration but to competing partial objects[20] that afford some of the previous effects and claims on the self.

CONCLUSION

The arrival of branding and sponsorship profoundly destabilized the relationship between the soccer jersey, its design, materials, and the non-circulatory, totemic manner in which fans related to it, where colors and materials were constantly held to be stand-ins for effort and courage. The unfortunate realities of soccer economy, with teams increasingly dependent on what they could generate from sponsorship and advertisement rights, meant that soccer fans had to adapt and make do with the new jersey having elements historically considered "matter out of place" (Douglas 1966), and find how they could have a relationship with the jersey that would still be about the team and its players, and not just about the brand. They had to find new strategies to express their love, and vicariously their masculinity, now that the jersey was a site not just of social relationships, but also for disputed allegiance and capital flows.

What is it that the new object affords? What can people do with the new object that they could not with the old one? The new jersey, with its changing branding and sponsorship, allows fans to make sense of its temporal and status location. The production and design of three new models of jersey every year allows fans to express their sacrifice and love for the team—and their special status among similar aficionados—by paying for the multiple variations of what the Boca jersey has become. The constant novelty opens up a new avenue for the demonstration of love,[21] which never closes; it is a particular kind of sacrifice: if you really want to be a good fan, buy a new jersey! This proliferation of Boca-associated objects includes also the special collector items issued to celebrate the team's anniversary and particular accomplishments (e.g., a championship), allowing fans to freeze a moment in time and commemorate it via the Nike branded jersey, thereby showing how nationalism and branding can combine instead of excluding each other.

On the other hand, the new jersey fabric did not pass a particular trial of strength; by disposing of sweat, it did not allow fans to see what can be inscribed on the material from human activity. One of the basic lessons of the nationalism literature is that even if presented as homogeneous and horizontal, the nation is embodied differently by different actors, in this case the players and the fans. If the body of the player was a metonym for the nation, with the jersey as armor, allowing fans to see the pain and feel it via sweat, tears, and blood, then what happens to the emotions awoken in those in the stands when they can't—because of changes in materials—see the signs of devotion from the player? What is there for fans to do? Changing the fabric, but not the color, is equal to denationalization, as the connection between player and spectators is weakened when sweat is no longer part of the game.

If objects are the felicity conditions of certain interpretations, what is it that a branded object allows for? Can there be a "We of Boca"—to paraphrase both Lee and LiPuma (2002) and Benedict Anderson (1991) talking about the nation—in a Nike branded jersey? We could say that the generic jersey worked within a logic of symbolization (this object stands for x) while it also anticipated the semiotic operations behind branding. This made sure a jersey with its colors not only stood for something for someone (in the case of this team, grit, as I've shown in this chapter), but was also distinct from the jersey of other competing teams. While in its continuity the object cemented, in a totemic way, the identification between the team and its supporters, it also presented an indexical logic in which the jersey stood not just for itself but rather as a representative of other meanings. The semiotic operations of branding extended themselves in such a way that for fans, Nike—after twenty years—counts as a legitimate part of what makes Boca unique and distinctive. It has become integrated into the narrative of the powers of the team, even if there are constant fights in the attempts to transform its designs and materials. Part of what explains this is that even if the generic version of the jersey prevented the existence of surfeits, the logic of branding and the logic of nationalism are not antagonistic (as is the case with the logic of commodity exchange) but are both producers of uniqueness and singularity. It is the fight over *how* Boca is unique, and how this can be read and expressed in designs and materials, where competing claims get imprinted.[22]

Scholars in cultural sociology have explored objects as totems (Durkheim 1995; Alexander 2008a,b; Collins 2004); as the site for the imprinting of competing claims (Zubrzycki 2013a); as fetishes that give out instructions of use which constitute the boundary between groups (Bourdieu 1984); or as highly contextual stabilizations of agents and resources (symbolic interactionism for which humans have the power of defining the situation unilaterally). The final plea of this chapter is to understand all of these conceptualizations as gradients of cases, in which even in totem-like situations there is always the potential for more than one affordance; always the potential for the correspondence between affect, individual, and object to be less than a one-to-one homology; and in which what we need to investigate—and never take for granted—is the work of holding those correspondences together.

NOTES

1. The team won the Intercontinental Cup in 1977, 2000, and 2003, and was a runner-up in 2001 and 2007. It won the South American Club Cup six times (and was a runner-up four other times). It has won the national first division championship twenty-four times.

2. "Camiseta nuevo modelo," *Clarín*, 17 February 2003.

3. River was founded in the Boca neighborhood of Buenos Aires in 1901, and because of that some people call Boca and River "cousins." After a few unsuccessful nearby moves, the team relocated definitively in 1923 in the northern and wealthier part of the city, leaving behind the tenements and the dock. To make the contrast with Boca even sharper, during the 1930s—the early period of professionalization of football in Argentina—the team became known as the "Millionaires" because of the money they paid for the transfers of several star players (like Carlos Peucelle).

4. As Mary Douglas and Baron Isherwood (1979) remind us, goods are used as a system of classification, help us make sense of the social world, and allow us to share those meanings.

5. Usually the vendors at the door of the stadium chant, "*Hay gorro, bandera, vincha!*"—Caps, flags, headbands!

6. On this, see Garriga (2007), and Alabarces (2000).

7. Paula Urien, "Este negocio es un golazo," *La Nación*, 10 June 2001.

8. Reebok—then provider of the equipment for the Argentinean national team—had a competing technology called Hidromove, in which a special chemical component worked as a sponge that absorbed perspiration.

9. Nike also transformed the way in which products are presented in stores, resulting in several tags attached to the jersey and written in English in order to demonstrate the originality of the product. This was pivotal, since counterfeited jerseys with fake Nike logos are sold on the street at a fourth of the price.

10. www.eblog.com.ar/7597/la-camiseta-polemica/#sthash.eYiSDcce.dpuf (11 August 2009).

11. www.eldiaonline.com/boca-presenta-su-nueva-y-polemica-camiseta-violeta/ (11 January 2013).

12. The team wore a pink jersey for one year before the establishment of yellow and blue as the club's colors.

13. Natacha Pisarenko, "Boca Juniors presenta color polémico," *Associated Press*, 26 July 2013.

14. "El club diseñará su propia camiseta," *Clarín*, 3 February 1998; "La falta de sponsors, otro dolor de cabeza," *Clarín*, 26 February 1999.

15. Daniel Ruchelsman, "Carrera atrás de la Plata," *Clarín*, 27 January 1998.

16. Out of 144 entries on Mercado Libre, Boca jerseys had roughly 40 references to the advertiser in its header.

17. This could be seen even though fans—as I've briefly discussed—had protested in 2009 the inclusion of a sponsor with the red color of archrival River Plate on the heart of the jersey.

18. Paradoxically, the totemic logic becomes restored via buying every variation of the jersey.

19. One-of-a-kind commemorative jerseys also belong to this group; for instance, one with Japanese characters on the back of the shirt to celebrate the team winning the world team cup in Japan.

20. I take the term *partial object* (or object *a*) from Lacan (2007). While I do not aim to inscribe this article within the logic of his work, I thought it worth pointing out how the intertwined logic of object and self-stabilization and that of the Lacanian *object a* largely overlap.

21. This continues by other means the account of the self that fans give to themselves and others as devoted to the team.

22. The two logics become intertwined in a few venues in which the club and the brand coparticipate: the annual presentation of new designs, where team players and models pose with the new jerseys; the museum and boutique store

of Boca where, like in most museums, you can both celebrate the history of the team and buy Nike items to mark the occasion; and in the fact that trademarks (like the swoosh), the sponsor, and the dry-fit technology are ways of producing patina for an object that (re)presents Boca to the fans and to others (even in copies).

CHAPTER 6

That Banal Object of Nationalism

"Old Stones" as Heritage in the Early Days of French Public Television

Alexandra Kowalski

In his 1995 classic, *Banal Nationalism,* Michael Billig argued that nationalist commitments are most often produced through the routinization of national symbols rather than through pomp and other spectacular and passionate displays. This is especially the case, he argued, in the more stable and richer countries of the Western world. In this chapter I move the inquiry away from banal *nationalism* as a social-psychological phenomenon (Skey 2009; Billig 2009; Slavtcheva-Petkova 2014; Koch and Paasi 2016), and onto the banal *objects* of Western European nationalism. Focusing specifically on ordinary objects that define "heritage" in the late modern period, I reflect on these objects' introduction into the repertoire of national memory, on their construction, meaning, and effect. I do so through a semiotic analysis of the popular television show *Chefs d'œuvre en péril,* produced and broadcast on French public television (the ORTF) between 1964 and 1974, at the dawn of the heritage age.

Actors' reflexive work on what counts as "their" culture (Surak, Chapter 8 in this volume) demonstrates the complexity of the symbolic relationship between the ordinary and the extraordinary in routine forms of nationalist practice—a complexity that defies religious analogies with the sacred-profane boundary. The theory of banal nationalism captured this complexity through the metaphor of "unwaved, unsaluted, unnoticed . . . unflagging flags" (Billig 1995, 40–41). The process of "heritage-ization" exemplifies the same paradox. It is a process that erects quotidian objects and practices to a new level of cultural worth, but it is also one that profoundly banalizes the experience of cultural specificity and national uniqueness, anchoring it in mundane acts and routine practices. The chapter shows that *Chefs d'œuvre* shifted the focus from traditional objects of national pride (great historic sites, famous châteaux and cathedrals) to the often unremarkable vestiges of the past such as farmhouses, rural churches, and other instances of *petit patrimoine*. Not only did the program redirect citizens' attention to ordinary vestiges of the past, but it also problematized the presence of these vestiges in the rural and urban landscapes of the present.

How do banal objects come to feature in national imaginations in addition to extraordinary ones, and how do these two categories relate to each other symbolically? What kinds of social bonds do these ordinary objects create and support? And what does an object-centric approach contribute, in return, to our understanding of everyday nationalism? These are the three questions I seek to answer more particularly through the following analysis.

THE SHOW CHEFS D'ŒUVRE EN PÉRIL: HISTORICAL AND THEORETICAL PERSPECTIVES

In 1962, a young French journalist and amateur historian dedicated to the cause of historic monuments, Pierre de Lagarde, launched a prize competition under the name Concours Chefs d'œuvre en Péril (Masterpieces in danger) to reward the efforts of private preservationists. Specifically, the prize was meant to distinguish private projects that successfully salvaged or preserved a historic site or building. Public television was used to publicize it. The first televised snippets were brief one-to-two-minute calls for nominations illustrated through images of ruins and narrated in Lagarde's voice deploring the neglect of ancient architecture throughout the country. The first two calls were broadcast on the evening news in December 1962 and in February 1963. From February 1964 on, similar calls were broadcast approximately every two weeks in the fall and spring. In May the prize awards were announced in the evening news, and around mid-June, just before the schools' long summer recess, an award ceremony was broadcast. In May and June 1964 longer features started to be produced, which were broadcast about once a month at a later time in the evening. Shorter ads and longer substantive shows alternated with the same frequency in the following year; after a break in July and August, long-form documentaries were broadcast at least twice a month until the following June, and competition announcements between January and May.

Both the short announcements and the longer shows featured abandoned sites, old churches and farms, empty villages, and neighborhoods threatened by developers, as well as the modest, everyday-life heroes who restored or took care of them. Broadcasting followed the rhythm of the nation's civil year and was closely associated with the events of French citizens' everyday life: the season started in September and ended in June for the summer recess. In an age when there was only one national TV channel, airtime meant that programs, especially the evening news, reached out to virtually every citizen in the country. Families without a TV set would often go watch television in better-connected relatives' or neighbors' homes. An informal poll of acquaintances who were twenty or older in 1964 indicates that young adults in 1964 remember the show, or at least its name, from that decade or the following. All this suggests that the show was one of the media institutions that made France into an imagined community after World War II.

The Ministry of Cultural Affairs, created by Charles De Gaulle in 1959 and headed by writer André Malraux, supported the prize and the televised advertisements. Support was both financial and symbolic, at a time when the French president and his minister of cultural affairs were committed to improving the condition of ancient buildings and sites (Laurent 2003)—a time (mostly since forgotten) when old buildings' fate was controversial and municipalities' modernization plans unavoidably consisted in razing historic centers to make space for beltways and new housing.

The partnership with the government broke down in 1969, the last year of De Gaulle's presidency, but by then *Chefs d'œuvre en péril* had become a popular show. It was continuously produced and broadcast on public television until 1991. Prizes were awarded until 1974, when the program was temporarily stopped owing to a restructuring of public television, which involved the creation of two new channels (bringing the number to an amazing three!). When it returned to programming two years later, the success of *patrimoine* ("heritage" in Anglophone countries, "*patrimonio*" in Italy and Spain) worldwide had made it unnecessary to promote its cause. The word became idiomatic after 1975 and came to mean what we still understand by it today (Kowalski 2012). New meanings included intangible, ethnographic, and quotidian forms of culture and identity. A new generation of museums developed to reflect these aspects (Vergo 1989; Lumley 1988). Old open-air museums such as Colonial Williamsburg adopted period costumes and all the paraphernalia of fabricated authenticity that have since become familiar parts of the "heritage industry" (Handler 1997). New functions of authenticity and profitability were added to the older ones of education and edification. "Heritage" was the new name for cultural tourism, the latter a key component of tourism, itself an established sector of the global economy (Hewison 1987; Graham, Ashworth and Tunbridge 2000; Meskell 2015). In other words, *Chefs d'Oeuvre en Péril* joined, in the late 1970s, the movement it had helped spark in the previous decade.

The early decade of the *Chefs d'œuvre* prize competition on which I focus here (1964–74) is thus one in which burgeoning cultural change can be observed as it happened. It is also a period when change owed less to economic factors than to cultural and political dynamics, which set the stage for later economic transformations. "Heritage" was not yet the commodity it later became. It was certainly being assembled in ways that later made it easy to trade for profit, and it circulated among audiences that resembled consumers as much as they did citizens. Old stones, ancient buildings, and abandoned villages, however, were still cheap in the 1960s and were mostly undesirable commodities traded for symbolic rather than commercial profit. Restorations were made by amateurs and volunteers, who were often students; ancient properties were bought by teachers, craftspeople, artists, and a few young professionals—all holders more of cultural than of economic capital. Preservation was not the tool of economic and urban development that it became in the 1980s: "historic center" was not a planner's concept and *vieille ville* (old city) only connoted the smell of stray cats, the sight of overcrowded apartments without toilets or water connection, and prejudice against the migrant and working-class families that shared these spaces with craftspeople, all in search of cheap rents. The terms connoted, more generally, a serious social problem in the context of the drawn-out housing crisis that followed World War II (Newsome 2009).

Preservationists and residents had to mobilize, protest, and alert the public in order to (sometimes) obtain the modification or cancellation of development plans cast as operations of *nettoyage des taudis* (sanitization of slums) (Newsome 2009). Glorious medieval city centers such as Avignon's were taken down by developers without eliciting serious opposition (Balle 1997). When historic sites were controversial, what was disputed was not *what* counted as heritage but the very notion that *any* less-than-exceptional *artifact* might be still valuable enough to preclude its replacement by something more convenient, more modern, and conforming more to a perceived idea of the common good. Old buildings and sites had to be defended in an age when patrimonial consciousness was only budding. Such was precisely Pierre de Lagarde's struggle in *Chefs d'œuvre en péril*.

Cultural sociologists, especially in the United States, have mostly analyzed heritage and historic places through the lens of "memory studies" (Olick, Vinitzky-Seroussi, and Levy 2011). In this approach, artifacts and images are studied for their "symbolic" value as well as the "social forces" that are supposed to have produced them. Accordingly, the materiality of ancient objects and places in the eyes of a cultural sociologist tends to be either a pretext to human activity (when ruins happen to stand as metaphors of a community's past, for example), or a plain and simple outcome of human activity (when a monument is erected to celebrate Lincoln's memory, for example, or when the ruins of the previous example are said to be "constructed" as heritage).

Over the past decade and a half, however, scholars of culture have called for greater awareness of the importance of practice and objects (Latour 2007b; Calhoun and Sennett 2007; Tornatore 2010; Zubrzycki 2010), registering the impact of the "material turn" in qualitative social sciences (Miller 2005; Hicks and Beaudry 2010). This approach has implied looking at the ways in which the dyad of media and matter create and transform the everyday reality of identities (Urry 1990; Bajc 2006). What precisely an object-centric analysis does for the study of nationalism in general, and heritage in particular, is still an open theoretical and methodological question. In this chapter I mobilize the object-driven approach as a contribution to the study and theory of "banal national-ism" (Billig 1995)—the kind of routinized nationalism found more par-ticularly in consumer-capitalist and information societies of the postwar era. The relevance of the new materialism to this specific case owes to the historical centrality of objects and devices in both consumer capitalism and information technologies.

The example of heritage nationalism, analyzed below, supports but also permits to refine the thesis of banal nationalism. On the one hand, it confirms that the peculiar efficacy of ordinary nationalism lies in the very ordinariness of repeated experiences of shared symbols, made pos-sible in particular by mass media. On the other hand, the analysis sug-gests that this efficacy owes less to symbols and images themselves, as ideological stimuli of sorts, than to the multiple, overlapping physical entanglements which "banality" forces onto experience. In other words, banal nationalism is not so much or not only effective as a function of implicit and subconscious "flags" stamped on our everyday experiences, as Billig's theory goes, but more fundamentally as a function of the fet-ters of material ties, both social and physical, into which everydayness and banality, in and of themselves, weave practices. A focus on objects brings the materiality out of the apparent symbol.

Banality and materiality in *Chefs d'œuvre en péril* are as much the attributes of the works of art that are represented as they are the televi-sual experience of the show itself. Symbolic objects such as works of art and "realms of memory" do not lose any of their sacral aura by being reproduced and circulated through technologies of information and communication (Benjamin 1986; Nora 1984). Quite to the contrary, as Benedict Anderson (1991) once famously argued: nations exist through and because of such technologies. Nations are defined by the banality and the concreteness of the practices mediated, enabled, conditioned by objects perceived, internalized, manipulated, shared, and consumed. It is striking that the materiality of experience is as central to these theories of culture and identity in the modern age as it remains implicit. Michael Billig's theory of banal nationalism is no exception. "Banal national-ism" is a state of consciousness and an attitudinal fact that presupposes practical attachments and entanglements in a world of things which the theory never really considers for themselves—unless they can be reduced to discourses, messages, and symbols. Material entanglements are par-ticularly important to keep in mind when accounting for the strength of the bonds that banal nationalism creates—not in spite of its everyday-ness and ordinariness, but because of it.

CASTLES AND CHURCHES: IN THE SHADOW OF THE ROMANTIC RUIN

The term *chef-d'œuvre* (masterpiece) signifies a work of art, typically one with decorative function, that is unique by the originality and the quality of its craftsmanship.[1] It is thus the opposite of banal. The term however was used in the title of the television show as a blanket concept for things that are not usually called by that name: vernacular buildings such as farms, architectural ensembles including technical infrastruc-tures, and neighborhoods as well as towns, cities, or landscapes. Other notions used in the show—*trésor d'art, monuments*—sound equally at odds with the contents.

This dissonance does not simply reflect the producers' obvious and awkward effort at producing new symbolic value. It also reflects a larger cultural shift that was starting to happen. Lagarde could not mobilize a repertoire of heritage that didn't exist. In order to "upgrade" his mate-rial symbolically he had to rely instead on old-fashioned but still com-mon notions borrowed from the fields of the fine arts, connoisseurship, and high-end antiquities collecting. Heritage is less today about excep-tional "masterpieces" than about representative or "typical" things and places. It is less about special *objets* than it is about "realms" or expe-riential totalities involving multiple things, places, people, and actions; and it is less about aesthetic value than about memory and community (Nora 1984; McCrone, Morris, and Kiely 1995). The show's use of classi-cal aesthetic categories to name new objects of interest such as vernacu-lar architecture or urban landscapes signals that representations were starting to change at precisely that historical juncture.

The treatment of châteaux and churches in the first years of the show illustrates the pervasiveness of this intentional paradox. Religious and mil-itary architecture were by far the main types of architecture it covered. This reflected a conventional take on the meaning of "monuments." Churches and châteaux have traditionally been the national "ancient monuments" or "historic landmarks" both in national imaginations and in European states' registries of protected sites since the nineteenth century. The spread of the "Gothic" as a central motif in Romanticism durably anchored cathedrals in public culture and national imaginations, from Goethe's eulogies of the of Strasburg and Cologne cathedrals in 1877 and 1815, through Victor Hugo's first tirades against "demolishers" in 1825, to Ruskin's and Morris's defense of ruins from the 1850s on, and to Riegl, Dehio, and Dvorak's theories of *Denkmalpflege* between 1890 and the Great War. Widespread interest in "Gothic" architecture led to the inclusion of medieval fortresses as well in the pantheon of national monuments (Choay 2001; Glendinning 2013). Churches, abbeys, and châteaux became the archetypes of the Romantic ruins celebrated in works of fiction, documentary or fictionalized travel narratives, catalogues of ancient architecture for amateur or professional audiences, and the first guidebooks for travelers. Descriptions were often accompanied with reproductions—drawings, and later photographs. Borrowing from the Germanic brand of primordialist Romanticism, images of solitary buildings standing alone in pristine wilderness stood witness to the decay and the fragility of civilization, and became a cliché, ready for circulation and made to stay.

The persistence of Romantic motifs is very visible in *Chefs d'œuvre en péril*. They were particularly dominant in the first year of the show, when the point was to represent the "danger" (*péril*) threatening monuments and to convince audiences to care for ancient sites. Whether showing a modest countryside chapel in Brittany's wilderness or the magisterial, fortified Abbaye de Jumièges (Figure 6.1), the pathetic grandeur of ruins was magnified through frequent use of low-angle shots, and the decay of materials and structures was magnified through a focus on collapsed naves, stand-alone arches, missing roofs, gutted rooms. The Germanic origins of the ruin-in-nature cliché is aptly illustrated by two short episodes featuring German (13 March 1966) and Alsacian (9 October 1966) castles on the Rhine, an archetypal obsession of nineteenth-century nationalism.[2]

It is tempting to interpret these images through the trope of nostalgia and of the aesthetics of authenticity that defined the Romantic Western cult of the past (Lowenthal 1985) and that is familiar to cultural analysts. A closer examination of objects in the show, and of the show as an object, brings up a very different dimension of heritage, however—a dimension that has little to do with ideology, representation, and beliefs and everything to do with materiality, practice, and entanglements.

Figure 6.1. Fortified Abbaye of Jumièges, "France's most beautiful monument," according to Pierre de Lagarde. *Source*: Institut National de l'Audiovisuel/ ORTF, *Chefs d'oeuvre en Péril*, "Jumièges" episode, broadcast 15 March 1964

BANAL MASTERPIECES AND MONUMENTS

Unlike the handful of Notre Dames and of Carcassones restored by Viollet-le-Duc in the nineteenth century, the "monuments" and the "masterpieces" of *Chefs d'œuvre en péril* were numerous, ubiquitous, and most often relatively unremarkable. Even when it came to the "noble" edifices mentioned above, attention was drawn to the modest ones that came in many exemplars—the small chapels and calvaries that dotted the Breton countryside, the plethora of Germanic fortresses in Alsace, and village churches everywhere. The monuments of *Chefs d'œuvre* were not all that monumental anymore. Vernacular architecture started being celebrated on the show already in the fall of 1964, the first season in which longer substantive features were broadcast independently from the short announcements advertising the prize competition. One of the features dealt with "ancient neighborhoods," one with Paris's Latin Quarter, and in December 1964 already the first feature about "abandoned villages" was broadcast.

The producers' gaze remained aestheticizing, shaped by the language and culture of "fine arts." The dominant regime of valuation through which they assessed the objects they introduced to the public remained that of the masterpiece, the "unique" artwork, rather than the representative one, or the "dear" one, as became common later. But it was now applied to ordinary, vernacular objects that were representatives of common types rather than inherently exceptional ones. In the same way that the ordinary tea culture in Japan acquires an extraordinary quality through the reflexive process that converts it into a national ritual (Surak, in this volume), the conversion of old farmhouses and small chapels into *patrimoine* through discourse and media representation projected some of the aura of "masterpieces" (the big monuments and sublime landmarks of national memory) onto what was otherwise commonly referred to as *les vieilles pierres* (old stones).

Such labor of apparently upward conversion of the audience's gaze was a key mission of the show. The host repeated it many times over the years: "the most humble houses," "the most modest objects of everyday life" were in some ways as important as the greatest "monuments," and deserved attention and care. At the same time, however, the audience was emphatically reminded of the modesty of the show's objects. The symbolic conversion of these unremarkable objects into heritage was thus not a simple upgrading of low-value objects into higher-value ones. The value hierarchy between important and "modest" objects was maintained. The latter were granted a value of their own however, a value that was paradoxically related to the fact that they had apparently none. They were valuable precisely because value was hidden and difficult to perceive. A new category of valuables was in the process of being created.

"The strength and influence of civilizations is not only measured through the strength and influence of the monuments they erect, but also through the skill [*art*] with which the most humble dwellings were built. . . . Their architecture is perhaps less spectacular, but how much closer it is to our hearts," states the host in the episode entitled "Les villages abandonnés" (8 December 1964). If the piece on ancient urban centers features the cathedral of Notre Dame de Paris, it is precisely as a counterpoint to the narrator's actual interest in "hidden cloisters and fountains," in "the charm and picturesque of Rouen's timber-frame houses," and in the ornamentation on facades. "Is it enough to save [Troyes's] churches?" asks the host at the end of the episode. "Is it even logical to spend millions for their restoration if the admirable houses that surround them are not also preserved? Don't these houses make the charm of the city too; aren't they inseparable from the important monuments—to quote Stendhal, as the soldiers around their captain?" ("Les quartiers anciens," 6 May 1964).

Great monuments are in the frame, and in a way even remain its center. Nonetheless the focus is on the totality they form with ordinary objects and nearby buildings. The latter provide architectural context, weaving them into a fabric that makes the "atmosphere" and the "picturesque" of a place. Together they constitute a historic landscape. Through the soldier-houses, the memorial function of the monument is overridden at the same time as it is enhanced by the atmospheric or experiential function of these new *chefs d'œuvre*. The show presents in this way the popular—one might say in this case populist—version of elite opinions that were made into policies around the same time: in 1962, the "Malraux law" provided a legal frame that enabled the state to register and protect historic areas (neighborhoods, old urban centers, and ancient villages). Picturesque village landscapes would become the centerpiece of French heritage policy (*politiques du patrimoine*) at the end of the 1970s, and of the economy of decentralization itself in the 1990s (Kowalski 2012). The 1960s was the time when they were mainstreamed through public TV.

The celebration of a banal past was anticipated in the 1960s in several ways. Besides the addition of new units of analysis (village, neighborhood, city) and new objects (farmhouses), ordinary objects were also celebrated as "beautiful" objects: a well, a fountain, a sink. Store signs were already an important part of the urban décor (e.g., in the "Rouen-Genève" episode, 28 November 1965), which later episodes[3] would extensively and repeatedly discuss.

Figure 6.2. Abbey of Hambye, Normandy. *Source*: Institut National de l'Audiovisuel/ORTF, *Chefs d'oeuvre en Péril*, "Hambye" episode, broadcast 27 February 1966

CONTEMPORARY OBJECTS IN ANCIENT LANDSCAPES, ANCIENT THINGS IN MODERN SETTINGS

Chefs d'œuvre en péril also gives a large place to the quotidian of the inhabitants of historic places. Farming tools and farm animals for example are a frequent motif, often placed in the foreground of a ruin. Their meaning in the camera's gaze is ambiguous. They partly signify the rural heritage that once made France into a major international economic player in Europe; a quainter and more authentic lifestyle; or simply a picturesque tableau. But the rusted harrows and carts look like they have been abandoned long ago and stand also as a kind of visual and material pollution. The latter meaning is particularly obvious when these things are featured in the path of the gaze toward a stone vault or stained glass, in uncanny harmony with the ghostlike buildings that are

Figure 6.3. Sausage stall, St. Pierre church, in "one of the most beautiful, one of the purest towns of France, Senlis, city of many belltowers," according to Pierre de Lagarde. *Source*: Institut National de l'Audiovisuel/ORTF, *Chefs d'oeuvre en Péril*, "Senlis" episode, broadcast 16 February 1964

the main objects of concern. There is just one small symbolic step separating the seemingly bucolic image of cows grazing in front of a derelict abbey eaten up by vines and grass (Figure 6.2) and an exercise in peasant shaming. That distance is crossed when commentary and traveling shots turn into a litany of clutter—live animals, clothes, cars, and sausages—in the mystical light of Senlis's Gothic churches, for example (Figure 6.3). From the 1980s, several episodes featured open-air museums, museums of agriculture, and other celebrations of "ye ol' times" that have come to define heritage. In the 1960s, the mundane parts of local culture had not all been transformed into valuable "realms of memory."

Urban landscapes exude similar ambiguity. Clothes hanging between the frames of mullioned windows, old ovens abandoned or maybe for

sale on the side of a street, the effervescence of a commercial neighborhood simmering with the activity of butchers and other merchants in the
early hours of the morning, and of course cars everywhere, the vehicles
of postwar modernity (Ross 1996)—these make the material environment in which "monuments" are set. A hasty cultural sociology could
again project nostalgia on these images of declining countryside and
destructive modernity. But nostalgia is only a fleeting nuance in a project that fundamentally and explicitly celebrates "life" and claims to pre-
fer inhabited, commercial neighborhoods to *villes-musées sans vie* (dead
museum-cities). As to the remains of the dying peasantry, their appearance is only briefly deplored and seems easily redeemed by the work of
enlightened locals to revive villages and restore houses.

There is indeed another mundane materiality that the show valued
positively. It is that of people who cared for ancient things. *Amateurs
de belles choses* (lovers of beautiful things), they were sometimes long-
time residents of these places, sometimes recent settlers: artists, craftspeople, or young couples from urban areas in search of patina, cheaper
real estate, or inspiration—"early gentrifiers" of sorts. This population
was the pool from which *Chefs d'œuvre en péril* drew its candidates and
prize recipients, a small crowd of modest and admirably down-to-earth
heroes. Contrast the orderly picture offered by the personal surroundings of amateurs of ancient things with the chaos of ruins and other
neglected "masterpieces" discussed above. Monsieur Julien, a deserving
farmer who restored "with his own monies" a "ravishing manor" in Normandy, is shown in a preppy gentleman-farmer's outfit among metal-
lic milk containers meticulously emptied, cleaned, and tilted against a
wood-framed house ("Manoir de Coupesarte," 23 October 1966). Unlike
the sausages hanging in bunches in the dirty disorder of the abandoned
Senlis cathedral's market (Figure 6.3), Madame Javosse's sausages are
lined up neatly against a background of clean tiles, under the wood ceiling she is praised for having restored (Figure 6.4).

The show consistently placed ancient objects, both noble and ordinary,
in the décor of "modern" banality and, conversely, "modern" paraphernalia in the décor of ancient houses and cities. In an era that preceded
the concerted uses of ancient architecture in gentrification programs
(and urban gentrification *tout court*), an era when the legal tools to preserve neighborhoods and villages were still new, this merging of tastes
and worlds was radically new. The rules of taste were not fully settled.

Figure 6.4. "Madame Javosse is a sausage maker in Dijon, which doesn't mean she's not an art lover." *Source*: Institut National de l'Audiovisuel/ORTF, *Chefs d'oeuvre en Péril*, "Maisons du XVème a Dijon" episode, broadcast 30 October 1966

But an avant-garde was there already, imposing its aesthetic and life-style choices and flaunting its stylistic audacity—with Lagarde's help and stamp of approval. In Lyon, for example ("Quartiers anciens de Lyon," 25 January 1970), a bourgeois couple exhibited "their" ceiling (a ceiling with exposed beams) paired with "modern" designer furniture. The vestiges of cities' commercial history (the heavy curves of cut stone arches, windows and their signs, underground storage spaces under metal doors) were insistently shown to be reoccupied by various consumer goods and their owners, from Madame Javosse and her hams to a designer store owner in Old Lyon.

In a 1964 episode featuring volunteers rebuilding villages, the latter are called "sincere people" [*des hommes de cœur*] who care about their art, and only their art." They were pictured as leaders and teachers of civilized manners: "Artists can show the right example," continued the host. "For example, a lot of farmers in Ardèche and elsewhere renovate their houses with roughcast, and that's quite a pity." All these individuals were pioneers of the new good taste, which required them to be also *amateurs de vieilles pierres* (lovers of old stones).

THE NATION REASSEMBLED
THROUGH THINGS

Chefs d'œuvre alludes on occasion to France's creative genius; cites a couple of famous preservationists such as Victor Hugo or Chateaubriand; and deplores French carelessness by comparison with the English, German, Italian, and Swiss meticulous watchfulness in matters of *patrimoine artistique*. Apart from such occasional "flaggings," or uses of overtly national(ist) categories, there is little allusion to or praise for national achievements. And yet the nation is present everywhere in the banality of its old stones. It is not a great nation of remarkable men and buildings. It is rather a tight fabric of modest and modern individuals with mundane and honest concerns, a crowd of old stones in ordinary landscapes. The show does not invoke great heroes' great feats; rather, it rewards ordinary people for modest gestures of painstaking labor. It does not teach hoi polloi about history, famous architects, the history of styles; instead, it shows people in everyday struggles with "beautiful" but badly damaged objects. No nationalist indoctrination is at work here. Instead, an ethics of work and entrepreneurialism directed toward unusual objects is offered as a model of behavior.

Banality is not just an attribute of nationalistic attachments in contemporary society. It also describes the very objects and channels of such attachments. Banality therefore works through bodies. It ties bodies through material practices. What then are, more precisely, the practices that tie humans to monuments and, through the latter, to each other? Let us discus briefly four practices which crucially brought the nation together in and through *Chefs d'œuvre en péril*: the production, the occupation, the consumption, and the performance of objects of heritage.

First, objects of heritage are produced through a *collective labor of restoration*. The appeal of the ruin according to *Chefs d'œuvre en péril*, if there is one, lies not so much in the derelict Romanticism of buildings falling apart as it does in the buzzing community life that the salvage, restoration, and reoccupation generate. The volunteer movement that is shown at work on restoration sites is the positive and true face of the ruin, says *Chefs d'œuvre* (Figure 6.5). Offspring of the 1960s' student culture, volunteers climb on roofs, shop, eat dinner, play guitar at the campfire, and cook together; they sleep in tents, work in teams, and open *chantiers* (excavation or restoration sites) in fanfares of brass instruments. Interviews by the television crew show that they mean well, want to pay society back for something they have received from it, and think highly of what they, like everyone else, call "beautiful things" and "old stones" ("Le Marais," 2 December 1967; "Quartiers anciens de Lyon," 25 January 1970).

The positive, forward-looking face of heritage is also embodied by virtuous individuals rather than by groups—individuals such as the Breton schoolteacher, the Norman priest, Monsieur Julien the gentleman farmer, and the Parisian aristocrat. The lone wolves tend to obscure the pack, however: either the groups of student volunteers they assemble and lead, or the diverse types of obstacles that make up their history—matter and geography, developers, municipalities, tourists, and other avatars of the ignorance, neglect, greed, and "vandalism" that *Chefs d'œuvre* makes a duty to finger-point and stigmatize. The historic site is a place of intense, disputed interaction.

If ruins are often depicted as lonely, deserted, miserable objects reminiscent of Romantic lithographs, their misery only makes sense in the context of its relationship with current human activity—such as that seen in the farms or the stores or the camps. As a result, the solitary ruin does not signify a passive state such as the soul's solitude or civilization's mortality, as in the Romantic trope. It is instead a presentist signifier of the culture of monument admirers and restorers advocated by the show. Ruins are primarily problems to be fixed through human labor; there is little complacency in the spectacle of dereliction they offer. And locals, when they are not part of the active crowds of restorers, are the human equivalent of ruins: asked about their memories and recent developments, they feature as passive witnesses of their own decline and of the countryside in an era of rural desertification and urban tertiarization. They are also sometimes cast as a category of vandals-by-ignorance, therefore as a nuisance.

Second, historic sites are occupied through a *process of physical discovery and settlement*. The "chef d'œuvre" of *Chefs d'œuvre en péril* is an

Figure 6.5. Student volunteers restoring a church in Brittany. *Source*: Institut National de l'Audiovisuel/ORTF, *Chefs d'oeuvre en Péril*, "Chapelles Bretonnes" episode, broadcast 1 September 1966.

object to be discovered and appropriated. The imperial-colonial trope of discovery might be a result of the process by which France "brought the empire back home" after decolonization, as argued by Herman Lebovics (2004), or an inheritance from nineteenth-century travelogue literature where the past was already a "foreign country" (Lowenthal 1985). In any case, new technologies of reproduction played a key role in spreading this motif and rooting it deeply in the rapidly expanding public of middle-class consumers after World War II.

With the spread of household cameras, movies and photographs became a staple of family life. As early as February 1965 the short-format prize advertisements asked candidates to submit applications "if possible with a photograph." In the summer of 1971, Pierre de Lagarde launched a print companion for the show, the illustrated magazine *Monuments en péril.* In 1973 the magazine launched a photographic competition with the alleged aim of completing a survey of France's architectural landmarks. The picture publicizing the survey showed two young figures, a boy and a girl, camera in hand, their backs to the viewer, bent forward as if peeking inside a forbidden or hidden zone. Each of them is pushing open one of the two panels of a heavy metal gate. Between these dark shapes, a beautiful abandoned manor sits in the back of a large garden.

The motif of discovery was central to the first long-form episodes on neighborhoods. The first one mentions "hidden cloisters and fountains," and "discovering in the back of the *traboules* [passages cutting through blocks] the marvelous palaces created for the pleasure of a few privileged individuals." Facades are interesting, but only as much as what lies behind them, beyond the public spaces of the streets. The imperative echoes many times: "one has to enter inside property lots" to be able to see the marvelous details that matter: the "excellent doors," the iron work on balconies, the "ravishing courtyards with harmonious scale," and "the flights of stairs, the iron work, the magnificent things that no one has the right to destroy" ("Quartiers anciens," 6 May 1964). Whatever is inside the lots "is what makes the history of Paris's architecture." And one of the commonplace stories about the rehabilitation of Old Lyon, generously echoed by *Chefs d'œuvre en péril*, is that of the discovery of *le plafond* ("the ceiling," pronounced with a slight stress on "the") by the lucky new owners of old apartments. *Le plafond* stands in eloquent simplicity for *plafond à la française*—a wood ceiling with exposed beams, a precious product of ancient craft previously hidden by the clutter of a plasterboard ceiling meant to hide messy entanglements of pipes and electric wires while making it more economical to heat the rooms in the winter.

Settlers are understandably an important part of this new world that is being discovered. They are their own category of middle-class heroes. In the December 1964 episode on abandoned villages, the latter's new occupiers are identified with interesting sociological sharpness: they are "the artists, the artisans, the antiques dealers [who] take over." In other instances they are called "pioneers" ("Maisons rurales de l'Aveyron," 16 March 1968). Several young couples are also featured in shows documenting new settlements in abandoned Provencal villages, and some of them are returning locals ("Villages abandonnés," 8 December 1964).

Thirdly, *heritage objects are consumed.* This happens, as far as the show is concerned, through cathodic transmission. In the 1960s historic sites were commodities in a limited, protocommercial sense—primarily as a reference circulated by means of "mechanical reproduction." *Chefs d'œuvre* participated in this process of early commodification. Beyond converting ancient sites into exchangeable, sharable images, mass media wove them into a world of already existing commodities—consumer goods produced and enjoyed by the large swaths of middle-class baby boomers born on the eve of the unprecedented economic growth of the *Trente Glorieuses*, the thirty glorious years that followed World War II.

The charm of this new bourgeoisie makes itself discrete in the first years of the show. It becomes less so in the course of the 1970s. At the end of the 1970s, the new taste for hybrid interior décors displaying modernity in a shell of patina surfaces frequently in the show. Advocates of historic preservation double up as defenders of neighborhood cleanliness and beautification, and their tone and syntax suggest that they belong to a privileged class of urban socialites. They praise the order and good taste of urban furniture in Swiss cities. They deplore architectural innovation and the allegedly "inhuman" environment of *nouveaux quartiers*. And discussion rolls at great length on the issue of the most desirable shape for Parisian trash cans ("Le décor de la ville," 12 June 1980).

Fourth and last, *heritage is performed*. During the period that interests us here mostly, the show was primarily a companion format to an award competition. As such it was not so much a *representation* of heritage as a *performance* of heritage, both in the dramaturgical and in the speech-theoretical senses of the term (Callon 2007; Butler 2010). *Chefs d'œuvre* offered the spectacle of people producing, occupying, and consuming heritage, and being rewarded for it (dramaturgical sense); and it performed itself the spectacle of heritage by producing, appropriating, and packaging ancient monuments for consumption and circulation in the new form of a TV show (speech-theoretical sense).

In this context, performing heritage refers not just to the broadcasting of images of monuments and to the production of "meaning," as classical cultural sociology would have it. "Performance" here means that citizens were physically enrolled, through the materiality of their TV sets on the one hand, and of their built environment on the other, in a new societal project. *Chefs d'œuvre en péril* was the name of a project through which the nation was brought together with cyclical regularity. Its aim was not to spread ideas or bind citizens through ritual but, more simply and more effectively, to teach new ways of dealing with an unremarkable but ubiquitous object that posed a number of practical problems, and solved a few others.

CONCLUSION

The "historic monuments" of yesteryear used to be objects of nationalist ideology. The banal monuments of the budding heritage age became objects of practice. No longer beliefs, they are the very stuff the nation is made of—material for a sustained relationship among a heterogeneous, large, and changing totality that was assembled and kept together through them. Not only the representation and symbols of the nation were transformed, but the very material and experiential reality of ancient sites was too.

Like tea in Japan (Surak, in this volume), old stones became part of the French nationalist imagination through a reflexive process that singles out cultural objects and practices and reclassifies them symbolically as remarkable ones. Information technologies were instrumental in this process. The use of mass media in our case reflects an educated elite's effort to enroll broad swaths of the population in the preservationist project. By calling objects of *petit patrimoine* "masterpieces" and "monuments," the show reallocated some of the aura of the great national monuments onto less significant ones. I have also argued, however, that the latter were made into a separate category with its own value and interest, altering the overall taxonomy. "Old stones" and other "modest monuments" have little individual worth but great value as a collective totality—as a landscape, a décor, or an environment through which "quality of life" and social solidarity can be improved.

The kinds of social bonds which these ordinary objects created and maintained were not only or primarily ideological. They were material. "Old stones" stood in the 1960s for the concrete problem posed by ancient real estate in the growing economy of the *Trente Glorieuses*. They were the object of debates, controversies, and policies. This puts the present analysis of heritage as an example of banal nationalism at odds with the bulk of historical and cultural analyses of heritage. The latter tend to look at the phenomenon as an ideational one, in which "identities" are "invented" and reproduced in the everyday life of gullible masses through rituals and other delusional tales of national greatness

(Hobsbawm and Ranger 1983; Lowenthal 1985). Object-driven analysis of the early heritage age shows precisely that these kinds of ideological mechanisms are secondary, if they define heritage at all. Heritage is primarily a practice-based and object-mediated culture.

The object-centric approach to heritage permits an explanation of the durability and strength of the heritage culture over the decades, and the latter's contribution to the durability of nations in general. In an age of commodities and information, beliefs and ideas have chances to be mediated and embodied through long and complex chains of things, images, practices, and social worlds. Such embodiments and mediations perpetuate and reinforce the nation as a form while making nationalist ideology often dispensable.

At a general level, finally, defining both heritage and banal nationalism by reference to the world of practice and matter that distinguishes them from nonbanal, "hot," celebratory, and explicit/textual forms of nationalism makes much theoretical sense. Banal nationalism is a cold nationalism that is supported specifically by commodity circulation in capitalist societies. If commodities make convenient supports for flags (Billig 1995, 41), the source of their specifically *banalizing* effect lies elsewhere—namely in the circulation, reproduction, and ubiquity of objects that inscribe them (and the flags they might bear) in a quotidian of taken-for-granted things and practices. The classical theory of banal nationalism muddied this basic fact when defining it as a set of "ideological habits" (Billig 1995). Within a world of commodities and circulation, some types of nationalisms are less banal than others in that they keep flagging objects (Molnar, this volume). In mainstream heritage nationalism the flags are often left aside or buried under mounts of other signifiers that perpetuate the nation indirectly. In the same way that archaeological artifacts contain ethnic identities that don't necessarily say their name when they speak through science (Greenland, in this volume), old stones in common heritage culture index an identity while talking about other things. The object-centric approach to banal nationalism opens up an entirely new agenda of cultural comparisons.

NOTES

1. All English-language citations from the show are my translation.

2. The titles of individual episodes are as listed in the databases of the Institut National de l'Audiovisuel public archive (INAthèque, Bibliothèque Nationale de France), where the *Chefs d'œuvre en péril* collection was viewed and researched for this chapter.

3. "Toulouse," 11 May 1968; "Les billes belges," 3 April 1977; "Quartiers anciens," 25 May 1978; "Les quartiers anciens de Lyon," 25 January 1970; "Le décor de la ville," 12 June 1980.

CHAPTER 7

The Mythical Power of Everyday Objects

The Material Culture of Radical Nationalism in Postsocialist Hungary

Virág Molnár

Scholarship on postsocialist nationalism has focused overwhelmingly on the dramatic post-1989 surge of ethnic nationalism that escalated into violent struggles of self-determination and civil wars in the Balkans and across former Soviet republics in Central Asia (e.g., Ignatieff 1995; Oberschall 2000; Oushakine 2010; Wimmer 2013). Less attention has been paid to other more mundane and less violent practices of postsocialist nationalism that emerged after the fall of socialism and can be characterized by strong symbolic and performative elements (Brubaker et al. 2006; Zubrzycki 2006, and this volume; Pilkington 2012). This chapter suggests that these new articulations and repertoires of symbolic nationalism warrant closer attention because despite their seeming banality, they have significantly contributed to the rise of new forms of radical nationalism across Central and Eastern Europe, particularly in countries such as Russia or Hungary (Feischmidt et al. 2014; Molnár 2016; Pilkington and Pollock 2015).

A relatively new development in the postsocialist context is also the rapid commodification of radical nationalist sentiments and the parallel emergence of a vigorous cultural industry that supplies a multitude of props for the expression and enactment of radical nationalist identities. The creation of cultural niche economies that carry political significance by reworking the symbolic lexicon and material culture of national and ethnic identification is an overlooked aspect of market transition in postsocialist countries. This is why the following analysis explores the intersections between markets, material culture, and new forms of nationalism in contemporary Hungary by looking at the manufacturing, sale, and consumption of radical nationalist commodities and services. It argues that the increasing right-wing radicalization of Hungarian politics and the growth of "uncivil" publics have been fueled by an expanding industry that effectively turns these attitudes into commercial products.

The larger research project focuses on four key areas of radical nationalist cultural production: First, *book publishers* that explicitly specialize in printing and disseminating nationalist literature. Second, *heritage tourism* to neighboring countries (especially to Transylvania, Romania) that aims to build bridges to diaspora Hungarians. Cross-border tourism strives to symbolically reintegrate diaspora Hungarians into the Hungarian nation and sustain the idea of a "Greater Hungary" which includes the territories that were detached from Hungary in 1920 as a result of the Treaty of Trianon.[1] Third, *national rock bands* that have codified a new, economically successful genre of political popular music. These bands are chief agents of updating historical motifs and narratives of mythic nationalism to fit contemporary social and political circumstances. And finally, *clothing brands* that market explicitly nationalist fashion items and have built extensive online distribution networks that also provide a platform for marketing other popular nationalist cultural products.

By showing how consumer objects play a significant role in giving expression to new forms of radical nationalism, the chapter highlights an important dimension of everyday or "banal" nationalism (Billig 1995; Brubaker et al. 2006; Edensor 2002; Fox and Miller-Idriss 2008; Löfgren 1989). This analytical lens helps to demonstrate that contemporary right-wing radicalism is not a codified political ideology but a more fluid subculture in which expressive symbols, material objects, rituals, everyday consumption, and lifestyle patterns are essential carriers of political convictions and markers of group boundaries. Everyday material objects also contribute to reconfiguring the boundaries between (official) politics and the public sphere, allowing radical nationalist discourse to penetrate mainstream political discourse.

The analysis proceeds by first engaging with various literatures that map how economic processes—most importantly, commodification—interact with and are shaped by national and ethnic identities. This survey shows that the commercialization of radical nationalism does not really fit any of the key categories discussed in the existing literature, and aims to suggest ways in which the conceptual framework of the literature can be expanded to accommodate this outlier case. To highlight this unique dynamics, the second half of the chapter develops in-depth empirical case studies of book publishing and clothing brands as key areas of radical nationalist cultural production.[2]

INTERSECTIONS OF THE ECONOMY AND NATIONAL/ETHNIC IDENTITY

Scholarship that probes the influence of nationalism and ethnicity over economic process covers a large interdisciplinary terrain from the political economy of ethnic nationalism to sociological research into ethnic enclaves to the anthropological study of nation branding. As this literature remains scattered across various fields, in the following sections I will bring disparate strands of scholarship into conversation with each other in order to build a conceptual apparatus mindful of the commercialization and material aspects of radical nationalism.

The relationship between the economy and nationalism is most extensively explored in the international political economy literature on economic nationalism (Helleiner 2002; List 1904). This body of scholarship examines the connections between nationalism and economic policies from a macroeconomic perspective and can be traced back to the late nineteenth century, to the work of the German economist Friedrich List, who was undoubtedly the most influential advocate and theorist of economic nationalism at the time (Helleiner 2002; List 1904). The term first became widely used in the interwar period in the twentieth century although its precise meaning remained diffuse (Helleiner 2002). In general, it came to denote a set of economic policies and practices including trade protectionism, statism, and autarky whose main aim was to champion the economic interests of individual nations. Economic nationalism, routinely contrasted with economic liberalism and the latter's dogged emphasis on free trade, treated the two as not simply competing but diametrically opposed economic doctrines (Helleiner 2002; Helleiner and Pickel 2005). Recently, there has been a revival among political economists in thinking about the relevance of economic nationalism in the context of globalization (Helleiner 2002; Helleiner and Pickel 2005; Nakano 2004). These scholars have argued for a renewed approach that takes the actual nationalist content of economic nationalism more seriously, instead of reducing it to a fixed set of interventionist policy instruments (Helleiner 2002; Nakano 2004). When changing meanings and techniques of national identity and nationalism are placed at the core of defining economic nationalism, such as food security or environmentalism, it becomes evident that this paradigm can be associated with a broad range of policy prescriptions and might even include policies that are not antithetical to neoliberalism, the most recent incarnation of economic liberalism (Helleiner 2002; Pickel 2005).

At first, preoccupations of the international political economy literature might seem fairly remote from the aims of this chapter with its focus on how consumer objects serve as everyday instruments for cultivating and reaffirming national identity. But recent studies that emphasize the greater diversity inherent in the repertoire of economic nationalism also draw attention to the importance of consumer sovereignty and cultural industries.[3] They highlight how economic nationalists rally around policy efforts that seek to protect and reassert distinct national cultures feared to be progressively undermined by globalization and neoliberal free trade. The political economist Patricia Goff (2005), for instance, examines two recent agricultural initiatives within the European Union: the restrictions on the circulation of GMOs (genetically modified organisms), and the elaborate system of geographical indications that give producers of artisanal foodstuffs exclusive rights to product names (e.g., Roquefort cheese, Prosciutto di Parma, Scotch whiskey). She shows that both initiatives go beyond just shielding local producers from international competition. They "seek to preserve and promote a set of shared understandings, cultural values, or social practices bound up with evolving notions of national security and held dear by a significant portion of a national citizenry" (183). National security in this context is increasingly understood not in terms of territorial sovereignty, but is reframed around notions of "food sovereignty" (safety, quality, and authenticity) and "cultural sovereignty" (protection of national cultures and local traditions).[4] Two other chapters in this volume explore these themes further: Alexandra Kowalski on the discovery of heritage, and Fiona Greenland on the state's use of potshards to claim sovereignty over a territory.

In a related vein, food production and consumption have for long constituted an important economic arena where questions of ethnicity and nationalism have repeatedly assumed center stage beyond mere discussions of protectionism. In fact nations are often imagined and consumed in everyday life in culinary terms either by declaring some aspects of their cuisine unique or associating national belonging with regular or ritual consumption of particular foods. Mark Weiner (1996) shows how Coca-Cola came to be cemented not only as an icon of American consumer society but of the American nation both in the United States and abroad during World War II, offering one of the best examples of what Roland Barthes (2009) has called a "totem-drink." Similarly, in a recent book on the historically evolving relationship between the tea ceremony and Japanese national identity Kristin Surak (2013) suggests that the iron grip of the *iemoto* system[5] over objects and practices of the tea ceremony is also bolstered by definite economic interests and constitutes a "set of modern business corporations invested in the Japaneseness of the practice they sell" (14). In her chapter in this volume, she goes further to argue that the spaces, objects, and practices of the Japanese tea ceremony offer a concentrated experience of Japaneseness by virtue of transforming the ordinary into the extraordinary. In the postsocialist context, the anthropologist Melissa Caldwell (2002) chronicles the immense popularity of nationalist food practices in 1990s Russia. She draws on an ethnographic study of food consumption in Moscow to reveal how Russians link their personal food experiences to a collectively shared idea of Russianness. She finds that "domestic food producers, store clerks and customers collaborate to classify foods and other products as either 'Ours' or 'Not Ours' and describe local goods as superior to foreign goods in terms of taste, quality and healthfulness" (295). The example of food nationalism thus underscores how, ironically, it is often consumer objects that serve the most fundamental and universal human needs that become essential markers of ethnic and national identity to function as crucial cultural signs.

The last strand of scholarly literature focuses primarily on ethnicity, exploring its economic significance in the context of contemporary migration processes, in the areas of immigration and tourism in particular. Economic sociologists produced a vast and insightful literature on ethnic enclaves that proved to be integral to the development of the entire subfield of economic sociology (Wilson and Portes 1980; Waldinger 1986, 1993). They demonstrate how ethnic niche economies, like the one established by Cuban immigrants in Miami, became a key vehicle for immigrant incorporation in the late twentieth-century United States (Wilson and Portes 1980). These enclave economies that are often built around immigrant-owned small firms do not only carve out distinctive niches in the labor market but also help to generate and maintain demand for distinctive ethnic products consumed by immigrants (and their families) employed in these industries. In some instances, like in the cases of Chinatowns or Koreatowns located in U.S. cities, spatially concentrated ethnic niche economies become attractive to local outsiders and even international tourists, giving way to a sort of second-order commodification of ethnic markers and identities that is now simultaneously aimed at members of out-groups (Lee 1992; Lin 1998; Zhou 1992, 2004).

It is precisely this twist that John and Jean Comaroff (2009) take under closer scrutiny in their book with the equally provocative and evocative title of *Ethnicity, Inc.* They explore how the politics of ethnicity was catapulted into the marketplace and how it is being transformed by the commercialization of culture at large as well as by turning ethnic groups into business ventures, or "ethnopreneurs" (Comaroff and Comaroff 2009; Surak 2010, 2012a). As a result, we see the proliferation of ethnic products and ethnic marketing, the rapid expansion of heritage industries and genealogical tourism (e.g., tourist tours to experience the Shipibo way of life in the Peruvian Amazonas), and the global circulation of handicraft items manufactured by indigenous artisans in the Global South (e.g., Wherry 2008, for Thailand and Costa Rica). A variant of this literature deals with the commercialization of national distinctiveness and heritage by focusing on the spread of nation branding and its entanglement with globalization and neoliberal corporatization (Bandelj and Wherry 2011; Kania-Lundholm 2014; Kowalski 2011; Rivera 2008).

While all of the above literatures illuminate crucial aspects of the nexus between the economy and nationalism/ethnicity and identify key mechanisms through which national and ethnic affiliation is infused with commodification and material objects, I argue that none of them captures the case of the specialized niche market of radical nationalism. Namely, radical nationalist consumer culture in Hungary commodifies national identity, not for outsiders—tourists, investors, or European Union bureaucrats—as is the case for nation branding or the corporatization of ethnicity à la *Ethnicity, Inc* (Comaroff and Comaroff 2009), but for local Hungarians. Yet it is not simply a form of economic policy protectionism that protects and promotes the production and consumption of locally made products. Simultaneously, it strongly ethnicizes national identity using commodification and material culture as an exclusionary mechanism against minority ethnic groups such as the Roma or Jews, thereby symbolically splintering the nation and undermining a civic understanding of national identity. Ethnicization, nevertheless, is simultaneously used as a boundary-bridging strategy toward ethnic diaspora Hungarians who live in neighboring countries as a consequence of post–World War I peace settlements.

This is why, theoretically, the commercialization of radical nationalism can be better understood by building on concepts and insights derived from subculture theories and from Viviana Zelizer's notion of "circuits of commerce," which both emphasize the significance of commodities and material culture as means of symbolic communication for social groups (Bennett 2011; Hebdige 1979; Zelizer 2010). Subcultural theory suggests that even seemingly superficial appearances such as clothing, language choice, music preferences, or leisure activities are politically meaningful and worthy of analysis, as Benzecry and Zubrzycki demonstrate in their respective chapters, and as a few others have in the past (e.g., Hebdige 1979; McKay and Goddard 2009). Close attention to the politics of style, that is how consumer goods are mobilized as everyday material objects to express group identities in relation to mainstream society and other social groups, sheds light on the relationship between the semiotic and the political. Subcultural studies, however, rarely take radical nationalism under scrutiny, as their analytical focus lies in youth cultures; but radical nationalism is not limited to youth and normally cuts across age and class groups.

In a related vein, Zelizer sets out to map how symbolic meanings that emerge through thick webs of social relations organize economic exchanges. Economic circuits are a distinctive and widespread form of interaction. They "embody and emphasize the centrality of negotiated meanings and social relations in the very economic transactions that analysts have often thought of as impersonal and detached from rich social life" (2010, 304). Some examples would include local currency systems, microcredit arrangements, barter groups, Internet peer production or what's often referred to today as the sharing economy (e.g., Airbnb, Etsy, Uber), and garage sales. Consumers of radical nationalism would constitute an economic circuit because both producers and consumers see commodities as constitutive of a material culture that effectively carries shared understandings of national belonging and moral value. Zelizer pays little attention to the political dimension of economic circuits, so the case of radical nationalism extends her scheme by highlighting how political convictions intersect with specialized economic transactions and consumer objects. The following empirical case studies build on these theoretical insights to capture the cultural and material logics of radical nationalist consumerism.

"NATIONAL BOOKSTORES" AND "NATIONAL BOOK PUBLISHING"

The so-called national bookstores and national book publishers provide one of the most important commercial circuits for the dissemination of radical nationalist print culture. It would be a mistake to imagine these bookstores as stuffy, low-end, hole-in-the-wall establishments tucked away in remote corners of Budapest and other Hungarian cities, peddling samizdat-style radical literature. On the contrary, they tend to be highly visible, airy retail stores located in the middle- and upper-middle-class neighborhoods of the capital and on the main streets of large urban centers in the Hungarian countryside. One of them, a bookstore called Anima, which is part of a Budapest-wide chain,[6] can be found in MOM Park, an upscale boutique shopping mall situated in the commercial heart of the well-to-do Twelfth District on the Buda side of the city. The district is a dominantly residential neighborhood with some of the city's most expensive real estate that has been a popular address both for the prewar conservative upper middle class and their offspring, as well as high-ranking Communist party officials during the socialist era (though the politically and culturally conservative bent of the neighborhood remains apparent). The mall houses high-end global fashion labels like Michael Kors or the Italian franchise Stefanel, classy restaurants and bars, a Multiplex cinema, and Budapest's most expensive butcher shop that supplies the city's Michelin-star chefs with their premium imported American Wagyu rib-eye and Argentine T-bone steaks. The bookstore is relatively small, located on the main level in a corridor that leads to one of the main side-entrances from the street. Most shoppers are therefore likely to pass by the store at some point. The store window already gives away the political leanings of the literature on offer. Next to the latest popular cookbooks and picturesque coffee-table books on horses and wildlife, there is a large magazine stand that displays "history" magazines. While these include the BBC's Hungarian-language popular *History* magazine, the lineup is clearly dominated by radical nationalist publications, most obviously the magazines entitled *Trianon* and *Greater Hungary*, but also *Dobogó: Hungarian Mythic History*, *Magyar Krónika* (Hungarian chronicles), and *Zsarátnok*,[7] which are less immediately identifiable as radical periodicals just on the basis of their titles (Figure 7.1). As the figure shows, the magazine stand also includes a copy of the Hungarian translation of Thomas Piketty's *Capital*. This is not simply a coincidence but indicates an important affinity between critiques of capitalism and radical nationalism.

Even as I idly browse the travel section of the store, I unexpectedly encounter some provocative material. The seemingly ordinary road atlas for Hungary I stumble upon turns out to be a political exercise in symbolic cartography. The atlas is entitled *Hungarian Habitat Road Atlas* (*Magyar Élettér autóatlasz*), where the Hungarian term used for "habitat" is a clear allusion to the German *Lebensraum* concept that was appropriated by Nazi ideologues in interwar Germany to justify their expansionist drive into Eastern Europe (Figure 7.2). In this specific case, the use of the term "habitat" is telling because the atlas covers the geographical territory of Hungary before the 1920 Treaty of Trianon (see note 1). Thus the atlas is used to symbolically rewrite and restore the "historical" boundaries of the Hungarian nation. The authors expressly formulate this intent in the preface to the atlas, entitled "Road to the Future":

> At first glance, this publication of the Hungarian Habitat Foundation looks like any other professional road atlas. The area encompassed by the map at the outset is divided into numbered squares, and the

Figure 7.1. Magazine stand of Anima bookstore in MOM park shopping mall, displaying radical nationalist periodicals. *Source:* Author, 2015

individual plates on subsequent pages display a detailed view of roads of various types, settlements of various sizes situated along the roads, and the enlarged city map of larger urban areas. *Everything, everything is in Hungarian.* Even just the map of the waterways of the Carpathian Basin amounts to a declamation about the past, present, and the future. . . . This is an unprecedentedly precise, boldly sincere, witty and incidentally useful road atlas that builds on the knowledge of the past and serves the needs of the present while pointing to a hopefully happier and more just future. *To a future in which things, objects and places regain their real names.* This atlas is one of the most beautiful and jovial testimonies to an emerging awareness. *It is not a nostalgia map but a map of the living past, a kind of intellectual and spiritual conquest.*[8] [emphasis added]

Hungarian memorial sites are also meticulously marked in the atlas including those "that were destroyed by the occupiers." According to the publisher, over thirty thousand copies of the atlas have been sold over the past four years, and an updated edition came out in 2014. While the atlas is evidently available in each "national bookstore," it is also

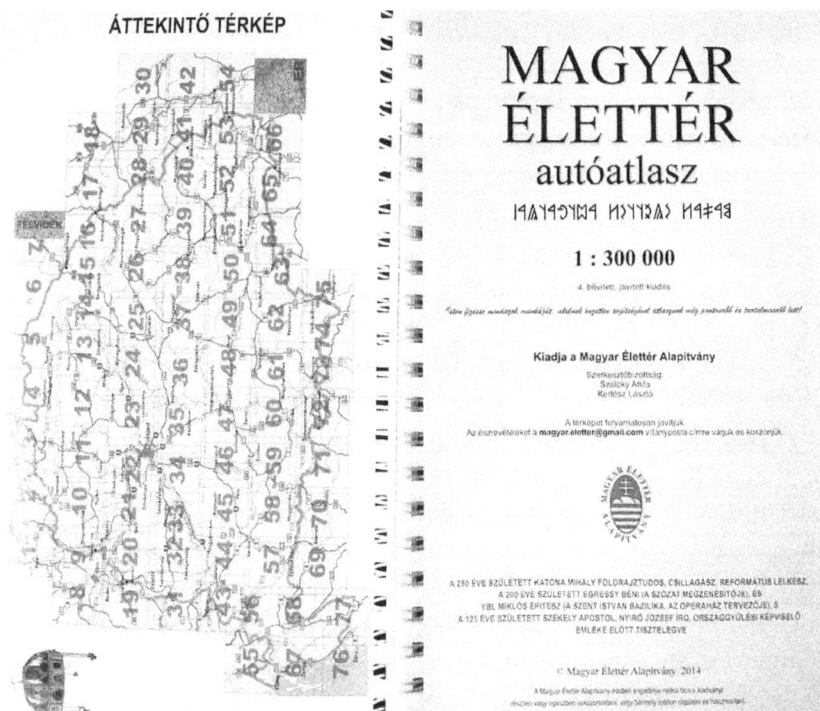

Figure 7.2. *Hungarian Habitat Road Atlas* for "Greater Hungary" with Runic script under the Hungarian title. *Source*: Author, 2015

distributed more widely: in 2014 it was sold in altogether forty-three stores nationwide while also being available via mail-order purchase. Note also the script under the Hungarian title for the atlas: the Hungarian Runic alphabet is said to be a rune-like script that was used in Transylvania in the ninth century. The popularity of Runic writing has seen a spectacular revival in the past decade. Almost all radical nationalist websites are "bilingual"; runic calligraphy is a popular motif in garment design; children learn it in after-school programs; and many villages and small towns in Hungary now display the name of the settlement in Runic script below the official Hungarian language sign.

In addition to specific products that turn mundane objects like a road atlas into a nationalist (and irredentist) political statement, there are entire categories of books that are characteristic of "national bookstores." The most common categories that organize the offerings include a vast sea of literature on the national trauma of the Treaty of Trianon, on Transylvania, on the Holy Crown of St. Stephen,[9] on Runic script, or on Arvisura, which is a modern reconstruction of the mythic origins of Hungarians rooted in Shamanistic spiritualism and recorded by a steelworker from the northern Hungarian city of Ózd over three decades in the postwar period. His writings were discovered in the late 1990s and have generated a large following since the turn of the millennium. Works on Hungarian prehistory which refer to the history of the origin of the Hungarian people, their roots in Central Asia, their migration trajectory, and the era of the ninth-century conquest of the Carpathian Basin make up another important category. Literature that investigates diverse, more or less speculative theories about Hungarian's links to various real and mythic people such as the Finno-Ugric, Hun, Scythian, and Sumerian, as well as theories that present evidence for Jesus actually being Hungarian, also features prominently among the offerings. In a similar vein, there seems to be an elective affinity between radical nationalism and a variant of new age spiritualism, as esoteric literature takes up an entire section in these stores and includes recent work that blends esotericism with more "traditional" Hungarian origin myths. The bookstores typically also house a large collection of fiction and nonfiction literature that deals with or is written by diaspora Hungarians from neighboring countries or the United States.

The pricing of books ranges from a few dollars to forty dollars with most books being in the ten-to-fifteen-dollar range. Purchasing these books is not a trivial expense for ordinary Hungarians whose expenditures on books had sharply declined in the postsocialist period, and customers are likely to come from a lower-middle-class or middle-class milieu.

Besides a significant number of independent bookstores that specialize in radical nationalist literature, there are two important chains of bookstores: one a nationwide chain called Scythia, and the other the previously mentioned Anima which operates six stores in Budapest and one in Northwestern Hungary. The Scythia chain is owned by journalist András Bencsik, chief editor of the conservative weekly *The Democrat* (*Demokrata*). In addition to the bookstore chain, he also owns a publishing house, the "Hungarian House Scythia." Bencsik was one of the founding members of the Hungarian Guard, a paramilitary group that was originally set up by the radical right-wing party Jobbik but was banned by the Hungarian courts in 2009. He also cultivates close ties to the conservative populist Fidesz government and has been the chief organizer of mass demonstrations in support of the government since 2012.[10] His private life similarly intersects with radical nationalist cultural circles, as his long-time partner is Zsuzsa Takács, a fashion designer whose nationalist clothing brand I will discuss below. In contrast, little is known about the owner(s) of the Anima chain.

Bencsik's main competitor in the radical nationalist niche of the book trade is the venerable and highly influential Püski Publishing House and Bookstore. The over seventy-year history of this family-owned and -operated firm aptly reflects the frequent turns and twists of twentieth-century Hungarian history and the importance of Hungarian diaspora communities. The publishing house was founded in 1939 under the name "Hungarian Life Publisher" and specialized in printing the fiction, poetry, and essay collections of so-called populist writers that both extolled and critically probed the traditional Hungarian way of life in a rapidly changing society. In 1950, after the Communist takeover, the press was nationalized and the owner was imprisoned, on false charges, in 1962. A few years later he was released, and in 1970 he emigrated with his wife to the United States, where he settled in New York City. They carried on with their publishing business, operating out of their apartment. They also embarked on organizing lecture-and-performance tours by Hungarian writers and artists for the Hungarian diaspora in the United States. In 1974 they bought a small, dilapidated bookstore named Corvin on Second Avenue in Manhattan, an area still at the center of Hungarian immigrant life in New York at the time. A year later they opened the Püski Publishing House through which they continued to publish the authors that made up their core list in the prewar period. They also began publishing authors who were banned in Communist Hungary and disseminated samizdat literature. The Corvin Hungarian Bookstore, which moved to a larger space on 82nd Street in 1984, became a focal point of Hungarian intellectual life among Hungarian immigrants as well as political dissidents. Once socialism fell, the Püski family returned to Hungary, reopened its flagship bookstore in Budapest's First District, and resumed its publishing business. Today the bookstore is run by the third generation of the family. Its publishing profile remains surprisingly consistent, although it has also added new titles by contemporary authors and expanded into more radical intellectual territory. The checkered history of this family publishing house draws attention to the countercultural cachet of radical nationalism in general that stems in large part from the oppositional role during the Communist era.

Obviously, today books are sold not exclusively in bookstores but also through online distributors. Each of the above-mentioned bookstores maintains a web shop and there are additional radical nationalist bookstores that only exist online; for example, "Gyepű: Nemzeti Könyvesbolt" (Hedge: National Bookstore, www.anemzetikonyvekboltja.hu). Online "general goods stores" that sell radical nationalist paraphernalia also carry many of these books in their regular catalogues. Significantly, these bookstores are not cookie-cutter institutions and they represent different gradations of radicalism. Anima is among the least radical bookstore chain partly because it also carries a mainstream inventory in addition to the radical nationalist literature. Püski and Scythia, on the other hand, specialize more closely in radical material and fall somewhere in the middle of the nationalist spectrum. The explicitly neo-Nazi publisher, the Gede brothers, occupies the far end of that spectrum. Neo-Nazi books constitute a separate subgenre within the field and are easily distinguishable from the indigenous Hungarian radical nationalist repertoire. There is little overlap in their respective catalogues: neo-Nazi books also tend to be more international and are often translations of foreign books, while the Hungarian radical nationalist literature is overwhelmingly Hungarian in every respect.

CLOTHING BRANDS: THE MILITANT, THE SPIRITUAL, AND THE FOLKSY

The close association between some fashion labels and far-right extremist groups has been widely covered in the media and scrutinized by some academic researchers (Miller-Idriss 2014; Turner-Graham 2015; Ventsel 2014). For a long time, members of far-right extremist groups across Europe favored brands like Lonsdale, Fred Perry, and New Balance, but following a considerable brand backlash, the brandscape of the far right has been undergoing a major transformation since the early 2000s. Currently, Thor Steinar is probably the best-known, and certainly the economically most successful, neo-Nazi-friendly clothing brand on the market. As the sociologist Cynthia Miller-Idriss (2014) noted, Thor

Steinar was the first to commercialize far-right identity by turning previously homemade-looking gear into expensive, high-quality clothing.

At a glance, Thor Steinar resembles waspy American pseudo-collegiate brands like Abercrombie and Fitch, Hollister, and Aeropostale, while displaying a distinctly Nordic aesthetics. A closer look, however, reveals a calculated use of subtle references to Nazi iconography. The brand's logo is an upward-pointing arrow with a zigzag and two small dots alluding to two illegal Nazi symbols. It was actually banned by a German court in 2004, but the company challenged the decision and won a reversal of the ban in 2008. In 2016, Thor Steinar operated forty-seven stores in nine countries with the most branches in Russia (twenty stores) and Germany (twelve stores). The brand was founded in 1999 and by 2007 was making two million euros in annual revenue, blatantly cashing in on the fact that neo-Nazis wholeheartedly embraced the brand (Rogers 2015). In recent years, however, it has begun to lose ground due to stiff competition from similar brands like Ansgar Aryan or Erik & Sons that employ more overtly political and directly neo-Nazi symbolism. These international brands are also available in Hungary primarily through online stores and a handful of local distributors. It is interesting, however, that Thor Steinar has no local branch in Hungary whereas it maintains three stores in the neighboring Czech Republic and five stores in Slovakia (Figure 7.3).

Radical nationalist clothing brands in Hungary tend to be more different than similar to their Western European counterparts. I focus on three brands—Harcos (Warrior), Szervető, and takács—as these represent the prevailing trends in the radical fashion scene in Hungary. All three brands came to life during the first decade of the twenty-first century signaling that radical nationalist sentiments began to percolate and crystallize shortly after the turn of the millennium. Harcos is in many ways the most similar to the international extremist brands. Its aesthetics resonates especially with the more explicit labels like Ansgar Aryan, though the themes highlighted by the design are again unequivocally Hungarian. The production is also more local and smaller-scale; it is a boutique brand that does not have its own stores. It is sold online and through mobile vendors at rock concerts and festivals, and is carried by small retailers. Nevertheless, Harcos is the most widely known and disseminated radical nationalist clothing brand embraced by many of the national rock bands like *Romantikus Erőszak* (Romantic violence).[11]

Figure 7.3. Thor Steinar logo on sweatshirt. *Source*: www.thorsteinar.de, accessed June 2016

The man behind the brand is Csaba Kis, originally a car locksmith from Balmazújváros, a small town in Northeastern Hungary—an area with a strong support base for Jobbik, the radical right-wing party—who started designing and printing T-shirts under the Harcos label in 2004 (Figure 7.4). He notes that he created the clothing line to assist those "who are willing to openly display their patriotism." He was also trying to persuade Hungarian radical nationalist youth, including previous skinheads who favored global brands like Lonsdale at the time, to switch to Hungarian labels. He first printed his clothing label in English, as "Warrior," which he gradually swapped for the Hungarian equivalent, Harcos, while also coming up with pieces on which the

Figure 7.4. T-shirt showing Greater Hungary by Harcos brand. *Source*: www. magyarharcos.hu, accessed July 2015

label is printed in Runic characters. He finds it particularly important to incorporate Runes (the calligraphic alphabet mentioned earlier that is visually similar to Nordic Runes and is believed to have originated in ninth-century Transylvania) into his designs because he believes that the usage of Runes practically marks out the radical nationalist camp.[12] Since 2009 each garment produced under the label includes the following "warning" to unequivocally proclaim the political message of the brand:

Warning: WARRIOR (HARCOS) is not only a fashion label, it is . . . a weapon against the system that is governed by the most harmful ideology ever, that of liberalism. We use HARCOS apparel to distinguish ourselves from the grey mediocrity, the slaves of the system who do not feel that the Hungarian people of the Carpathian Basin are one and indivisible regardless of the present borders. For us it is natural to express *love for our homeland* and appreciate our ancestors who made unforgettable sacrifices so that we can still raise our

head with dignity *in the heart of Europe*. We who wear HARCOS
apparel are fighting for a country in which the national interests
of Hungary triumph above all. I recommend my clothing line,
THE RADICAL PATRIOTS' WEAR, to everyone with no age limit,
but only to those who identify with the above values. [emphasis in
original]

Kis also experimented with a career in politics, first by running as a can-
didate for a parliamentary seat to represent the Hungarian Life and Justice Party (MIÉP), the right-wing party of the 1990s, and then for Jobbik,
although he never formally joined Jobbik as a member. He was actually
elected in the 2010 local government elections on Jobbik's ticket but he
gave up his seat after a year in office because he was deeply disgruntled
with professional politics. He returned to his mission of spreading radical nationalism by other—cultural and economic—means.

The second brand, Szervető, represents a different take on radical
nationalist fashion. Creators of the brand also stress the importance of
employing Runic script as part of the design, and locally produced gar-
ments, but favor an aesthetics that highlights the spiritualist strain of
radical nationalism. Its website is "bilingual," printed both in Hungarian
and Runic script just like its brand logo. Extensive explanation is offered
on the origins and symbolic meanings behind the name of the brand,
which sounds like a real word but was actually invented "to evoke the
magical beauty of the word formation and connotational power of the
Hungarian language." The root, *szer,* is an archaic term that is only used
today in some parts of Transylvania and Western Hungary to refer to
being part of a local community. Nevertheless, it is an important component of many important and ancient Hungarian words including
those for love, method, structure, organization, and ritual. The name
was picked "to elicit the idea of community and unity and to call for
a new alliance that unites all Hungarians in synthesis with tradition.
Szervető thus stands for the dissemination of this idea of solidarity in
the Carpathian Basin." Moreover, "the brand uses symbols that are
exclusively Hungarian, that embody ancient emblems that reflect the
fore-mentioned values [of unity and solidarity] and inevitably build on
Hungarian folk art." The clothing line mixes the pan-Hungarian theme
with strong Eastern mysticism, especially Central Asian shamanism,
which is clearly reflected in its T-shirt designs. The Scythian warrior rid-
ing on a horse while shooting backward with an arch, or the image of

Figure 7.5. T-shirts by Szervető brand with mythic motifs such as the Scythian warrior. *Source*: http://szerveto.hu, accessed June 2015

the miraculous deer, are fundamental motifs of this mythical vocabulary supplied by popular legends about nomadic tribes including the Huns, Avars, and Scythians that Hungarians were believed to have come in contact with during their long migratory journey from Central Asia to Europe (Figure 7.5).

The company is a small family-owned firm that has been active in the garment business for the past twenty years making everyday wear, primarily T-shirts. The owner notes that they launched the Szervető brand because they did not understand "why everyone should wear T-shirts that say 'I love N.Y.' or apple sauce in Chinese characters. We were really annoyed by the fact that as young adults we could not find everyday wear that was Hungarian, unique and carried a meaningful message while it was also affordable and comfortable." They also emphasize that the symbolism of the brand demands that each product is Hungarian-made in every respect: design, manufacturing, and distribution. The T-shirts are silk printed and embroidered in small artisanal shops; one of the signature designs, the "sun worshipper," takes ten hours and sixty thousand stitches to make.

The last brand, takács, exemplifies yet another variation on using fashion design to assert Hungarian cultural uniqueness and superiority.

The label carries the last name of its designer, Zsuzsanna Mária Takács, who was mentioned earlier in connection with András Bencsik, the owner of one of the main radical nationalist bookstore chains. She in fact also designed the uniform of the Hungarian National Guard, the paramilitary wing of Jobbik. Takács is a graduate of Hungary's preeminent art and design school, the Moholy-Nagy University of Art and Design and previously called the University of Applied Arts, and launched her clothing brand in 2008.

The symbolism of the brand owes its origins to both Hungarian folk traditions as well as the visual and material culture of the time of the Hungarian conquest of the Carpathian Basin between the ninth and eleventh centuries, often referred to in Hungary as the Árpád Age after the name of the dynasty that ruled the country in this period (Figure 7.6). There is, of course, nothing inherently nationalistic about embracing the aesthetics of this period. But radical nationalists uphold the material culture of the times of the conquest as evidence of the cultural superiority of Hungarian settlers over other ethnic groups (such as Slavs) in the Carpathian Basin. As the history of this era can only be reconstructed from archaeological sources, chiefly material artifacts, there is plenty of room for interpretation, which has spawned speculative and unsubstantiated theories about the kinship between Hungarians and various Near Eastern ancient cultures like the Scythians and Sumerians. These theories emerged roughly in the late nineteenth century and have prevailed ever since, constituting a linchpin of the radical nationalist cultural canon. The designer of the takács brand seems to share these views, as the brand's website contains a lengthy essay that openly endorses these ideas.

According to the main argument put forward by this interpretation, the material artifacts that have been dug up from this period are more intricate and sophisticated than could be expected on the basis of Hungarians' status as a nomadic tribe at the time. Moreover, continues the reasoning, the material remnants of the period suggest that "the technological-civilizational development of Hungarian settlers can be considered to be almost on par with that of 20th century societies" (www.korszeruviselet.hu/hagyomany.php). These arguments dramatically overstate the uniqueness, cultural superiority, and length of "Hungarian civilization." The centrality of this spirit to radical nationalist mythology is clearly reflected in the praise of the designer by the

Figure 7.6. Apparel by takács brand using visual motifs associated with material artifacts from the time of the ninth-century Conquest of the Carpathian Basin. *Source*: www.takacszsuzsa.hu/takacs.php, accessed June 2015

journalist and right-wing ideologue András Bencsik on the brand's website. Bencsik raises the rhetorical question, "How many thousands of years must it have taken for such a highly developed formal design vocabulary to emerge if it had taken European product design two thousand years to mature?" suggesting that Hungarian civilization is much older than other European civilizations. He also scolds Hungarians for forgetting this heritage and technical know-how, while commending the designer for reintroducing these ancient motifs into contemporary Hungarian wear.

CONCLUSION

This chapter has argued that the recent rise of radical nationalism in Hungary has also benefited from the vigorous commodification of radical nationalist sentiments. It examined this thesis in light of a sprawling interdisciplinary literature that probes the intersections between markets, material culture, and nationalism. It showed that radical nationalism does not really fit the existing categories of analysis in the literature, and thus turned to subcultural theory and Viviana Zelizer's cultural approach to economic exchange to explain the cultural and material dynamics of radical nationalism. In-depth case studies of radical nationalist niche markets, including book publishing and clothing brands, were used to empirically substantiate the main argument. These illuminate how everyday material objects in the form of commodities propagate representations of a mythic past, thereby increasing the visibility of and domesticating radical nationalist discourse. Markets clearly serve as an important conduit for the dissemination of radical nationalist ideas, and commodification facilitates their mainstreaming. Mundane consumer objects produced in a wide range of domains from book publishing to clothing brands make up an interlinked system of signs that also intersects with mainstream cultural production, again blurring the line between niche and mainstream consumption. Finally, the steady presence of a diverse radical niche economy in a low-wage country like Hungary signals the support of a strong middle-class base for radical nationalism that in turn ensures the long-term viability of these cultural markets.

My chapter thus extends other contributions in this volume that demonstrate the diverse ways in which nationalism is entangled with mundane objects, while highlighting the mediating role of markets in this process. Claudio Benzecry, for instance, draws attention in his chapter to how the branding practices of transnational corporations inadvertently lead to the trivialization of the soccer jersey as a key proxy for national devotion, through the manipulation of its colors and materials. My analysis, by contrast, shows how markets can amplify the reach of radical nationalist sentiments precisely by turning them into banal but symbolically coded objects that can effectively circulate and spread through simple market transactions and consumer preferences. This chapter, with other contributions in this volume, thus emphasizes the need to more carefully map the multiple logics that link material cultural and materiality to nationalism.

NOTES

1. The Treaty of Trianon, the formal peace agreement that ended World War I between the Kingdom of Hungary and most of the Allies, was signed on 4 June 1920 in the Trianon Palace in Versailles, France. The Treaty of Trianon and the consequent partitioning of Hungary remain one of the greatest collective traumas of Hungary's twentieth-century history. The treaty reduced Hungary to a mere one-third of its pre–World War I size and turned it into a landlocked country, cutting off its access to the Adriatic Sea. The country's population was halved as the result, and most importantly, nearly one-third of all ethnic Hungarians were stranded beyond the new borders of Hungary in neighboring countries. With the detached territories, Hungary lost its largest urban centers, with the exception of Budapest, and virtually all of its natural resources. The implementation of the new borders triggered a massive migration and refugee crisis. Between 1918 and 1924 about 350,000 ethnic Hungarians migrated to Hungary from the detached territories, putting huge strain on a new country already gravely destabilized by the aftermath of not only the war but a Communist revolution in 1919 and the violent failure of the short-lived Hungarian Soviet Republic. Revisionist claims dominated Hungarian foreign policy in the interwar period and were largely responsible for Hungary entering World War II as a German ally. The post-1920 borders and status of diaspora Hungarians have continued to be a cause of political tension with neighboring countries.

2. Because of space constraints, the current chapter focuses only on two areas while the larger book project covers all four areas enumerated above.

3. Eric Helleiner (2002) and Roman Szporluk (1988) also note that in some parts of Europe, especially in the multiethnic states of East Central Europe, consumer and consumption-oriented forms of economic nationalism have a much longer history that can be traced back to nineteenth-century consumers associations.

4. Similar cases are also discussed by DeSoucey (2010) for foie gras in France, and by Bowen and Gaytán (2012) for tequila in Mexico.

5. The *iemoto* refers to the traditional Japanese certification and licensing system that is in effect in many areas of traditional Japanese arts including the tea ceremony, Go, *ikebana*, and Japanese dancing. It is characterized by a strong hierarchical structure where the *iemoto*, the "Grand Master," inherited the secret traditions of the school from the previous *iemoto* and is endowed with supreme authority.

6. It also has one store in Győr, the largest city in Northwestern Hungary, which is an economic powerhouse for the region.

7. The title is an archaic term for a fire/flint striker, and the magazine is dedicated to "Hungarians with ancient beliefs" (*"Ôshitű magyarok lapja"*) drawing attention to the strong links between neo-paganism (rooted in Central Asian ancient pre-Christian religions) and radical nationalism.

8. The text uses the Hungarian word, *honfoglalás* (the conquest).

9. The Holy Crown is both the symbol of the Hungarian state and the actual crown that was gifted to St. Stephen, Hungary's first Christian king, and had been used in coronation ceremonies from the twelfth century to the demise of the Austro-Hungarian Empire in World War I. It also denotes a peculiar brand of conservative constitutional theory unique to Hungary called the Holy Crown doctrine that attributes personhood to the crown, and suggests inter alia that as a legal entity it is identical to the state of Hungary and superior to the ruling monarch. This doctrine has enjoyed a remarkable renaissance in recent years. See Scheppele (2012) for a critical analysis.

10. Békemenet, since 2012.

11. There is also official sponsorship between the brand and three key national rock bands, Secret Resistance, Romantic Violence, and Hungarica. According to the sponsor agreement, the musicians wear Harcos apparel during their concerts, interviews, and on CD covers. Csaba Kis, the creator of the Harcos label, claims that he was approached by the bands about the possibility of sponsorship and not the other way around, although he is certainly happy to support them.

12. To him Runes express a yearning for a strong connection to the "glorious past": "Runes are a link to our ancestors; they represent a bond among people who do not want to just barely eke out a living in a colony but continue to dream of a homeland in which we can be our own bosses and still enrich ourselves."

PART III

Places, Practices, and Performances

CHAPTER 8

Engaging Objects

A Phenomenology of the Tea Ceremony and Japaneseness

Kristin Surak

To the outside observer, few cultural practices in Japan appear more ineluctably Japanese than the tea ceremony. In its most iconic form, a master wrapped in kimono kneels on tatami mats and prepares the frothy beverage in an earthenware bowl with an esoteric yet elegant series of carefully choreographed movements. From the opening bow to the final words of gratitude and humility, the experience resonates with much of what is defined as "Japanese culture," a label that foreigners are perhaps the most ready to apply. Yet the precisely timed trains, delicately organized bento boxes, and quirks of fashion that may convey a Japaneseness to foreigners are hardly relevant to a local population pushing through the daily grind of getting dressed, getting fed, and getting to work. The tea ceremony, however, stands out among these mundane activities, for even the locals readily proclaim its national resonances. Students will commonly cite an interest in taking up the study of "Japanese history"; pamphlets promoting internal tourism will proclaim that a moment in the tea room will afford an experience of "Japanese culture"; and public demonstrations will declare a hope that participants will feel in their "own heart the sprit of the Japanese."[1]

How does this work? How is it that even for Japanese within Japan, who might take the nation for granted, the tea ceremony operates as a site for experiencing Japaneseness?[2] The question, so posed, almost occludes part of the answer, for indica of nations do not exist in isolation. Rather, they are situated within an assemblage of similar cultural phenomena that can be considered a national "cultural matrix" (Edensor 2002, vii). The term captures an uneven and loosely bounded terrain populated by elements that vary in degree of centrality, legitimacy, and connection to—or friction with—other elements. Though the items people understand to be representative of "national culture" can vary, patterns in the heterogeneity can also be discerned. Broad consensuses might elevate certain components to a dominant position—few would question the claim that jazz is a distinctively American form of music, for example. Clear-cut disputes may emerge around others, as debates about headscarves or religious symbols in France may illustrate. And some items may simply occupy an ambiguous or liminal position. How French are precisely displayed hams (Kowalski, this volume)? How Polish is Jewish culture (Zubrzycki, this volume)?

Seen in this light, the tea ceremony occupies a secure position within the Japanese cultural matrix. If it holds little in common with the self-sacrifice of the "samurai way," let alone anime or cosplay, the practice incorporates domains as varied as architecture, cuisine, pottery, clothing, scrolls, calligraphy, lacquerware, poetry, and design. All are part of a formal tea gathering and are understood to constitute Japanese traditional culture. These material elements make connections across the domains as they inhabit multiple spaces—the scroll in the tea room could be a scroll in a temple. So too do homologies in their aesthetic expression; for example, a preference for the asymmetrical is common across spheres. But if commonalities help to bind a set of items into "Japanese traditional culture," the tea ceremony occupies a privileged place among them. Frequently termed a "cultural synthesis" (*sōgō bunka*), the tea ceremony combines a rich array of traditional objects, practices, and places. Densely interlinked within the cultural matrix, its standing within the field is rarely questioned, whereas the putative Japaneseness of train commuters' quiet obsession with their telephone screens, for example, might be challenged.

The complex associations among elements of the matrix, taken as a whole, constitute a changeable crystallization—a "nebulous condensation," to borrow Roland Barthes's formulation (2009, 43)—that is Japaneseness. Yet they do not float free. Sustaining the national meanings are the institutions and authorities, such as schools, museums, and the media, that declare these associations to hold and thereby institute cultural practices and products as indica of the nation (see Bourdieu 1991, 168–70; examples include B. Anderson 1991, 163–85). Their prerogatives may be accepted or disputed, but even contestation and conflict over the position or inclusion of elements within the matrix enlivens national meanings as it challenges the definition of the nation (e.g., Verdery 1991; Zubrzycki 2006, 2013a). Either way, institutional connections lend the cultural matrix validity, utility, and comprehensibility.

These would remain mere cognitive associations without a second axis of connection and contrast that enlivens the national inflections in practice: nation-work (Surak 2012b). Making tea is at once connected to the ordinary lifeways within Japan and aloof from them, simultaneously ordinary and extra-ordinary (Surak forthcoming). If tea drinking and socializing are unquestionably mundane, the ceremony hones these unreflexive actions of ordinary existence into rarefied form as an objectified expression of "Japanese tradition." These parallels to and contrasts with everyday customs in Japan—enlivened in the making of tea—enable the ceremony to appear as a purified and condensed version of Japaneseness. The operation recalls Barthes's (2009) reaction when encountering Basque houses in different contexts. In their home region, they might be identifiably "Basque," but they never struck—rather "attacked," as he puts it—him as particularly ethnic. Reproduced in Paris, however, in simplified form and without the details—the barns, the dirt, the external stairs—that made them functional rural dwellings, they called out to him as Basque, imposing their "Basquity," as he terms it, on him (148–49).

In a modern Japan, putting on a kimono and kneeling on tatami mats to whip up a bowl of tea encourages a similar reaction. The practice can be experienced as quintessentially Japanese, even within the country, because it is different yet not completely removed from mundane life. The deliberateness of the tea ceremony refines and concentrates elements of the everyday, yielding an extra-ordinary version of the ordinary.[3] In Barthes's vignette, it is the concept "Basquity" that has agentive power. It "seeks" him out, "calls" to him, issues an "imperious injunction" (149), which is all the more powerful for the physical adjustments made in the house's reconstruction. In his case, the material alterations suppress the history that has caused the house to be there. Within the tea ceremony, by contrast, the objects are full of history—at least of a certain sort. They draw a line to a past constructed as tradition and refined into elegant, if mythic, form. They take on individual personae that mediate the interactions in the tea room. They structure the tempo of the ritual, smoothing the flow of these extra-ordinary exchanges and naturalizing the unnatural. How does this work?

TEA IN JAPAN

Little in Japan is more commonplace than preparing tea, had any time of day as a refreshment or accompaniment to meals. Indeed, the dining room of a house may be called—if with slightly musty tones—the *chanoma*, or "the tea space," if the term is taken literally. Of the varieties on offer, green tea may predominate, but barley tea, buckwheat tea, and tea accented with toasted rice are frequently found too. Alongside them, English tea—more commonly known as "milk tea"—as well as a range of nouveau blends like "matcha au lait" no longer raise eyebrows. And if canned sodas supply an alternative to the steeped, they are rarely to be seen without an equally wide range of bottled teas in any of the ubiquitous vending machines.

But the drink prepared in the tea ceremony stands out from among them. Made from pulverized rather than steeped tea leaves, the liquid *matcha* appears as an opaque and very green suspension. A "thin" variant is most common, prepared by whipping a scoop of the powder with some hot water in a small bowl until a frothy head forms. Still, it is not so easily had. If one splurges on *kaiseki* haute cuisine, it may appear in a final course, though perhaps a more common experience is a bowl of tea bought at a traditional tourist site like a temple, or served at a national Culture Day celebration or town festival. The beverage's exotic qualities have been encouraged as the taste has spread more widely through a boom in *matcha*-flavored products, with items from ice cream to cakes, crackers, chocolates, donuts, and coffees rolled out to lure new customers. All are typically marketed with Japanese inflections and catchphrases like "taste the tradition." Yet though such products can be found in most convenience stores, actual bowls of *matcha* tea remain an uncommon, if familiar, drink for most.

Nonetheless, in the tea ceremony—known in Japanese as *sadō/chadō* (the way of tea), *chanoyu* (hot water for tea), or simply *ocha* (tea)—the beverage itself is of secondary importance. A full formal tea gathering is a four-hour social affair with the largest stretch of time spent enjoying a *kaiseki* meal with a dozen or so courses, accompanied by the formal preparation of thick tea and thin, as well as two formal preparations of the charcoal in the hearth, broken by stints in the garden. The most palpable difference from other ritualized feasts, like wedding parties, is the degree to which not norms, but highly scripted rules govern nearly all actions, gestures, and even conversation within the setting, down to the paths participants trace when walking in a room, how the lids on the soup and rice are opened, and the extent fingertips touch the floor when guests exchange greetings among each other. If routine activities of eating, drinking, and socializing motivate the tea ceremony, the ritualized and aestheticized versions that constitute it ensure that the ordinary is keyed into the extra-ordinary within the tea room (see also Goffman 1974).

OBJECTS IN TEA

Tea practice turns around objects. Though the ritual preparation may entrance a novice, the utensils are the main draw for the seasoned practitioner who will have seen the standardized procedure hundreds of times.[4] It is not unusual for the host at a tea gathering to spend weeks or months assembling the profusion of tools employed—the bowls, tea containers, scoops, scrolls, water containers, kettles, trays, vases, incense containers, and the like—selected and combined with care (Figure 8.1). Of the array of objects, the most honored are more than mere drinking implements. Tea utensils are not only a common item in museums (the national museum dedicates a room to them); some have even been named national treasures. But practitioners will consider these pieces, stored behind glass, to be "dead." It is use that enlivens them, ensuring that an object remains a tea ware rather than a relic, and even the most expensive and ancient pieces will still be taken from their boxes and given occasional exercise in the tea room.

To understand where the great value of such tools derives from, one can take tea bowls as an example. About twelve centimeters across and nine high, they look more like rice bowls than the smaller teacups commonly used for steeped tea, and novices will typically fumble a bit with uncertainty when drinking from such a large-mouthed vessel for the first time. Tea bowls can be found in a range of shapes and styles, from delicate porcelain pieces to finely painted Kyoyaki or the uneven yet intriguing asymmetries of Shigaraki ware. Iconic of the practice, however, is the rough and thick style of black Raku pottery.

A tea bowl's value, however, derives from sources beyond its design and composition. What distinguishes tea utensils from everyday objects

Figure 8.1. Objects for making tea, including a kettle, portable brazier, tea bowl, scoop, whisk, thin tea container, ladle, and water container. *Source*: Author, Tokyo, 2008

is less their use in tea preparation than their housing. Not all implements employed in the tea room are purpose-made, and—within limits—the incorporation of found objects into a tea performance is welcomed. A tray picked up on a holiday to Turkey might be rallied to carry sweets, or an antique pillbox used as an incense container. Yet to transform found objects into tea utensils, another object is required: a box. Any article beginning a new life in the tea world will take up residence in a commissioned case when not engaged in a tea gathering. These finely crafted cedar repositories are tied with a thickly woven ribbon and sometimes housed in a yet larger box, and no utensil worth its salt goes without one. As such, the value of the object is not to be found merely in its use-value or exchange value, but in its relationship to other objects. It is an object-in-use—a protective box, also on display—that readies an ordinary implement for a novel role within the tea room and testifies to its new identity.

Though the container may protect the implement, it is the lid that is valued most. The top or its underside will often carry the name and origin of the utensil, penned in fine calligraphy. In some cases, an inked signature of approval from a grand tea master, past or present, may grace the box as well. The brushstrokes lend a pedigree and identity to the object, all the more important when the value of the implement is not immediately recognizable. The tea world places great importance on a "wabi" aesthetic, favoring the rough-hewn, withered, eroded, and repaired and rejecting the glitziness that might advertise an object's worth, which may remain obscure to the untrained eye. Indeed some tea bowls began life several centuries ago as common dishes for rice before becoming national treasures. The inscribed provenances, as well as endorsements by tea masters, elevate the objects from humble origins and render them valued treasures in a tea room. They are a "technology," to borrow a concept from Alexandra Kowalski's chapter, that transforms the mundane into the extra-ordinary. Thus box covers of significance are, as a rule, displayed at tea gatherings for ogling participants. And they are closely guarded as well—it isn't hard for a slim tea scoop case to end up in a kimono sleeve. If the box names a utensil, its loss renders a piece anonymous, and since two tea scoops can look remarkably alike, they offer little resistance to the easy transfer of persona (Figure 8.2).

Giving the utensil a unique identity, however, is its name, written in the center of the lid. Typically, these are evocative phrases, often taken from poetry, that hint at the seasons, a historical occurrence, or even make oblique comparisons to everyday objects—"daybreak," "one meeting," or "burst bag" are examples—that not only attach symbolic significances to the utensils, as will be discussed below, but contribute personality as well. Utensils that are centuries old may carry with them letters from prior owners or written records of possession that establish a genealogy of historical hands through which it has passed. The unique biography, attesting to the character of the piece, lends it identity and import that, as some practitioners may proclaim, overshadow the mortality of individuals. Yet this human element, too, becomes simultaneously implicated and elevated each time the list of prior owners is read. Present tea masters may see their relationship to the object not as one of ownership but as a custodianship of the item on its historical journey. As

Figure 8.2. Tea practitioners admiring the inscriptions on box lids at a gathering and pointing at the signature of a tea master. *Source*: Author, Tokyo, 2007

one aficionado described of an ancient bowl she possessed, "I am merely the caretaker at this moment."

The genealogy and identity do more than simply add to the object's worth; they are incorporated into the flow of the tea preparation itself. After drinking the beverage, the guest will be presented with the opportunity to take a closer view of the bowl, and will—without fail—ask about its provenance. Separating the master from those of lesser experience is the ability to go beyond the ritualized questioning and converse naturally about select points. An adept might, for example, recognize the potter's seal at the bottom of the bowl and contribute a story about him even before eliciting the name of the maker from the host, who may respond with more information about the hands through which the bowl has passed. On such occasions, the object becomes the pivot point linking the host and guest through the interaction it channels.

For this chance, however, the owner will have paid royally. While a basic tea bowl can be had for less than one hundred dollars, a high-quality vessel of the sort used at formal gatherings will typically carry a price tag of a few thousand dollars. And ancient wares accompanied by seals, letters, and stamps of approval can easily find two zeros added to that figure. Even if whipped *matcha* is something of a rarity, tea bowls nonetheless occupy a lofty position within the hierarchy of pottery in Japan. They are hardly ever absent from a ceramics exhibition, and the ability to produce a viable bowl is assumed of any potter of note. Indeed, most ceramicists will have spent a bit of time learning the tea ceremony to gain a sense of the form and handling required of "good" pieces.

Not merely an esteemed pedigree conveys value, but symbolic significances do as well, and any seasoned practitioner will be well versed in reading these, unprompted, off of the pieces. If a tea container is lacquered with striped bands of red, yellow, and black, an expert will know that the design recalls a spinning top and was favored by the sixteenth-century warlord and tea aesthete Toyotomi Hideyoshi, who carried the emblem on one of his family crests. Copies of famous wares lend a historical bias to the cultural knowledge required. A student may be told that a paddle-like incense container resembles the equipment used in the ancient game of battledores, played at New Year's in the past, and that its top is lifted in a certain way. In summer, a tall and narrow water container made of lacquered wood might appear in the tea room, bearing as a lid not a wooden slat, but a large kudzu leaf. As the students learn how to delicately dispose of the top, the teacher may explain that the plant was historically associated with the Tanabata Festival, still observed at the beginning of July, and may recite a few lines from the standard canon of ancient poetry in which both appear. A replica of the ceramic tea caddy "Spindle Tree," known by its amber-colored glaze, may evoke talk of the verse from the *Kokinshū* collection of premodern poetry—the source of its name—or of the powerful Hosokawa family that owned the piece during the Tokugawa Period. A teacher may then encourage her students to visit the original in the Nezu Museum. As students acquire the skills for handling utensils, they simultaneously develop a repository of historical and social learning—knowledge of a distinctively Japanese high culture. Deployed for manipulating and reading the utensils, this knowledge is the grease smoothing the interactions of the gathering. As one practitioner explained, "If the guest doesn't know about history, then it's not interesting. If you see, for example, that the scroll is by [a famous historical leader], then you should know that he retired to Kumamoto and took up drawing. That is then referenced in the choice of the incense container using *higo* inlay, which Kumamoto is famous for. This is all just the assumed background knowledge. You need to have a deep understanding of Japanese history and art history to truly enjoy utensils." As in Geneviève Zubrzycki's analysis of food or dancing in ethnically Polish groups performing Jewishness, or Claudio Benzecry's examination of soccer players and their fans, we find that in the tea room too, interaction between participants, mediated through objects, enlivens the national associations. The performance of the nation is no pantomime. It requires not merely actors but also sets and props to define and mediate the action.

In addition, a keen awareness of seasonality is required for the appreciation and appropriation of utensils. Many parts of the world mark the calendar according to seasonal changes, but in Japan such sensitivity is claimed as a national hallmark. Training starts early, and schools are a key site. Like many textbooks, one popular volume produced by the Ministry of Education informs students in a section on patriotism, "Nature in our country has distinct seasons of spring, summer, autumn, and winter, and a beautiful climate. Each season has sights, sounds, colors, and winds that reverberate in our hearts" (Kokoro no Nooto 2002, 125). English textbooks regularly contain sections on seasonality as an important part of intercultural exchanges—something that Japanese must be prepared to explain to foreigners. Adults can brush up on their seasonal knowledge by exploring any of the numerous books and magazines on "Japan's seasons" available at bookstores. Indeed, such expertise is deemed so important that even manners manuals regularly include a section on seasonality. One produced by the leading family of etiquette experts, for example, begins: "There are few countries that have such clear changes between the four seasons as Japan. Japanese culture is distinctive in that it does not oppose nature, but adeptly brings in and coexists with nature in everyday life" (Ogasawara 1999, 176).

As a rule, the utensils used at a gathering will make reference to the season. A tea caddy lacquered with a few glistening points suggesting fireflies may be used in June when the insects appear. A tea scoop named "fresh water on rocks" might be taken out during the hot summer months. Autumn could provide an excuse to use a utensil stand made of persimmon wood—just the time when the fruit is ready for harvest. The ever-shifting combinations create opportunities for conversation about the choices, or instruction in the references made, which may be obscure to initiates. Choices are not made with complete freedom, and most seasonal associations have been fixed to the calendar. Even if the summer comes early or winter lingers long, plum blossoms appear in the tea room only in February. Similarly, June is the month for hydrangeas, August for cicadas, and September for chrysanthemums. The associations are codified, and books will give voice to the rules of what goes when. If greenhouses ensure that eggplants are available year round, not only tea dictionaries but even general letter-writing guides will inform the novice that, historically, they reached the plate at the beginning of June—the same time that the finest *kaiseki* restaurants still serve them today.[5]

The tea utensils, as such, are valued not merely for their individual properties, but for how they work together as a whole, both meaningfully and aesthetically. Indeed, this *toriawase*, or combination of utensils, is a primary resource for creative expression in the tea room. A seasoned practitioner is expected to be able to deftly mix utensils to evoke a sui generis theme, while the seasoned guest should be able to read the meaning without much intervention. In early March, a tea scoop carved from cherry tree wood might be paired with a tea container bearing on its lid a schematic design in gold leaf of hills recalling those in Yoshino, an area made famous in a tenth-century poem in which the author confuses its blooming cheery trees for snow. These might be used to prepare tea underneath a scroll reading "one flower opens," which an experienced practitioner would know is the first part of the Zen phrase that ends "under heaven is spring" and refers to the cherry blossom season.

Utensils are typically polyvalent—indeed, their cost increases with the number of meanings that may be attributed to them. It is their combination as a set that does the work of determining what is meant and not meant. Thus, the hills on the tea container mentioned above could, in another setting, suggest the distant mountains that appear in winter. If the tea scoop bears the name "daybreak," it might be used at New Year's, a time when many stay up through the night to catch the first rays of sun, with little mention made that it was carved not from bamboo but from cherry wood. Used in March, however, along with other objects recalling the season of cherry blossoms, "daybreak" would recede and the cherry wood material would rise to prominence. As such, the implements are seen twice, both in their singularity and as a constellation, which narrows the range of possible readings while producing an additional layer of value and signification. At the same time, successfully communicating the theme chosen for the day through the selection of utensils is dependent on the extent of the guests' background knowledge—training in a distinctively Japanese high-cultural knowledge—needed to decipher the intended message.

OBJECTS ENGAGED: TEA PERFORMANCES

But what does this mean in practice? A condensed account of the preparation for thin tea offers some insight. In the idealized form—though not far from actual practice—a host will serve tea to three guests, all kneeling patiently on tatami mats in a Japanese-style room.[6]

The first few minutes are devoted to setting up the space with the tea bowl, a water jar, a small tea container, and other utensils that will be used. As the host enters and leaves the room to fetch and position each object, all attention is concentrated on the quiet gestures of standing, sitting, turning, and opening and closing doors, none of which can be taken for granted. Bowing, for example, is a ubiquitous part of everyday interactions in Japan, found in greetings, apologies, requests, displays of comprehension, or even simple acknowledgment. So common is the reflex that even people talking on the phone can be caught genuflecting slightly. Textbooks used in schools for English classes commonly introduce greetings with images of foreigners shaking hands and Japanese bowing. Yet being able to bow naturally, unthinkingly, does not mean that one knows how to bow correctly or formally, and it is typically one of the first things that a tea novice learns. Initiates will commonly curve their back and bend their head to only centimeters above the floor to suggest formality and respect. In response, the teacher will demonstrate how to maintain a straight torso and bend only at the waist as the hands move smoothly from lap to floor, the fingertips landing in a caret. Following a strict form, similar to that found in Japanese-language etiquette books and business manuals, students are taught to count to

three as they bow down, and then to hold the position for the same dura-
tion before returning upright, again to a count of three (see, e.g., Tokio
Narejji 2013, 26–27). They also learn three levels of formality, each grade
distinguished by the depth of the bow, as well as the amount of contact
between the fingers and the floor. These publications commonly flag the
Japaneseness of such greetings, and it's not unusual to find statements
like the following: "Bowing is the action used for greetings if one is Japanese" (Shiotsuki 2005, 26). Employed during the greetings that com-
mence and conclude lessons, as well as throughout the tea preparation
proper, these bows over time become second nature to participants. But
unlike the genuflections in everyday life, the far more elaborate rules
structuring the tea room greetings must be explicitly taught, with mis-
takes made along the way. New students, and even some experienced
ones, may forget how deeply to dip on a given occasion, and consistent
precision may take several months to master—curved backs and hasty
returns are easy lapses.

Not only are mundane movements like standing, walking, and sitting refined within the tea room, but they are typically channeled by
the dictates of a kimono, with its long sleeves, open flaps, and tubelike
bottom. Teachers alert their students to these exigencies, for most will
have worn this increasingly archaic garb only a handful of times, college
graduations and weddings offering rare opportunities. In the tea room,
one stands without spreading out the legs at the hips—a motion that the
straight bottom of a kimono fights against.[7] Whether or not in the garment, one walks by small sliding steps with the legs separating at the
knee rather than the hip. And no one merely sits on the floor: all kneel.
This posture, *seiza*—literally, "correct sitting"—is widely considered both
the most formal way to position oneself on the floor (it's assumed, for
example, at funerals or when making weighty requests), and a distinctively Japanese way of sitting (see, e.g., Akashi 2007, 34). Books on the
Japanese body will typically contain an entire section devoted to *seiza*
and its putative benefits (see, e.g., Yatabe 2007; Tei 2009), even if it is so
rarely assumed in an age of tables and chairs that the threat of kneeling
for an entire tea gathering is enough to worry, even turn off, many of the
uninitiated. Learning tea prepares students for natural movement in a
kimono, as learning how to move in a kimono does so for tea—two symbols of the nation enlivened through a homology of gracefully retooled
comportment.

After arranging the space, the host will begin the preparation proper by symbolically purifying the utensils with a close eye to the effect she conveys as she handles them. Exhaling, she moves the tea bowl to the front of her body, grasping the costly object close to the front (Figure 8.3).[8] With her thumb balanced straight on the lip, hand curved around the side, and fingertips aligned at an angle, she shifts her grip between the two hands before setting it down. The small tea container made of finely lacquered wood must be moved closer as well, and she traces with it a smooth arc to the front of her lap, navigating around the bowl to avoid the danger of a kimono sleeve—real or imagined—dipping inside. Removing a heavy silk cloth from her belt, she folds it and wipes the lid of the tea caddy with a few stately gestures and a light touch that preserves the textile's cushiony billow.

The movements, though distinct, flow in a controlled rhythm from one into another. To purify the small bamboo tea scoop, for example, the host refolds the silk cloth and grips it lightly in a rounded left hand, but the action is not finished until the cloth-holding hand comes to rest on her lap. Only once the left hand has returned does she extend the right to pick up the tea scoop, shifting forward her center of balance by tilting her torso rather than casually stretching out her arm. The right hand, holding the scoop near the bottom, remains steady while the left sweeps the silk cloth along its body three times. The first is decisive, and the second proceeds somewhat more swiftly. The third and final time, however, moves at a slower pace and suggests a concentrated note and closure, ending with a slight pause at the tip of the scoop as the cloth leaves the item. After the left hand, still grasping the cloth, comes to rest on the lap, the right replaces the tea scoop. Exhaling, the host sets down first the curved cup and then the handle before relaxing the grip slowly and moving her hand back to the body as she inhales.

The object's importance sets the rhythmical flow and lays down an economy of movement (though not of total moves). The result is a calming cadence that catches the participants in its motion. Indeed, skilled teachers may use irregularities in the flow to correct unseen movements. A slight difference in speed may alert an attentive teacher to whether a student turned to the right or left upon exiting a room—even if she is already out of sight. At a class where a student stumbled between moves, the teacher cautioned, "If you don't have a good rhythm, then the guests won't be relaxed. You need to place that rhythm into your body." Later

Figure 8.3. A tea practitioner measuring powdered tea into a tea bowl during a tea gathering. *Source*: Author, Tokyo, 2006

she corrected the student while wiping the tea scoop: "You need to watch it when you take your hand away; otherwise the guests will feel uneasy. Not stopping, but doing it slowly is the most important." Closing her eyes, she recited the steps to the student, whose gestures accompanied the words, until her eyelids suddenly flew open, disturbed by an unevenness to the gentle rustle of gestures, and she broke in, "Wait, you put that down too fast. Do it again."

Yet the rhythm is more than a mere pedagogical tool. First and foremost, it enacts—literally marks out—the regard for the utensils. The slight form of a tea scoop, a mere sliver of bamboo about the size of a pencil curved at the tip, belies its great value within the menagerie of tea objects. Its handling must project its worth, and to suggest gravity and importance, the host lifts the light piece as if it were heavy—first raising the handle of the scoop and then the curved cup. The attention projects an aura onto the utensils, which teachers encourage by cautioning students to remove their hand from objects "as if leaving a cherished friend." One teacher tried to train this skill by instructing a student to pretend that her inexpensive practice utensils were far more important: "You have a very valuable and famous bowl there, and you don't want to hit it. You need to take your hand away slowly. The movement *after* setting down a utensil is extremely important. That's what experienced practitioners notice most." As such, fluency in handling must also be tempered, and a well-trained student manipulating the implements with swift efficiency may be told: "You must create a mood that makes the guest focus on the utensils by projecting respect for them. You need to think about how important the tea caddy is and let your body move in that way. As your hand moves closer to it, you should immediately change due to its importance."

This instructional moment captures the dual role that rhythm plays. As it projects respect for the utensils, it simultaneously sets down a beat that aligns the movements of the host and guests. The object's aura, enlivened in the action of making tea, also delineates a refined sense of coordinated activity crucial to maintaining flow and tempo. If some imagination is necessary for students to learn how to physically embody and project such reverence when handling cheaper utensils at lessons, verbal reminders are rarely needed at formal gatherings, when much-valued objects are removed from their many wooden containers and cloth wrappings, and their handwritten pedigree certificates or inked box lids are placed on display. Crucial, though, is how the utensils are handled, which defines a cadence that structures the interaction among the participants, carrying them in its stream. It fluidly sweeps them from one point and deposits them at another, smoothing the social experience in this unnatural ritual. And in the course of it, the host—with the same precision—will examine the tines on the tea whisk, open the lid of the kettle, and warm the bowl.

Finally, the host prepares the tea. Picking up the tea scoop, she humbly touches her fingers to the floor, and with a slight bow of the head, invites the first of the three guests to try one of the sweets brought out before the procedure began. Lifting the tea container with a circular motion that would keep a kimono sleeve from catching on the bowl, she brings it around to her left knee and measures two heaping scoops of green *matcha*. With a dignified yet quiet gesture, she taps the scoop on the side of the bowl to remove the remaining clumps of tea, careful not to rap with a force that might leave a hairline crack, or to make too loud a sound, which might worry knowledgeable guests about such potential damage. The host then adds some hot water to the bowl, ensuring that the ladle hovers slightly above the bowl to avoid a sense of contamination or danger to the pottery that might be conveyed to the guests if it were to sink below the rim. Picking up the bamboo whisk, she mixes the tea into a frothy suspension, and turning the bowl twice so that its front, perhaps decorated, faces outward, she sets it out for consumption.

The moment her hand leaves the container, her eyes flick toward the first guest, who slides up to retrieve the tea only at that moment—anticipation would convey greed and slowness suggest inattention. If the role of the host is highly scripted, that of the guests is no less choreographed. Returning to his place, he sets the bowl between himself and the second guest, and with his fingertips only partially on the floor in a semiformal bow, he apologizes for being the first to drink. Then moving the bowl to the front of his knees, he offers the host a much lower formal bow and thanks her for preparing the tea. Finally he lifts the container onto the left palm, and while grasping the side with the right hand, raises the tea and lowers his head in a final show of gratitude. Turning the bowl twice so that its front faces away, he drinks from the back as an indication of humility. After the first sip, the host inquires about the taste, and the guest responds, without fail, that it is delicious.

As such, the flow of the gathering is marked and guided not merely by the handling of the objects, but by the interactions between the participants in managing them, all carried off with an attention to the effect on others. This careful coordination of action is encoded not only in the formal procedures—turning the bowl to drink from the back or apologizing to other guests—but also in the stylistics of action. The guest, for example, will finish the two ounces of tea in a few sips without setting down the bowl, careful not to take too much time, as the other guests are waiting. Though it's hardly unique to Japan, active consideration for others is commonly hailed within the country as a distinctively national trait. Not unusual is the best-selling book of 2006, *The Dignity of the Nation*. It sold more than two million copies in its first year by defining what is to be valued about Japanese culture. At the top of its list of particularly Japanese traits were "unspoken understanding, intuitively knowing what others are thinking, non-verbal communication, respect for one's elders, duty, and mutual obligation" (Fujiwara 2006: 3). Not only has the vast *nihonjinron* literature on Japanese uniqueness perpetuated the notion that Japanese culture is matchless in its regard for others, but cross-cultural manuals for Japanese businesspeople working with foreign clients are rich with such examples as well (Yoshino 1992, 9–38). Unsurprisingly, practitioners may remark that they "learn Japaneseness" in mastering the anticipation of others' needs within the tea room.

CONCLUSION

The tea ceremony offers a place for a concentrated experience of Japaneseness within Japan, self-evident yet intense. From the moment of entry into the tea room, little can be taken for granted. Even the elementary actions of walking, sitting, bowing, and standing are relearned to conform to the "correct" standards dictated by etiquette books and business manuals and the demands of a kimono. If an attention to seasons and seasonal associations is a regular feature of everyday life in Japan and claimed as a national hallmark (see also Shirane 2012), the tea room heightens this awareness and supplies training in the vast array of codified references. The rule-governed ceremonial preparation may risk formalism and divorce from the everyday, but its flow softens the stiffness. Setting this rhythm are the utensils and their import. The host handles them in a way that both projects an aura of respect onto the objects and marks a cadence that draws in the guests in attendance. The tempo sweeps the participants along, naturalizing what might otherwise seem a very unnatural ritual.

But a delicate keying of the ordinary does not carry the Japanese resonances of the practice on its own. Connections to other elements of the national cultural matrix contribute as well. Within this, the tea ceremony occupies a prominent position, for it incorporates many of the items deemed indicative of a distinctly traditional version of Japanese culture, from the kimono worn, to *kaiseki* meals, to the "Japanese rooms" employed. At issue are more than mere static homologies that might be read from the component parts. Rather, it is the action of making tea that enlivens the associations in practice. Learning how to handle a particular tea container, for example, may involve also learning a piece of ancient poetry from which its shape derives. The student of tea thus acquires a distinctively Japanese historical, social, and cultural knowledge that is put to work in the tea room. If serving as a host, she will deploy this in the artful selection and combination of utensils, or if sitting as a guest, she will draw on it to decode the theme of a gathering meant to emerge as sui generis from a distinctive combination of polysemous utensils.

Behind the Japanese label often linger variants deemed Western or modern that serve as a foil for defining national qualities—the handshake versus the bow that makes ubiquitous appearance in textbooks, for example. These divisions, once well established, can recede into the background to be called up directly only when needed. Sustaining them are institutions and actors—school systems, museums, instructional manuals, business guides, among others—authorized to instate just what *is* Japanese. They reach into the tea world as it reaches out to them.

If the tea ceremony holds a secure place in a national cultural matrix, sustained by interested institutions, then a delicate interplay between the ordinary and extra-ordinary is what enlivens the Japanese resonances in practice. While tea drinking and socializing are unquestionably mundane, the ceremony hones these actions into rarefied form, retooling the body and transforming perceptual awareness. In so doing, it recasts the unreflexive patterns of ordinary existence as an objectified expression of "Japanese tradition." If objects and the performances around them serve to reify the nation and a specific notion of Japaneseness, Geneviève Zubrzycki shows, in the next chapter, that performing Jewishness acts to deconstruct and expand the notion of Polishness.

NOTES

1. All of these statements were produced in Japanese for a Japanese audience. The analysis presented here draws on several years of ethnographic and historical research on tea practice in Japan, including extended participant observation of four classes, shorter visits to over a dozen additional classes, and participation in numerous demonstrations, tea gatherings, events, meetings, and training sessions, alongside more than one hundred interviews. The presence of an obvious foreigner like myself would, on some occasions, encourage locals to stress the Japaneseness of the practice, in consonance with its prominence as a self-reflexively identified symbol of the country. Striking, however, is that such flaggings readily appear in contexts without an immediate foreign presence, including popular magazines, public demonstrations, advertising pamphlets, museum plaques, collected essays, and the like. My analysis focuses mainly on these internal claims, made by Japanese for Japanese, of the Japaneseness of tea practice.

2. This chapter addresses only the contemporary manifestations of how already-constituted national symbols or icons operate. For an examination of the origins

of such significations—the motives that the myth naturalizes, to use Barthes's terms—see Surak (2011). Surak (2013) provides an analysis of how this operates in the cases of the tea ceremony (57–90) and of the gymnastics movement (174–80).

3. In Japan a little over two million people claim to do the tea ceremony as a hobby, and 90% are women (Shakai Keizai Seisansei Honbu 2006). "Doing tea" means, for the most part, attending weekly lessons where the teacher instructs a group of typically four to eight people in the hundreds of ways of preparing tea, which vary according to the utensils used, architecture of the tea room, and season. A few times during the year, practitioners may attend formal tea gatherings, which last up to four hours, or shorter public demonstrations. Lessons are most commonly held at the homes of teachers, though they are also offered at most community centers, secondary schools, and universities. See Surak (2013, 135–38).

4. To stress the centrality of objects is not to suggest that spiritual elements do not matter to practitioners. Many will recite Zen phrases and tea mottos commonly found on the scrolls hung in the tea room to underscore the importance of focusing on the present moment, thinking of others, feeling at peace, being at one with nature, and the like. Some will state that only a whisk and a tea bowl are needed for the tea ceremony, and the most esoterically oriented will claim that not even those objects are required: all one needs is a sense of gratitude. The "actual existing" tea world, however, revolves around utensils. These are not only thematized at all lessons and tea gatherings; they also are the key means through which status and power are displayed and contested. For further reading on status competition in the tea world, past and present, see Surak (2013).

5. Kyoto, still considered the capital of traditional culture, is commonly used as the reference point.

6. These "Japanese rooms"—literally *washitsu*—typically possess walls of a clay mixture, sliding paper doors, tatami mat flooring, and a decorative alcove, and can be used for eating, sleeping, or receiving guests. Semantically, they stand in contrast to "Western rooms," or *yōshitsu*, which in contemporary Japan refers to run-of-the-mill modern constructions, but also stand out as much rarer. As modern structures now predominate, the term *yōshitsu* is used with far less frequency, while a *washitsu* remains marked as a separate space, often carrying a sign outside the door marking it as such. An apartment advertisement would read, for example, "two bedrooms, one kitchen, one living room, one dining room, and one *washitsu*."

7. Less-experienced men will often wear *hakama*, or a large, pant-like cover over the bottom of their kimono that enables them to spread their legs more widely. Men certified to teach usually wear a standard male kimono, whose shape closely resembles that of the more familiar women's kimono.

8. For readability, I use a female host and a male guest in this example. Of the over two million tea practitioners in Japan today, most are women. Men, however, dominate the upper echelons.

CHAPTER 9

Traces and Steps

Expanding Polishness through a
Jewish Sensorium?

Geneviève Zubrzycki

Historical narratives and national myths are mostly learned and experienced in visual depictions and other material forms like the built environment, landscapes, and embodied practices and performances. This repertoire of materials and performances carries with it a set of cultivated techniques for the proper discernment of national histories. I call this assemblage the *national sensorium* (Zubrzycki 2011). Understanding the sensorium of any given case is crucial to the sociology of nationalism. Only through the sensorium does the abstract notion of the nation become concrete and real to subjects, such that "nationals" come to feel the nation and feel *for* it. The national sensorium's multiple and diverse sites of material expression facilitate the convergence, exchange, and intersection of sensory perceptions, often weaving a dense tapestry of "national feelings." The creation and maintenance of a national sensorium is thus a crucial skill honed equally by nationalist actors and by those who seek to alter or subvert a given national identity.

Polish national identity and its national sensorium are articulated around myths of martyrdom and Poland's intrinsic Catholicity. For reasons beyond the scope of this chapter, that vision of the nation has been increasingly contested since the fall of communism. The critique is articulated in various spheres of public life: in political discourse, constitutional debates, historical narratives, and artistic production (Zubrzycki 2001, 2006, 2011). I argue that the current "Jewish turn" in Poland, characterized not only by the revival of Jewish communities but also by the phenomenal interest of non-Jewish Poles in all things Jewish, is part of that project of national redefinition (Waligórska 2008; Lehrer 2013; Zubrzycki 2016a). In this chapter, I show how socially conscious and politically engaged actors and institutions are reviving Jewish ruins and resurrecting Jewish culture to integrate Jews into the Polish national sensorium and, in so doing, expand the symbolic boundaries of Polishness.

For many activists involved in these acts of salvage remembrance and performance, post–World War II Jewish absence has come to represent the loss of a multicultural Poland (Zubrzycki 2013b, 2016a). Their activities, I argue, are meant to re-member: not only to recall past Jewish presence on Polish lands but to attach a prosthetic Jewish limb to the Polish national body. If certain Polish social milieux now experience Jewish absence as a form of phantom limb pain, knowledge of the prior existence of the limb is a prerequisite for the pain of amputation to be felt. For absence to be meaningful and perhaps even experienced, in other words, an absent presence must be brought back to the surface; erasure itself is being newly refigured. To demonstrate this process of creative historical salvage, I first discuss the material creation of absence. I then focus on the material discovery of Jewish traces and the recovery of Polish Jewish history through museums' material and phenomenological modes of storytelling. The chapter concludes with a discussion of the performance and consumption of Jewishness.

My analysis is based on a varied body of data collected through archival and ethnographic research between July 2010 and March 2016 in several Polish cities, towns, and villages.[1] Ethnographic research included participant and nonparticipant observation in religious events, popular festivals, historical commemorations, political demonstrations, touristic excursions, and museum visits. My data include formal and informal interviews; primary texts (e.g., political speeches, inscriptions on monuments, newspaper editorials); iconographic documents (e.g., photographs, graffiti, ads, pamphlets); audiovisual materials (e.g., films and amateur videos, radio broadcasts, music and soundtracks); and artifacts (e.g., mementos and souvenirs). Although space constraints preclude my referring to all these materials in the present chapter, they do inform my analysis.

THE MATERIAL CREATION
OF JEWISH ABSENCE

Before World War II, Poland had the largest Jewish population in Europe. Ten percent of the Second Republic and one third of Warsaw's inhabitants were Jewish. After the Holocaust, Jewish life all but disappeared from Poland.[2] In Warsaw, only the old town was rebuilt as a faithful copy of the original; other districts like the former Jewish neighborhood disappeared under new streets and buildings that told new stories. With socialist districts built over the rubble of former Jewish spaces and large avenues paved over sinuous streets, material traces of past Jewish life and death were mostly erased. The very memory of Polish-Jewish history was gradually effaced.[3]

Indeed, postwar Warsaw became so different from its prewar incarnation that the Jewish absence could only be felt by those who knew the former space, or with the help of physical markers indicating what was once there. To help conjure the specters of this past, during the past decade the city has been dotted by such historical signposting. The signposting project, however, has not been left to the typical fare of rather banal memorial plaques. Rather, it carefully features significant material markers, and in ways that engage the senses of passersby. The most prominent initiative is one that traces on the ground the vanished walls of the former ghetto (Figure 9.1).[4] Twenty-two monuments were also installed along its perimeter, each made of concrete and embellished with a bronze map and a Plexiglas plaque that gives its history in Polish and English.[5]

The commemorative path not only marks the location and extent of the former ghetto but also provides a powerful reminder of the absent walls, whose trace crosses streets and parks and is sometimes interrupted by postwar buildings. By stepping onto the commemorative path, the passerby stumbles onto three realities: that of the past, that of its erasure, and that of its reemergence through new spatial imaginaries in the

Figure 9.1. Commemorative path that marks the emplacement of the vanished Warsaw Ghetto wall. *Source*: Author, 17 May 2014

present. Signposting the former ghetto wall highlights the Polish experience of absence (of Polish Jews) on two levels, as it reminds viewers of both the extermination of Jews during the Holocaust and their erasure from memory after the war.

Another form of signposting signals the different experiences and fates of Jewish and non-Jewish Poles during World War II. A street-art piece by the artist Adam X (Adam Jastrzębski) titled *Here Was the Footbridge* in Polish, Hebrew, and Yiddish shows the location of the wooden footbridge that linked the small and the large ghettoes during World War II.[6] It highlights the different experiences of the war for Jews and non-Jews: packed crowds of Jews are depicted on the stairs and on the bridge crossing Chłodna Street, while a few gentiles appear to walk nonchalantly on the light and airy "Aryan" street (Figure 9.2).[7]

The mural was ceremoniously unveiled by Marek Edelman, the last surviving leader of the Warsaw Ghetto Uprising, on 21 April 2007 to commemorate the sixty-fourth anniversary of the event.[8] Meant to be

Figure 9.2. *Here Was the Footbridge*, by street artist Adam X. The art piece's title is given in Polish, Hebrew, and Yiddish. *Source*: Author, 17 May 2014

a temporary piece, as street art often is, it eventually led to the establishment in 2012 of a formal, permanent monument to the footbridge in the form of an art installation called *The Footbridge of Memory* (*Kładka pamięci*) (Figure 9.3). The installation, created by Tomasz Lec, consists of two large steel pillars that mark the sites of staircases to the footbridge, linked by wires above the street. At night, the wires are illuminated, creating a virtual bridge. The wires not only represent the platform of the bridge but are also reminiscent of *eruvim,* the wires or cords strung outside ultra-Orthodox Jewish homes that symbolically extend the private domain to allow the residents to carry objects on Shabbat and Yom Kippur, when they are not allowed to perform any work. At the foot of the pillars, at eye level, are historical inscriptions and visual materials, including bronze 3-D viewers showing photographs of life in the ghetto. The juxtaposition of the monument's contemporaneity and the archival photographs assails the spectator with the (virtual) weight of absence.[9]

Other mnemonic projects also focus on signposting the world that has been lost. The Great Synagogue is a case in point. Opened on Rosh

Figure 9.3. *The Footbridge of Memory* (*Kładka Pamięci*), by Tomasz Lec, at the corner of Chłodna and Żelazna Streets, Warsaw. *Source*: http://wiadomosci. onet.pl/warszawa/70-rocznica-otwarcia-drewnianego-mostu-laczacego-duze-i-male-getto-w-warszawie/6xbvq, accessed 16 November 2015

Hashanah in 1878 for Reform Jews, the majestic building could seat 2,400 people, making it at the time the largest synagogue in the world. It was blown up by the Nazis at the end of the Warsaw Ghetto Uprising on 16 May 1943, and the site lay vacant until it was designated as the location for a modern skyscraper. Construction started in the 1970s but was not completed until 1991.[10] On 16 May 2013, the seventieth anniversary of the destruction of the synagogue, the Jewish Historical Institute in Warsaw "brought the synagogue back to remembrance," as it announced several weeks in advance. Part memorial happening and part artistic installation, the event, called "The Great Absentee" (*Wielka nieobecna*) consisted primarily of a 1:10-scale plywood replica of the synagogue situated in a plaza adjacent to the Jewish Historical Institute and the former site of the Great Synagogue. The architect Jan Strumiłło also built walls around the structure on which he plastered photographs of prewar façades of the square where the synagogue stood, in order to give visitors "the feeling of strolling in the authentic square before the war"[11] (Figure 9.4).

The temporary installation was perhaps less successful than other projects, as its scaled-down, papier-mâché appearance did not truly

Figure 9.4. "The Great Absentee" (Wielka nieobecna), by Jan Strumiłło,
Warsaw, 2013. The art installation/commemorative happening was part of the
seventieth anniversary of the Warsaw Ghetto Uprising. The Great Synagogue,
represented here by a plywood model, was burned down by the Nazis as the
final act of crushing the Uprising. For a short film about the commemorative
event, see www.youtube.com/watch?v=JI_VoVvroFQ&feature=youtu.be.
Source: Jan Dybowski for Jan Strumiłło, http://janstrumillo.com/built/the-
great-synagogue/; printed with permission

enable visitors to experience the space "as it once was." But if the space
could not be felt or experienced, it could at least be intellectually grasped,
especially since it stood in the shadow of the Blue Skyscraper (as it is
nicknamed) that now towers over the area.[12]

THE DISCOVERY OF MATERIAL TRACES

Another strategy of memory activists has been to transform sites of
rubble left after the Holocaust and render them visible as distinctively Jewish ruins. In doing so, "empty" things like bricks and beams
are animated; they begin to exert power and act as historical agents.
A key case is Próżna Street, the only remaining block of Warsaw's

former Jewish district, which had been left to fall into ruins (Figure 9.5). The street's former apartment buildings were crumbling away, to the degree that metal nets were suspended over the sidewalks to protect pedestrians from falling debris. In 2008, on the occasion of the sixty-fifth anniversary of the Ghetto Uprising, memory activists covered the boarded-up windows of the Próżna Street buildings with large prewar portraits and candid photographs of Polish Jews. Photographs were collected through a campaign called "And I Still See Their Faces," initiated in 1994 by the Shalom Foundation, headed by the prominent Polish-Jewish actress Gołda Tencer.[13] By the time the exhibit and installation opened on the anniversary of the Ghetto Uprising in 2008, over nine thousand photographs of Polish Jews had been collected.

The giant photographs on Próżna Street transform the buildings from a faceless, decrepit space into a meaningful, if ephemeral, Jewish place. It became the heart of "Jewish Warsaw" and an important site of Polish attempts to remember Jews and celebrate Jewish culture.[14] The material juxtaposition of the large sepia photographs of individuals and the dilapidated building with giant weeds growing in its gutters created a potent testament to the fate of Polish Jews, long forgotten, and of a new generation of Poles now trying to remember them. It also returned a quality of individual dignity to Jews whose lives and deaths were lost in the anonymity of the Holocaust's mass destruction and its commemoration as the extermination of the Six Million.

Yet unlike the street-art piece *Here Was the Footbridge,* which led to a permanent commemorative installation on Chłodna Street, the Próżna Street project has so far not produced such permanent markers. The tenement houses on the south side of the street have been completely renovated in recent years, transformed from Jewish ruins into office and retail spaces and bourgeois *apartamenty* unselfconsciously called Le Palais. A plaque on the immaculate building at the south corner of Próżna and Grzybowski Square now explains that "this building—a witness to the history of Jewish Warsaw—was renovated and preserved for future generations thanks to the support from the Jewish Renaissance Foundation, Mr. Ronald S. Lauder and Warimpex. TRIUVA as current owner contributes to the revitalization process of Próżna St." The buildings on the north side of the street are currently being renovated and the large portraits of Jews have been removed.

Figure 9.5. The last standing building of the former Jewish Warsaw, on Próżna Street. The ruin itself has become a monument with its marking as a Jewish edifice. A metal "net" wrapped around the building's first floor was installed to catch falling debris. *Source*: Author, 6 July 2010

The situation of Kraków in southern Poland differs sharply from that of Warsaw, since the city was not destroyed during the war. Though its Jewish district, Kazimierz, was left in a pitiful state until it underwent a slow process of gentrification in the 1990s, its seven synagogues, two Jewish cemeteries, and its Jewish street names remained.[15] The neighborhood is now the stage for the largest festival of Jewish culture in Europe, and boasts cafés, hotels, and music clubs where Jewish culture is performed and consumed year-round, as I discuss below. While much material Jewishness in Kazimierz is obvious and evident, there are also hidden traces that remain invisible to the untrained eye. It is precisely that training that designers-cum-memory activists Helena Czernek and Aleksander Prugar, founders of Mi Polin ("From Poland" in Hebrew), seek to provide.[16] In their early thirties, the couple creates what they call "tangible Judaism"—modern Judaica design, commemorative objects— and hosts commemorative and pedagogical design workshops. At one such workshop, sponsored by Kraków's Jewish Community Center (JCC) during the Festival of Jewish Culture in 2014, the designers distributed empty frames to participants, giving them the task of roaming through Kazimierz to find and mark Jewish traces. The exercise was meant to "train the eye"—to change the way one looks at one's surroundings; to look for, to see, and then to render visible the Jewish traces that remain. Absence, in this case, is rendered through the act of noticing past presence (Figure 9.6). The ultimate goal is not to uncover new Jewish elements in Kazimierz per se, but to cultivate a different way of seeing and looking that participants can then take with them to the four corners of Poland to discover—and uncover—remnants of Jewish life that tell the story of a different Poland. The participants were mostly young adults, some with children, from different regions of Poland. They expressed interest in learning how to discover traces of Jewish presence in their own towns, asking what they should look for and where. Many saw discovering those Jewish traces as an important step in recovering a multicultural Poland. As one young woman told me as we were walking down a street in July 2014: "This [Jewish] culture was taken away from us. First by the Nazis, then by the communists who transformed old synagogues into storage facilities or neglected to care for cemeteries. Finding some of it again today is a bit like finding pieces of ourselves."

THE RECOVERY OF JEWISH LIFE

So far I have discussed small-scale initiatives by individual memory activists, NGOs, and city planners that focused on framing and animating absence; either by signposting what has vanished or by marking anonymous ruins or invisible or ill-defined cultural remains as Jewish. In this section I focus on major state-sponsored or -sanctioned projects like museums, which also play an important role in the Jewish revival and in the creation of a Jewish sensorium.

History museums, like schools, play a key role in the creation and maintenance of collective memory and national identity. In posttotalitarian societies, they acquire the additional social function of demystification and re-education.[17] The current terrain is thus extremely fertile for history museums, as is evident throughout Eastern Europe: old museums are being redesigned, their narratives revised. Most obvious in the

Figure 9.6. Paper frames on stones (fragments of *matzevot*, or tombstones) used in the wall separating Jakuba Street from the old Jewish cemetery in the Jewish neighborhood Kazimierz, Kraków. Participants in the workshop looked for—and found—Jewish traces. Marking the stones brings attention not only to them but also to their fate, squeezed between fieldstone blocks and bricks, and held "in place" with mortar. *Source*: Author, 5 July 2014

revised historical narratives of Eastern Europe is the emphasis on the Holocaust, which prior to 1989 had been mostly effaced or diluted as but one part of a broader history of fascist aggression. In the decades since, new museums are being opened every year, and many more are in the works.[18] As museums are privileged sites for the transmission of historical narratives and the construction of collective memory—because they are usually legitimized by state authorities—they typically have significant resources that allow them not only to affirm and promote a historical discourse, but also to transmit that knowledge with unusually dynamic and technologically sophisticated pedagogical tools. New Holocaust museums increasingly try to impart knowledge not only by relaying information, but also by cultivating emotions. Intellectual recognition of a new history is achieved through sensation: in that sense, these newly opened facilities are "phenomenological museums" where the visitor's body directly encounters and engages the recreated history. The goal is to have visitors "feel" and "experience" the past.[19] In the Polish context, Kraków's Schindler's Factory Museum does just that: it plays with visitors' vision and orientation (crossing a narrow, dark passage), hearing (music, archival radio broadcasts), touch (walking on uneven surfaces), or smell (in the musty, damp, and smoky hiding place), creating bodily sensations in the visitor to generate a multidimensional impression of the historical situation.

While Schindler's Museum focuses on wartime Kraków and thus deals primarily with the Holocaust, Warsaw's POLIN Museum of the History of Polish Jews, inaugurated in October 2014, focuses on everyday life, specifically rejecting the tendency to reduce the long and complex history of Polish Jews to their destruction in the Holocaust. The museum stands at the center of Muranów, the former Jewish neighborhood and wartime ghetto, in front of the monument to the heroes of the Warsaw Ghetto Uprising. Financed through a transnational public/private cooperation, POLIN's core exhibit tells the story of one thousand years of Jewish life on Polish lands, narrated through a series of multimedia scenarios and interactive props. The core exhibit is exceptionally rich, impressing upon the visitor the diversity and complexity of Jewish communities over centuries before the Holocaust. It relies largely on digital magic. Built without a collection, and thus with very few artifacts, the exhibit relies on strong visual and tactile cues to engage the visitor in a specific virtual scene. Its primary mode of communication is storytelling, but always from the perspective of those who lived at a given time, creating an intimate link between a given narrator and the visitor, transporting the visitor through sound, sight, and touch to different places and times, from sacred spaces like the replica of the Gwoździec Synagogue to the shtetl's marketplace, to the city street, the dance hall, and the cinema (Figure 9.7). By the time the visitor enters the Holocaust gallery, she has been trained and equipped to grasp the variety of worlds that were annihilated during World War II and the challenges of rebuilding a many-faceted Jewish life in communist Poland.

By focusing on mundane life, the museum makes two important narrative correctives. One is oriented to foreign visitors as the exhibit emphasizes that Poland is not only the graveyard of European Jewry but also the place where it grew and where it nourished rich and diverse

Figure 9.7. Replica of the seventeenth-century wooden synagogue from Gwoździec (now in Ukraine) damaged during World War I and destroyed by the Nazis in World War II. It was reconstructed using traditional methods and hand-painted with natural pigments by artists/volunteers from Poland and the United States. POLIN Museum of the History of Polish Jews. *Source*: Author, 28 October 2014

communities, important religious and secular movements, and histori-cally significant political projects. This emphasis on life before death is important in and of itself, but also because it presses guests to fully grasp the tragedy of the Holocaust and its aftermath. After the visitor passes through that section of the exhibit, she exits the museum and encounters—not only visually, but also aurally and viscerally—the void of Jews and Jewish signs, sounds, and symbols in the streets of War-saw. The second challenge proffered by the museum is to the dominant mythology of Poland's intrinsic Catholicity and ethnonational homo-geneity. The museum pointedly and irrefutably shows that the current demographic makeup of Poland is the exception instead of the rule in Polish history. Polish visitors therefore learn an important lesson by vis-iting the museum, namely that Poland was once different from what it currently is, *and can be made so again.*

Kraków's Kazimierz is a living testament to that diversity, and it is prolifically used as such. Inspired by the ever popular "Museums at Night" events when museums open their doors free of charge until early morning, Jewish Community Center (JCC) initiated "7@Nite" in 2011, opening Kazimierz's seven synagogues to large crowds of Krakovians eager to learn about the past and present religious landscape of Polish Jews. In the first year of 7@Nite, over ten thousand people flooded the narrow streets of Kazimierz. The event was such a success that it became a yearly tradition, attracting similar numbers. Each synagogue hosts lectures or workshops or gives tours during which visitors/guests can meet the local Jewish population, talk to rabbis, and get a "feel" for places they otherwise rarely or never enter. In a way similar to that of Kraków's Festival of Jewish Culture, non-Jewish Poles, through events like 7@Nite, revisit and at least momentarily recover part of Polish history. As Janusz Makuch, the cofounder and director of Kraków's Festival of Jewish Culture, told me in one of our conversations: "Whether people know it or not, it is a *fact* that Jews, for many, many centuries . . . made tremendous contributions to Polish culture. So when we're talking about Polish culture, we're equally talking about Jewish culture. Without the contribution of Jews, true Polish culture couldn't exist. Forget it! [. . .] What I'm trying to do . . . is to help Poles realize what is theirs" (1 March 2012, original conversation in English). What the Festival of Jewish Culture, JCC's 7@Nite, and the POLIN Museum of the History of Polish Jews are working toward, Makuch explained, is not merely to bring non-Jewish Poles in contact with the past Jewish presence in Poland, but to instill an intuitive knowledge in Poles that Jews and Jewish culture are part and parcel of Polish culture, and must be recovered and reintegrated as such.

These multifaceted initiatives undertaken by individual artists, NGOs, and state institutions are creating an ideological climate where Jews, Jewish culture, and Judaism can occupy and even thrive in public space. Since the mid-2000s, for example, a giant outdoor Hanukiah is lit in Warsaw on the first night of Hanukkah by Chabad Rabbis, accompanied by city and state officials. The Chief Rabbi of Poland, Michael Schudrich, also lights a Hanukiah at the presidential palace. Both events are photographed and widely publicized on television and in the press.[20] In 2012, to give another example of Jewish traditions carried into public space, Warsaw's Joint Distribution Committee (JDC) foundation invited architectural firms to exhibit their contemporary interpretations of *sukkahs*, temporary structures built on the occasion of the Jewish holiday of Sukkhot, on Grzybowski Square.[21] Half a dozen were built and exhibited in the square, near Próżna Street, described above. The local population was invited to attend, meet members of the Jewish community, and learn about the tradition. I asked a (non-Jewish) commuter walking by what those structures/sculptural installations were; he correctly explained that they were contemporary interpretations of sukkahs, adding that he was very happy that the tradition was being revived. "You know," he told me, his eyebrows raised, "Poland is more than the traditional nativity scenes of Kraków."[22]

Jewish markers, whether religious or secular, create visual and material diversity in the cityscape, "monumentally" if modestly, diluting Catholicism's sensory dominance. Aneta, a longtime Kraków JCC volunteer who is expressly anticlerical and declares herself an atheist, expanded on this during a Shabbat dinner: "I think it's great to see all of that [Jewish religious activity]. I'm not religious but I think it's good to see that there's something else than what we already know, and frankly speaking, we're sick of . . .processions, pilgrimages here and there, crosses everywhere."

EMBODIED JEWISHNESS: WALKING THE WALK AND DRESSING THE PART

Marek Edelman, the sole survivor of the Warsaw Ghetto Uprising until his death in 2009, used to commemorate the onset of the Uprising, on 17 April 1943, with a bouquet of yellow daffodils. After his passing, the tradition was taken up by several of his close friends and members of the Jewish community. And in 2013, on the occasion of the seventieth anniversary of the Uprising, designer Helena Czernek created for the POLIN Museum of the History of Polish Jews a yellow paper daffodil to be worn as a pin. Some forty thousand were made and distributed by volunteers, and the paper daffodil could be seen worn by Poles for weeks after the commemorative events. The memento was effective because it linked the commemoration of the Uprising with the memory of Marek Edelman, a much-respected figure. It was also semiotically complex. Once pinned, the yellow paper flower opened up and looked much like a star.[23] Many affixed the flower/star to their lapels, others to their sleeves, replicating the branding of Jews during the Nazi occupation. Special commemorative marches and bike rides were organized, retracing the now vanished traces of Jewish Warsaw.

The paper daffodil has now become a tradition. On 19 April 2016 over one thousand volunteers distributed sixty thousand paper daffodils in Warsaw alone. Eight hundred schools in various regions of Poland made additional daffodils and distributed them in their small towns and villages.[24] While the daffodil flower has come to symbolize, over the years, the memory of the Uprising, its paper incarnation that mutates into a yellow star has acquired an additional signification, that of the Holocaust and the fate that separated Jewish from non-Jewish citizens of Poland. Wearing the paper daffodil/star has therefore become a commemorative act as well as a posthumous act of resistance to the distinction made by Nazis (and by many Poles) between Jews and non-Jews (Figure 9.8).

While events commemorating the Holocaust in Poland are not new, their scope and frequency have dramatically changed since 1989, to the extent that they are now commonplace. In Kraków, for example, the March of Memory commemorates the liquidation of the Jewish ghetto every year. Participants walk from the Podgórze neighborhood, where Jews were relocated in a ghetto, to the Płaszów work camp. It takes on meaning for its participants as an embodied practice attempting to replicate the forced migration of Jews; as practiced and walked history. These embodied and publically performed rituals simultaneously allow Polish-Jewish history to be phenomenologically internalized by individuals, and externalized onto the material cityscape. The material and performative remaking of public space in turn motivates political discourses about citizenship and what constitutes Polishness. While the march is conducted in silence, speeches are made at the departure and arrival points. In the multiple marches I participated in since the early 2000s, the theme of citizenship has been uniformly prominent, with the emphasis laid squarely on the fact that Jews were Polish. The effect is to not only materially and performatively but also discursively reject a vision of ethnic Polishness narrowly predicated on its association with Catholicism.

Dressing the Part

Many of the practices I discussed in previous sections are ritual-like (e.g., commemorations, perambulations), educational (e.g., museums,

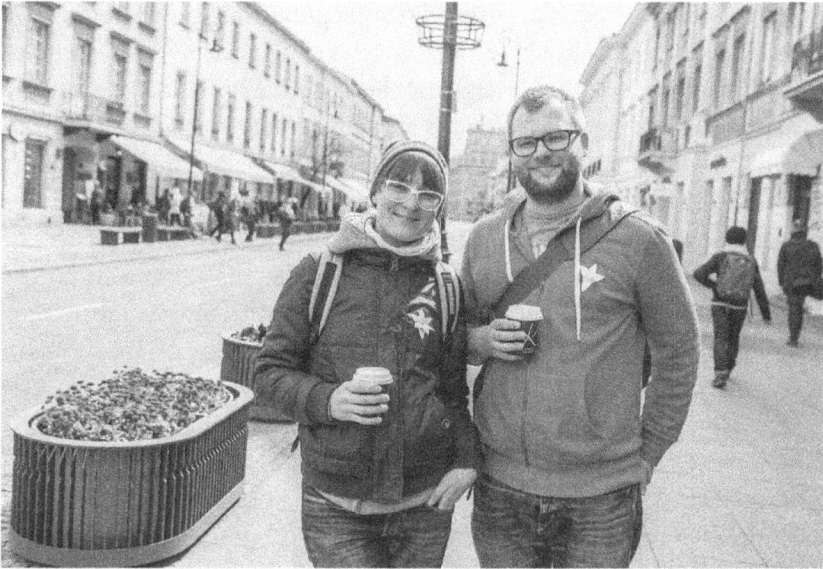

Figure 9.8. Young couple strolling on Nowy Świat Avenue in Warsaw, proudly wearing the daffodil/yellow star. On the man, the daffodil; on the woman, a "bloomed" version of the flower, transfigured into a star. *Source*: Alicja Szulc, POLIN Museum of the History of Polish Jews, 19 April 2015; printed with permission

workshops), or festive (e.g., holidays, festivals). Many Poles however engage in daily, mundane "Jewish" activities: they listen to Jewish music, from modern klezmer to Israeli hip-hop; they eat in Jewish restaurants and drink kosher vodka (rumored as "purer"); and some even "dress Jewish." What do consumption patterns and individual practices mean to those engaging in them?

A fashionably contemporary clothing label in Warsaw that launched a new "Jewish" line called "Risk Oy" may offer clues. Initially targeted at young Jews, Risk Oy produces pricey T-shirts and hoodies with slogans such as "Thanks to my Mom" (in English), adorned with a variety of Star of David designs and Hebrew inscriptions. The owner of the brand told the *Times of Israel*: "What we really want . . . is to rebrand Jewish identity. We want to show the modern, positive aspects of it. What we are doing is showing that being Jewish is cool and sexy."[25] The clothes are not bought and worn by Jews alone, however. One non-Jewish customer quoted in the story, a forty-year-old lawyer living in Warsaw, explained,

"Wearing [Risk Oy] is like taking part in a public discussion about Jews in Poland—that Jews live here and that Jews can live here." This is a noteworthy comment on two levels: first, because it emphasizes that public discussion about Jews in Poland is actually one about the very identity of Poland and a critique of the still dominant vision of the nation as ethnically Polish and (nominally) Catholic; and second, because it indicates that this public discussion is taking place not only in the pages of newspapers and the discourses of public intellectuals, but also on the streets among hoi polloi and the clothes they wear (or the music they listen to, or the bars they patronize). The NGO Foundation for Freedom several years prior (2010) had produced "I'm a Jew" T-shirts as part of a campaign that consisted in "spreading . . . slogans signaling the existence of . . . discriminated social groups in Poland," including Jews, atheists, and homosexuals.[26] Hence liberal, leftist youth wore T-shirts and brandished posters in protests against clerical nationalists, subversively claiming that they were "Jews." With this display they mocked anti-Semitic conspiracy theories of the right claiming that Jews rule Poland, but they also called for a different kind of Poland, one in which the right's distinctions between "real Poles," "Jews," and "bad Poles" would have no political traction.

Consuming Jewish food, whether in its Ashkenazi form or in its contemporary Israeli versions, is also a way to acquaint oneself with either the "known" and recognizable (Ashkenazi cuisine, very similar to, because in part constitutive of, Polish cuisine) or the mysterious and exotic (Israeli cuisine). It is that mix of "ours" and "other," of the familiar and the exotic, that likewise attracts many (non-Jewish) young women who take part in an Israeli dance group. One of the dancers, a young Protestant woman who majored in Judaic studies and art history and is now a museum educator in a Catholic institution, explained to me:

> On one hand, [Jewish culture] is, let's say, "Oriental." But on the other hand, because it developed in Poland, in spite of everything it's somehow very much tied with Poland, yes? It's kind of an exotic element in our environment. It's not something like . . . Swahili somewhere far off in Africa, but [rather] something that is different from Polish culture yet at the same time related to it, inseparable even.

Performing various forms of Jewish dances—Ashkenazi, Sephardic, or contemporary Israeli—brings those young women (and, one presumes,

Figure 9.9. Members of the dance troupe Kachol, rehearsing at the Popper Synagogue in Kraków. *Source*: Author, 5 March 2012

their audiences) closer to a different side of Polish history than the one exalted in Polish national mythology and its sensorium. At the same time, as this woman's explanation suggests, the dances transport them to faraway, exotic, "Oriental" (yet, paradoxically, more "Western" than Poland)—places like Israel (Figure 9.9).

CONCLUSION

Wearing a "Jewish" sweatshirt, dancing to Jewish music, eating Jewish foods, and drinking kosher vodka become embodied practices meant to challenge a restrictive definition of Polishness. These practices do not serve to *reproduce* an existing national identity but to *de-* and *reconstruct* identity along new lines. Polishness is being challenged and redefined by activists and artists as well as by ordinary people in their mundane activities. Multiple forms of memory work such as graffiti art, walking tours of formerly Jewish spaces, commemorative marches, or the cleaning and restoration of cemeteries all serve to undermine the political claim and the dominant view that Poland is essentially, primordially ethno-Catholic. Ordinary Poles become involved in the revival and assimilate Jewishness, to the extent that it becomes "Polish," through embodied and repeated actions. They remake Polishness by learning how to "cook Jewish" or how to serve and consume Jewish foods during a festival, at a café all year round, or at a Sabbath dinner at the JCC; by singing and dancing; by learning Jewish paper-cutting techniques; or by donating their time and energy to Jewish individuals and organizations.

Evocative as these examples are, we should ask whether they reach large enough audiences to be significant, or to constitute a bona fide social movement. Do they remain elite practices by artists and activists that do not quite resonate *en masse*? How successful are the mnemonic recovery of material traces and the embodied practices rehearsed by attempting to follow the footsteps of Jews who no longer live in Poland? From a sociology of nationalism perspective, it is not yet clear how to define the "success" of attempts to attach a prosthetic Jewish limb to the Polish national body, at least symbolically. One way to adjudicate or at least gain perspective on the issue, I suggest, is to give close attention to the Polish national sensorium. We can speak of a revived Jewishness in Poland to the degree that Jewish histories are discovered, named, and animated and to the degree that the proper attunement to their material traces is cultivated—not only among memory activists and cosmopolitan consumers, but also as a matter of public pedagogy and city planning. By this measure, I have shown, the so-called Jewish revival is well underway, though its effects in reforming Poland's national identity, or the manifold ways it is subjectively internalized, are still unclear.

NOTES

Research for this article was funded by grants from the University of Michigan's Office of Research, the Rackham Graduate School and LSA, and the Society for the Scientific Study of Religion. A research leave at the University of Michigan's Frankel Institute for Advanced Judaic Studies allowed me to complete the writing. I'm grateful to the fellows of the Frankel Institute for their comments on an earlier version of this chapter. Special thanks are due to the many in Poland who opened their homes, shared their thoughts, and invited me into their worlds so that I could make better sense of the Jewish revival in that country.

1. I conducted most of my fieldwork in Kraków and Warsaw, where the ongoing "Jewish turn" is strongest, but I also conducted research in Lublin, Wrocław, Oświęcim, Chmielnik, Szydłów, and Jedwabne.

2. Approximately 3.5 million Jews lived in pre–World War II Poland, of which 400,000 inhabited Warsaw. Ninety percent of Polish Jewry was exterminated in the Holocaust, and many survivors chose to rebuild their lives elsewhere in the immediate aftermath of the war. Postwar pogroms and anti-Semitic purges in 1968 forced the emigration of thousands more Polish Jews, further diminishing the number of Jews in Poland. In 1989, the *American Jewish Year Book* reported that approximately two thousand individuals were registered members of Jewish communities. By the beginning of the new millennium, the number of Polish Jews registered with communities, belonging to Jewish organizations, or receiving aid from the American Jewish Joint Distribution Committee had nearly quadrupled, to between seven and eight thousand. In the most recent Polish census, seven thousand Polish citizens self-identified as Jewish (Główny urząd statystyczny 2015*)*. Yet it is estimated that approximately forty thousand Polish citizens have some Jewish ancestry without necessarily being conscious of it (*American Jewish Year Book* 2002, 2003). When asked how many Jews currently live in Poland, the chief rabbi of Poland, Michael Schudrich, often responds: "How many do you think there are? Take that number and double it. And now add one. There's always one more coming out of the closet" (informal conversation, Warsaw, 22 March 2013).

3. For an outstanding comparative study of the postwar treatment of Jewish ruins in Poland, the German Democratic Republic, and the Federal Republic of Germany, see Meng (2011). For incisive studies on the fate of Jewish ruins in Warsaw, see Janicka (2012) and Chomątowska (2012).

4. This initiative is akin to that of stumbling stones (*Stolpersteine*) in Germany, as the brick and brass pathway visually and sensorially interrupts the walking surface to tell a story to the casual walker who steps on, over, or beside it.

5. For a list of the monuments' locations, see https://pl.m.wikipedia.org/wiki/Pomniki_granic_getta_w_Warszawie (accessed 18 April 2016).

6. To the (rare) onlooker who can read Hebrew, the inscription in that language (top line) is most interesting, as a small diacritical mistake on one of the letters in the word *bridge* transforms it into the word *void*. Thus "Here was the bridge" becomes "Here was the void." The mistake was most likely accidental—a spelling correction has been added underneath the misspelled word—but acutely captures the meaning of the artwork. My thanks to Efrat Bloom for pointing this out to me.

7. Chłodna Street was excluded from the ghetto because it was an important transport and communication axis.

8. http://puszka.waw.pl/tam_byla_kladka-projekt-pl-52.html (accessed 23 October 2014). Before his death in 2009, Marek Edelman was the last surviving leader of the Warsaw Ghetto Uprising. He remained in Poland after the

war, became a noted cardiologist, and was an active member of the Solidarity opposition.

9. This effect is perceived, of course, only to the extent that the passerby stops, looks, and views the photos on the monument: its potential phenomenological effect is necessarily limited by the viewer's ability and desire to engage with the installation in the first place. The installation nevertheless imparts some knowledge of the past presence and current absence even with minimal engagement.

10. One of the reasons for the delay, Varsovians like to say, was that the rabbi of the Great Synagogue placed a curse on the site when the Nazis blew it up. Absence often comes with rumors, stereotypes, and ghost stories. I address those more fully in a chapter of my book *Resurrecting the Jew: Nationalism and Philosemitism in Contemporary Poland* (in progress).

11. www.sztetl.org.pl/en/cms/news/3327,the-70th-anniversary-of-the-destruction-of-the-great-synagogue-on-tlomackie-st-/. More photographs of the replica and the square can be viewed on Strumiłło's webpage, "The Great Absentee," www.janstrumillo.com/built/the-great-synagogue/ (accessed 21 September 2015), and on the website of the design firm that executed the project: www.pracownia-tryktrak.pl/portfolio/wielka-nieobecna/ (accessed 21 September 2015).

12. These comments are based on conversations I had with many Poles and foreign tourists who visited the installation.

13. For a description of the project, consult the webpage of the project "And I Still See Their Faces" on the Foundation Shalom website, http://shalom.org.pl/en/projects/i-ciagle-widze-ich-twarze/ (accessed 26 April 2016).

14. Próżna Street and Grzybowski Square is where Warsaw's Jewish festival, "Singer's Days" (after Isaac Bashevis Singer), is celebrated in August every year since 2004.

15. The gentrification of Kazimierz is related to the filming of *Schindler's List* in the early 1990s, the subsequent development of Holocaust tourism, as well as hipsters moving in because of low rent. See Kugelmass and Orla-Bukowska (1998); Murzyn (2006); and Lehrer (2013).

16. I interviewed Czernek and Prugar on 26 October 2015. See also their website, http://mipolin.pl/.

17. That process, however, is not always easy because museums also *objectify* memory and identity, which means that museums in such societies must first *undo*—deconstruct some of what they had previously done—before they can reconstruct. This is sometimes easier said than done and of course this does not mean that new or revised museums do not engage in a remythologization of another kind. See my analysis of the Auschwitz-Birkenau Museum in Zubrzycki (2006, 98–140).

18. In Poland alone, and specifically on Jewish history and/or the Holocaust, over half a dozen museums have been inaugurated in the past decade: Kraków's *Galicja Jewish Museum* was founded in 2003; *Schindler's Factory Museum* on occupation in World War II Kraków opened in 2010; the Museum of Kraków's

Ghetto, *The Eagle Pharmacy,* opened in 2013; and the POLIN *Museum of the History of Polish Jews* in Warsaw opened its building in April 2013 and its main exhibit in October 2014. There are many other smaller museums and educational centers throughout Poland, such as the "*Świętokrzyski shtetl*" in Chmielnik, which opened in 2014.

19. This experiential strategy has been important elsewhere as well. The Holocaust Museum in Washington, DC, presents the museum-goer with an identification card as she or he enters the premises to foster a temporary, virtual identification with a person whose fate the visitor does not know until the end of the tour. The visitor is supposed to live the uncertainty of the war through this historical avatar. This creates a certain emotional investment in the story being told to the visitors, the materials they see, and the facts they learn.

20. Such practices cannot be cynically seen as mere electoral strategies by non-Jewish politicians, since the "Jewish vote" is of little significance given the small number of Jews in Poland. But they are certainly addressed as much to international audiences as to national constituencies. The Polish state has been keenly aware of the need to rebrand Poland abroad and there can be little doubt that its support of Jewish-related initiatives is part of that process. A prime example is the recent opening of the POLIN Museum of the History of Polish Jews, which the Ministry of Culture advertised and promoted throughout the Western world.

21. The event was meant to mark the opening of the Warsaw Jewish Community Center (JCC); www.jccwarszawa.pl/galeria/170/g/9https://vimeo.com/55538006.

22. This interaction should not be overgeneralized. A cabbie driving me from Grzybowski Square had no idea what the installations were, and when I told him he embarked on a vitriolic anti-Semitic monologue.

23. Czernek told me she had never intended the daffodil to be a yellow star; that it was a material flaw caused by nothing more than poor glue and problematic execution by the volunteers who had assembled the forty thousand paper flowers. It is however precisely that additional, accidental signification that made the small paper memento such an impactful one. This is an excellent example of "cultural entropy," the ways objects take on new, unintended meanings as they travel and are brought into novel contexts (McDonnell 2016).

24. www.polin.pl/en/news/2016/04/22/4th-edition-of-the-daffodils-campaign (accessed 13 July 2016).

25. At: www.timesofisrael.com/polish-fashion-entrepreneur-makes-being-jewish-sexy/?utm_source=Newsletter+subscribers&utm_campaign=0c5a586595-JTA_Daily_Briefing_1_31_2014&utm_medium=email&utm_term=0_2dce5bc6f8–0c5a586595-25416689 (accessed 1 February 2014).

26. Other T-shirts part of the 2004 campaign included, "I don't go to church," "I don't want to have kids," or "I'm gay." See www.tiszertdlawolnosci.tiszert.com/ (accessed 22 July 2012).

CHAPTER 10

A Temple of Social Hope?

Tempelhof Airport in Berlin and Its Transformation

Dominik Bartmański

> Most banal externalities are bound up with the final
> decisions concerning the meaning and the style of life.
>
> — GEORG SIMMEL, *METROPOLIS*

In the fall of 2008 one of the oldest city airports in the world, Berlin Tempelhof, was closed and with it an eventful chapter of German history. The airfield was reborn in the spring of 2010, albeit in a different capacity of a public park. The architecture assumed other public and private uses. The closure of this centrally located airport turned out to be the beginning of Berlin's new urban commons. What may have seemed at first to be yet another temporary top-down project quickly morphed into a lasting bottom-up social mobilization to keep the park intact. The unique leisure area has been instantly embraced, celebrated, and successfully defended against any developing plans in a democratic plebiscite.

How was this remarkable transformation possible? Where do the collective feelings for the park stem from? In particular, what made the former airport amenable to this change and so much lasting social support? It is not accidental that I ask here about *what* rather than *who* underpinned this unique reshuffling of social meaning. Although individual and collective actions of Berlin authorities and citizens were important for social, political, and legal reasons, I wish to refocus analytical emphasis from political intent to phenomenological content. How do the winning reasons make sense to Berliners? What emotional content propelled the mobilization? Officially articulated reasons count and are easily accessible to sociologists as data, but they *make sense* only in broader experiential and affective contexts. Thus, one needs to comprehend what framed the political enunciations and actions. One key dimension of the experiential context I have in mind comprises material affordances of built environment. As the old phrase goes, people shape their cities and then the cities shape them in turn. The story of Tempelhof's transformation exemplifies this observation. In what follows I focus on how a set of experiential relations between Berliners, their city, and the former-airport-turned-park engendered this transformation. Any prominent urban site is a spatiocultural environment conducive to a range of embodied experiences. These experiences become meaningful vis-à-vis other experiences and correspond with the discursive surround of the era (Wagner-Pacifici and Schwartz 1991). The very matter on which social facts depend matters. It is to be conceived of not as inert *material* but as "vibrant matter" that constitutes a "political ecology of things" (Bennet 2010). I approach it here as a meaningful, sensuous conglomerate of substance, form, dimension, and scale, each of which features relational affordances. Some of those material constellations can jointly shape an urban place in which certain emotional attachments and intellectual commitments are likely to occur and subsequently cherished, articulated, sustained, or even performatively mobilized as political force. Such places form meaningful social topographies invested with feelings. They are sociotopes.

The case of Tempelhof is a story of materially mediated collective feelings, their emplacement, embodiment, mobilization, and public projection. Those feelings and actions are simultaneously being made by that site and are making it too. The present chapter shows that the turning and developing of Tempelhof into a public park was a decision about the meaning and the style of life, as the epigraph from Georg Simmel posits. It was a collective decision-making process rooted in and informed by seemingly banal externalities of that place, not just in ideological internalities of politics. In fact, the latter were significantly conditioned by the former. Cultural sociology's traditional approach of privileging codes of political communication over materially constituted experiences could hardly flesh out this reflexive position. To approach a more balanced epistemic vantage point, a nexus of new concepts is proposed.

THE CONCEPTS

The analytic shift to include the phenomenological and affective aspects of meaning foregrounds two salient but sociologically undertheorized things. First, the relational materiality of social symbols considerably shapes their cultural power and potential for social resonance. What a given signifier *is* matters for what it can possibly *mean* and *do* to people under particular circumstances. Whether a given social symbol is a tool, a picture, or a building makes a huge difference. Where a given symbol is put to work matters as well because it entails a particular set of experiential and semiotic relations. While this may seem uncontroversial, the standard take on material symbols has treated them as social mirrors regardless of what they were. Symbolic things were reflections of power, not its sources. However, objects and sites of social importance do not just *stand for* something. They are not mere screens of discursive projection. Their material constitution is an integral part of significatory and social power. That is to say, they are not just *place holders* for something else, but *place makers* whose relational features partake in generating uniquely calibrated possibilities of shared experience, collective feelings, and social agency.

Second, although relatively open-ended, the meaning of the material signifier emerges neither fully arbitrarily nor purely conventionally. It takes place partly due to specific relations of the human sensorium to the world, and partly by dint of specific relations of a given material object to other signifiers. We relate to objects and places not randomly but in patterned and phenomenologically ordered ways relative to those relations. Cultural scholars today call these relations *affordances* (cf. Hodder 2012; McDonnell 2010; Harré 2002). Unlike Rom Harré, who strongly prioritizes discursive action over material relations, I posit that the two are mutually constitutive. In fact, urban sociology and new material culture studies provide arguments that enable us to transcend this old dualism altogether (Miller 2005; Bennet 2010; Bartmański 2012; Beauregard 2015).

For a long time, modern cultural sociology bracketed this understanding of materiality. Constructivist methodology turned objects into negligible props in meaning creation. A kind of triple conflation ensured this perspective, namely equating (1) meaning with symbolic meaning, (2) cultural symbols with arbitrary signs, and (3) arbitrary signs with linguistic signifiers. Although problematized even by structuralists, notably by Castoriadis, Saussure, and Lévi-Strauss, respectively (see Bartmański and Binder 2015, 502), this paradigm dominated many cultural sociological works and construed cultural meanings as discursive forms. Dominated by discursive analysis of official archival documents, public media narratives, and interviews and surveys, sociology has neglected its phenomenological traditions. As a result, it has had comparatively little understanding of how place-specific and object-specific processes of meaning making crucially *inflect* collective feelings and social narratives, not just *reflect* them. In short, culture has been commonly modeled with language, especially in semiological and structuralist fashion.

The problem is that human cultures do not work simply *like* language or only *through* language. We now know that discursive frames and tropes are deeply enmeshed in experiential features of life and given material conditions (e.g., Lakoff and Johnson 2003). Some contemporary sociological analyses of the causal power of motivations and discursive meanings continue to make semiotic conception of culture more nuanced (e.g., Reed 2011; Tavory and Timmermans 2013). But these theories ultimately offer no systematic understanding on how objects and spaces coordinate our perception and correspond with our feelings, that is, how materiality impacts meaning making, not just the other way around. No wonder then that they fail to account for the fact that places are not mere "containers" but complex conditions of meaningful action. Put differently, little work in cultural sociology has so far been dedicated to sociologize a key phenomenological insight, namely that experiences and discursive articulations are reciprocally conditioned aspects of meaning making rather than separate or hierarchically related domains of social reality. "Discourse never exhausts reality," and it is the inseparability of humans and materiality that defines culture, not any one aspect (Beauregard 2015, 6, 10). Thus, nowadays cultural anthropologists tend to see human-object assemblages as key elements of meaning making, whereby cultural significance emerges contingently out of topological, material, and temporal structures (e.g., Weszkalnys 2010, 7). In other words, meanings are not mechanically "attached" to places, or merely conventionally "attributed" to artifacts, as standard culturalist language goes. Rather, they are an emergent dimension of social life, always materially mediated. As I demonstrated elsewhere (Bartmański and Woodward 2015, 139), social spaces are punctuated and energized by copresence and the arrangement of objects within them, whereby an interpretive field is engendered. It is in such fields or assemblages that affordances are clarified, bodies placed, feelings made visible and shared, and thus social. This is conducive to the emergence of culturally significant sites that can be understood as both quasi-totemic focal points and nodes of social life.

This perspective is gaining increasing traction in sociology only today, but it is not entirely new. A conception of restricted arbitrariness of object-based meanings is explicit in the classic sociological works of Georg Simmel (2008, 384) and Karl Mannheim who distinguished between *sign-meanings* and *form-meanings* (Mannheim 1964). Similarly, reflecting on the meaningfulness of architecture, Theodor Adorno argued that certain key ideas are derived from experience and that our "sense of space" is not arbitrary (1965, 12). Durkheim too famously urged sociologists to treat social facts *as things* but did much less to treat things as meaningful social facts in their own right (Steets 2015). To redress this problem, contemporary Durkheimian cultural sociology has turned to the concept of cultural icon. Icons are material condensations of meaning (Alexander 2008b), symbols to be experienced not just decoded, surfaces that have depth. Icons are not mere representations; they are experiential entities and building blocks of lifeworlds. Social meanings, traditionally approached in sociology as "inherently 'invisible'" (Tavory and Timmermans 2013, 689), or as autonomous "depth" capable of "infinite resignification" (Reed 2011), are in fact materially precoded and existentially grounded (Merleau-Ponty 2012, 126). Therefore, as Mannheim already observed, "the range of emotions and experience available to a given epoch is by no means unlimited and arbitrary" (1964, 55). Nonrepresentational aspects of symbols are salient (Keane 2005; Miller 2005). For this reason, as for instance archaeologists demonstrate, meanings of objects are always traceable to their affordances (Hodder 2012) and their aesthetic design "constitutes community identity rather than simply reflects it" (Feldman 2014, 9). Cultural sociologists also join the call for going "beyond the cultural arbitrary" (Smilde and Zubrzycki 2016) and develop this perspective by showing how interpretation of meanings in contemporary societies is always afforded by particular properties and constellations of objects and their settings (McDonnell 2010; Griswold, Mangione, and McDonnell 2013; Bartmański 2011, 2012; Bartmański and Woodward 2015). Thus, prominent objects, sites, or events that concretize massive social sentiments are not just a matter of discursive power. They are not infinitely open-ended, wholly based on conventional "semiosis." Rather, their power and resonance is a matter of a complex fit between given concerns, bodily experiences, available material objectifications, and semiotic patterns that coordinate one another. Objects and sites indispensably crystallize social meanings.

In short, when it comes to the emergence of social meanings of iconic places and objects, their form, substance, scale, design, appearance, and relational positioning are all important factors. They all stir and shape our interpretative processes. In addition to historical connotations, they have their signature feel and mood (Silver 2011) and atmosphere that can sociologically be defined as "the external effect of social goods and human beings realized perceptually in their spatial ordering" (Löw 2008a, 44). Their very presence matters, framing, disabling, and enabling what's happening here and now. Distinguishing between certain key sociomaterial conditions that define urban atmospheres, Durkheimian cultural sociologists developed a basic typology of elementary forms of place going beyond the basic binary of sacred and profane. Philip Smith (1999) introduced the category of the *liminal* and defined the liminal place as "sustained by quasi-ritualized carnivalesque playful forms of behavior." Such places defy easy classification and can therefore play a role of vehicles of alternative or special practices. Smith notes that especially in the postrevolutionary periods, they provide social stages for "frivolous and ludic micro-rituals of anti-structure," in Victor Turner's sense. They are liminal not just because they happen to emerge as political signs at "unsettled times" (Swidler 1986), but because they coproduce playful, relaxed, experimental, or even subversive sensibility in people through experiences and an atmosphere of freedom they foster. In what follows, I propose to approach the Tempelhof airfield-turned-park as an instantiation of an iconic liminal place.

THE CASE

Background

Upon its creation in the 1920s, Tempelhof was the biggest civilian airport in the world. Back then it signified the development of German modernity. Further expanded during the National Socialist period in the mid-1930s, it grew by the giant crescent building—the main terminal and the architectural interface between the airfield and the city. The sheer scope and ambition of that construction may still impress. One can regard it as a historic apotheosis of the authoritarian, high-modernist practice of "seeing like a state" (Scott 1998). When in 1948 the Soviet authorities imposed the blockade on West Berlin for over a year, Tempelhof stood for its lifeline. As Bryan Ladd (1997, 21) observes, "More than any other event, the triumphant Berlin Airlift made the city a symbol of Western resolve in the Cold War." Until the fall of the Wall in 1989, Tempelhof retained this symbolic capital.

However, as an aging inner-city airport, Tempelhof's prime utility was gradually supplanted by the suburban Tegel Airport in the northwest of the city. Tempelhof's commercial operation was temporarily shut down in 1975. After the reunification of Germany in 1990, Tempelhof tentatively reopened but Tegel's own obsolescence began then to be discussed too. Eventually, the decision was made to construct a new airport in the diagonally opposed corner of the city's southeast suburbs. A quarter of a century after the fall of the Wall, the new facility was finished but not launched due to severe mismanagement and subsequent delays which made it unlikely to open before 2018. Meanwhile, Tempelhof Airport reached an age at which it was claimed to have much history and little future. Born out of a zeitgeist of innovation and grand demands of the day, it now seemed to have no choice but to succumb to the current pressure of the same progressive social forces. It was therefore irrevocably closed down in 2008, at a time when the profound banking crisis affected Western economies. While some financial institutions at fault seemed notoriously too big to fail, Tempelhof proved too big to go unnoticed as an enormous urban, economic, and social asset. The significance of this temporal overlap should not be underestimated. The deep economic recession and global criticism of financial institutions that caused it defined the context in important ways. Among other things, it accentuated that "we increasingly live in divided, fragmented and conflict-prone cities. How we view the world and define possibilities depends on which side of the tracks we are on. . . . The results are indelibly etched into the spatial forms of our cities, which increasingly become cities of fortified fragments, of gated communities and privatized public spaces kept under constant surveillance" (Harvey 2012, 9). It is within this frame that a constitutive narrative of Tempelhof Park as a "public space of freedom," inherent in its official name Tempelhof Freedom, was formulated. At the same time, that economic crisis meant "a fatal crisis for the idea of stateless or largely state-independent cities" (Therborn 2011, 282) and thus restored the cultural and social importance of the nation-state for framing the city and taking responsibility for its life quality. Finally, like many other disused sites in post-Wall Berlin, this one too was bound to undergo cultural transformation and broach controversial questions of repurposing and meanings of national heritage (Ladd 1997).

A more local dynamic is salient too, and a personal experience can help describe it. Around the time of Tempelhof's last days as an airport, I lived in a building at Leinestrasse in the not-yet-gentrified district of Neukoelln, whose south-oriented backyard windows faced the tree-lined approach to the airport. It could still get quite noisy at times, as planes were landing literally a stone's throw from the buildings. When the airfield reopened in May 2010 as a public park, the approach strip was also turned to a park. This meant that the low-rent area very quickly became a battleground of gentrification. Now the backyard balconies like mine were sunny places of repose overlooking calm greenery. Soon many local apartments became subject to increasing rents and developers' interest. This social effect is just one among other similar examples of how a single act of spatial repurposing can affect the local communities in manifold ways. It is rather ironic that the locally supported urban transformation of Tempelhof Airport into Tempelhof Park might have jeopardized the very possibility for some tenants to enjoy its peaceful results. Because many other disused and open spaces had experienced the encroachments of developers, Tempelhof came to be seen as the last space of its kind, worthy of the widest and most dedicated support. Due to the steadfast commitment of various civil parties, Tempelhof managed to persist and insist on its tentative urban identity as a public park. That has been established as its default unassailable identity, one to develop and promote further rather than defend. That it would be hard to impose on it even comparatively moderate plans for commercial development became clear in 2014. Having consolidated its meaning as a huge urban leisure site seen as a "space of hope" (Novy and Colomb 2012), the Tempelhof Freedom organization officially precluded any further change through an act of direct democracy. Berlin residents unprecedentedly blocked any redevelopment possibility with over 180,000 signatures. The experiential meanings of the park overrode a series of historically rooted narratives of the place, as well as potential predicaments of gentrification. A social hope for lasting leisurely space materialized as a concrete space of hope. Yet the symbolic power of that singular event can gloss over the fact that we are dealing here with a materially mediated process that stretched over years. This process could take place because various kinds of meaning structures defined Tempelhof, notably the national context, that is, the current situation of Germany as a polity manifest in Berlin's status as its progressive capital; the urban context, that is, the relational position of Tempelhof within the city; and the local context, that is, specific affordances of the site itself. Below I consecutively zoom in on these closely intertwined aspects.

The (Capital) City of a (Nation) State

Berlin has often been described as the epitome of grand urban transformation engendered by the changes of 1989 and its being the capital of reunified Germany. Although not fully representative of postcommunist transformation due to its half-Western condition, or even downright "particular" situation (Bernt, Grell, and Holm 2013, 14), Berlin has showcased a mix of processes often found in the "postsocialist city" (Kliems and Dmitrieva 2010; Bartmański 2011; Grubbauer and Kusiak 2012). Simultaneously, it has also been said to evince "typically Western" concern for historical preservation and spatial rearrangement (Ladd 1997, 2). Contemporary Berlin faces also contentious dilemmas of being a rediscovered artistic and entertainment center. This poses a range of unprecedented pressures and opportunities, many of which are related to Berlin's increased political importance that shifted Europe's power gravity eastward (Schlögel 2008), its newfound status as a "tourist city" (Novy 2010, 196–97; Richter 2010), the efforts (and counteractions) to brand it (Novy and Colomb 2012), and its ascendancy to the status of "Europe's cultural metropolis" (Simmen and Heinze 2010).

Undeniably, all this contributed to making Berlin "a model city of change" (Bodenschatz 2010, 5), replete with iconic sites of urban transformation. But "change" is a rather generic term. More precisely, Berlin is a "synonym for change *and* modernity" (Visscher 2008, 6), a capital city in a state of perennial becoming. While still broad, the term "modernity" has relatively clear and well-entrenched connotations in the collective consciousness of the German educated public. Berlin is popularly claimed to embody both the substance and spirit of modern life, and its architecture features numerous monuments of modernism. In short, when it comes to architecture and planning, Berlin's division and subsequent transformation endowed it with a uniquely eclectic heritage of iconic forms whose particularities clash along the East/West binary (Udy 2012, 71). For example, the Bauhaus legacy is mixed with postmodern forms that refer to it stylistically, and with layers of socialist aesthetics sometimes described in Germany as *Ost-Moderne*—East Modernism (Flierl 2008). Yet even this overarching modern eclecticism combined with the preservation and reconstruction programs may not suffice when it comes to understanding what distinguishes Berlin's own mix of the unique and the archetypal. After all, experts nowadays assert that despite an abundance of (re)construction, "one looks in vain for the visionary, modern plans that once seemed to be so programmatic in this city" (Wittmann-Englert 2008, 20). What are, then, the sociocultural tropes and material features that could help us comprehend Berlin's contemporary specificity?

When asked why Berlin is special, experts tend to agree "certainly not for its beauty, rather as a city of bold gestures and startling incongruities" (Ladd 1997, 3). They point to its being "a city of extremes" (Tichar and Peters 2004, 8), an "imperfect" city *in statu nascendi* (Boros in Hegenbart and Mündner 2012, 19), a "dramatic" space of urban renewal and restructuring (Weszkalnys 2010, 1). The key trope, however, is that of urban *laboratory* replete with voids, relics, ruins, and spaces of experimentation and liberty. Typically, it is such disused infrastructures and abandoned sites that are subject to aestheticization and reappropriation. Although Berlin is gradually leaving its "wild East," post-Wall reputation behind, those spaces of apparent freedom and social hope continue to mark its fabric and therefore make it a unique national capital. While current neoliberal pressures are certainly a vexing and imposing reality, it is also the case that Berlin has resisted such pressures to a considerable degree and sustained constructive solutions and opportunities that set it apart and can help explain its social mood. In particular, unlike other sizeable West European capital cities, Berlin still possesses a "large number of informal spaces" (Lanz 2013, 1320). Moreover, quite a few of them can be found in the central parts of the city, not just at its distant forlorn outskirts. Those spaces have distinguished Berlin's relatively dense urban fabric even though "the reunited city has come of age and most of its decrepit areas have been renovated" (*Monocle Magazine* 2009, 26). These sites, dubbed by some "spaces of uncertainty" (Cupers and Miessen 2002) or "spaces of hope" (Novy and Colomb 2012), comprise a variety of urban assemblages, including open lots and disused or decaying infrastructures which tend to disappear as (re)development projects take off. Importantly, these spaces have been credited with inducing and supporting Berlin's open-ended "style" (Reiter 2004) and its "creative atmosphere" connected to "the edginess and inventiveness of underground scenes" that thrive in such material conditions (Tichar and Peters 2004, 9). Perhaps the best-known catchphrase to reflect that trait of Berlin is mayor Klaus Wowereit's slogan *arm aber sexy* (poor but sexy). From the general phrase of "laboratory situation" (Heyden 2011, 64) through to the journalistic descriptions of a "vast laboratory for cultural production" (Goldmann 2011) and more technocratic, official visions of "a laboratory for the business of temporary use" (Junge-Reyer 2007), the notion of Berlin's experimental intensity and vast urban potential prevailed, earning it a description as an unpredictable and free "city of the future" (Visscher 2008, 6) that still tends to defy or at least question mainstream urban expectations. As anthropologist Gisa Weszkalnys (2010, 12) writes, the reunified Berlin has exerted "incredible attraction. Berlin spelled adventure and 'cool'; it offered space for exploration and, perhaps, for taking part in a big social and cultural experiment." The altered appearance of Tempelhof's vast space in the landscape of Berlin perfectly instantiates this character of the city.

In conjunction with relatively low rents and formidable liberal and countercultural traditions, Berlin achieved a fusion of attractive cultural factors and thus quite quickly became a city with a critical mass of young residents from the world over, especially from other countries of the European Union, who made it their preferred base. This happened despite the fact that only a very low percentage of Western Europeans migrate and settle in other European countries (Favell 2008). This influx of people and cultures in turn sustains and perpetuates a cultural myth of Berlin—something usually "much easier to visualize than describe" (Fischer 2004)—the elusive but ongoing *"Mythos Berlin"* (Hegenbart and Mündner 2012), a collective feeling of Berlin being the "Babylon" of the post-1989 era (Siegert 2001). Arguably, it is this "permanent laboratory situation that cannot be directly applied to other cities" (Heyden 2011, 64) which contributes strongly to Berlin's progressive experiential logic (Strohmaier 2014; Löw 2013) and its new "outstanding international reputation" (Bodenschatz 2010, 5). Importantly, these discursive and experiential tropes have not only cosmopolitan sources but also strong connection to the national German context. Many national and international economic forces, especially financial conditions, cease to be abstract and numerical when refracted by specific experiences and quite literally grounded in space. The story of Tempelhof also needs to be linked to Berlin's pre- and post-1989 economy and national politics, especially the strains of reunification, the city's comparative financial poverty (Bernt, Grell, and Holm 2013, 14), and an increased stream of visitors and new residents, which brings revenue but burdens the infrastructure. Without these references, it would be difficult indeed to understand both the logic of rent seeking and vehement resistance to it. And yet isolating these factors of national economy would skew our view. They need to be relativized. For example, at least within the European Union, "urban population development does not necessarily follow strictly national lines" (Kabisch, Haase, and Haase 2012, 1326). Second, while national-demographic urban factors may be harder to pinpoint, the dimensions of national-cultural and historical factors are more directly relevant; for example, the fact that Berlin is the historical and current capital of Germany (Tuck 2013, 32). Third, "there is deep-seated national organization of life in even the most internationalized of cities" (Favell 2008, 1). Importantly, despite—or perhaps precisely because of— the currently turbulent and economically challenging times, the nation-state remains a key institution (Therborn 2011), whereby contemporary Germany has emerged as one of the most stable nation-states in the European Union and as a whole its most powerful economic unit. Berlin may be comparatively poor but it is also one of the main beneficiaries of the German federal redistribution program (*Länderfinanzausgleich*).

This very circumstance makes Berlin much more socially attractive than other dynamic capital cities, both in Western Europe and in the region—for example, Warsaw (Bartmański 2012). This comparative social advantage is self-consciously cherished, watched, and fought for in the city. The story of Tempelhof's transformation is inseparable from the struggle to gain, preserve, and protect public assets.

In short, the context of German federal stability and national identity can hardly be ignored when the meanings of Berlin's progressive and experimental character are scrutinized. Berlin's ongoing budget troubles may be relatively threatening in financial terms, yet even this objective aspect makes political sense in a broader context and is mostly articulated in comparison to richer West German metropolitan areas that in turn belong to the wealthiest EU municipalities, for example Hamburg, Frankfurt, or Munich. Berlin may be relatively disadvantaged vis-à-vis those cities, yet it also profits from being directly entangled with them at all levels, while having more symbolic cachet than them, and certainly more international visibility than such rich regional centers as Stuttgart or Düsseldorf could ever dream of. Even if some of those cities are stages of momentous contestations and healthy cultural markets, it is Berlin that tends to host the vast majority of key actors on a regular basis. The national narratives—the historical and political kind—framed the transformation of Tempelhof in their own right too. As Borzou Daragahi (2010) observes, keeping the park as a low-key liminal space of play is "in tune with a nation that continues to move away from its stern militarism of the early 20th century and the hard-working asceticism of the postwar years." The cultural significance of this frame is considerable, for it sheds light on why the initiative of military veterans to keep the airport intact failed: it was not only "too small" to exert considerable influence but also too divergent from the current national self-understanding, prominently staged in Berlin and predicated on searching for legitimate dissociation from the authoritarian culture of the past. The field itself was not only "too big" to not be noticed as a perfect playground; it was also in tune with the experimental counter- and multicultural mood of the city's adjacent districts of Kreuzberg and Neukoelln that are also epicenters of creativity and cutting-edge social projects.

Thus, it is Berlin the German capital where the powerful thrust of the main symbolic energies of Germany is most palpable and where various historical and current notions of German national identity are routinely trialed and tested. Berlin is inexorably one of the most intensely national spaces in the country despite the fact that it is also one of the most intensely antinationalist German metropolises. Berlin is energized by the tense binary of the national and the cosmopolitan. The two aspects are in fact intertwined, feeding off each other, with Berlin being the special stage for their everyday unfolding and resonant rearticulation. Berlin's citizenry has become highly diverse, comprising many international communities and supranational institutions, but the city's status as a social magnet and free place is in significant part due to the relative stability and strength of the nation-state it both represents and keeps at bay.

The Site: Liminal Topography and Its Atmosphere

As I have tried to show, the defining liberal and experimental features of Berlin are not free-floating arbitrary meanings. Let us now provide a close-up view of the present case to understand how it generates and refracts the meaning structure outlined above. The sheer presence of Berlin's ill- or undefined urban sites counts as a key condition from which the city's "laboratory situation" emerged. Those sites directly inspire and galvanize rather than merely re-present the city's meanings. Disused spaces and their relationally constituted properties are performers of sorts. They afford specific types of social actions and gain new meanings through localized contrast and networked associations with other such spaces elsewhere. Once recognized and reappropriated, they create an urban landscape of cultivated dilapidation that may be amenable to nonstandard or nonprofit repurposing. In the Berlin of the 1990s the very persistence of the undefined and uncontrolled spaces contrasted starkly with the hyperefficiency of Western capitalism and relentless for-profit land use. It created a relatively anomalous urban context that many local communities championed as rare specificity rather than abnormality. It fitted Berlin's anarchic lifestyles and fueled the collective feeling of "zero gravity" so often recalled by the city's cultural agents and their audiences (Defcon and Dax 2014, 81).

The case of Tempelhof as an unconventional space of leisure and fun is no different. The collectivity of supporters of Tempelhof Park is not simply "made out of speech acts by mere conventions" (Latour 2007b, 34). They practically embraced the park as a liminal place of free fun.

The way this development unfolded has been a rather familiar Berlin scenario: a place ceases to perform its prescribed social role, is subject to organizational inertia, and enters more or less protracted stages of abandonment and repurposing, inspiring controversy and excitement regarding its future. It's a place in limbo. After the closing in late 2008, Tempelhof stood unused throughout 2009. What distinguished it from other such spaces was its sheer size, the open space that reportedly could contain five hundred football fields. As the last planes left and the sixty-million-euro redevelopment plans including a park design were unveiled, a brand-new opportunity structure had been opened.

Predictably, the project encountered dissent. In particular, plans to transform the land around Tempelhof Airport into a park have been strongly criticized by a group of aviation professionals and Berlin Air-lift veterans. The dissenters, led by Claudia Jaekel and supported by Cal Korf, the last president of the Berlin US Military Veteran's Association, made a critical petition, emphasizing that Tempelhof is "an historical icon, perfect as it is," and claiming that the very idea of having a park there is "disrespectful," "absolutely upsetting," and "a slap in the face of all Berlin Airlift Veterans" (cited in Welling 2011). The leader of the redevelopment project, Daniel Reiser, also saw Tempelhof as perfect but for a different purpose, which he deemed "one of the most important and unique projects in Europe" (ibid.). Thus, Tempelhof reemerged as a space whose original identity and value may have been interpreted in two different ways but whose iconicity and uniqueness were unanimously agreed upon.

The controversy seemed closed when Martin Pallgen, a spokesperson for Tempelhof Projekt GmbH, pointed out that the movement of dissenters was small and in no way expressed the public opinion of Berlin, especially the directly adjacent residential neighborhoods. Those, when asked, welcomed the idea of the park. Importantly, "Most wanted to keep the wideness of space to keep the area visible as a disused airport" (Welling 2011). This was a way of saying that Tempelhof is "perfect as it is." This time, however, its traditional *function* was questioned, not the very existence and appearance which in fact seemed to lend itself effortlessly to other social uses. The popular acceptance for the park project cherished the basic affordances of the actual space right from the start. Local Berliners effectively refused to be held hostage to any historical event, no matter how important. The experiential features of the site itself began to count for more. For similar reasons, Tempelhof witnessed another kind of protest at that time, a demonstration of thousands of people who tried to occupy it when rumors of privatization surfaced (Goldmann 2011). One-third bigger than the famous Tiergarten in the west part of the city, it was easier for the place to remain a single public unit for all. The physical dimensions and a sense of open space it exuded were officially underscored by the very name of the place, "Park der Tempelhofer Freiheit"—the Tempelhof Park of Freedom. The treeless expanse could, of course, be described in various ways, depending on one's imagination, although certain imageries have always been more plausible than others. In the past, the conservative chancellor Konrad Adenauer saw Berlin's vicinity as marking the beginnings of the "Asian steppes." To some contemporary critics the "unused" character of this fallow emptiness might perhaps signify decadence rather than freedom, reckless abandonment rather than social purpose, a liability not an asset. Indeed, as *The Independent*'s writer Jess Smee (2008) reported, one German newspaper even joked that Tempelhof should be renamed "Tempelhof Wasteland."

However, it was precisely this feeling of Tempelhof as something that now stands outside the overpowering logic of capitalist order that made it amenable to liminal experiences of freedom. Hans Korfmann would go so far as to say that Tempelhof's field "lies outside space and time." Not only writers or anthropologists but also regular visitors to the park seem to have shared that feeling. Borzou Daragahi's report about Tempelhof Park for the *Los Angeles Times* quotes a local woman, Sarah Hartung, a forty-year-old psychologist: "It needn't be turned into anything. Just leave it as it is. It doesn't have to be such an organized thing. It's a nice place to chill—a *purpose-free* environment" (Daragahi 2010, emphasis mine). Here Tempelhof and its fallow, wide-open ground iconizes freedom from the relentless regimentation of everydayness and the discipline of for-profit development. In the eyes of the quoted Berliner, it offers a particular, relaxed, and soothing ambience. Moreover, once it is regularly available in this capacity, it makes visitors more cognizant of the value of a purpose-free environment, which they now see as coming under pressure and threat. And being outside the nexus of daily routines may indeed mean being outside time in a quite explicit sense, or at least resisting the flow of standard time. As public city life becomes increasingly the dominion of assiduous closed-circuit TV surveillance and subject to ongoing privatization of public spaces, the disused airfield provides an increasingly desired respite from omnipresent techniques of control. Gilles Lipovetsky referred to this condition as "hypermodernity"—a situation of modern metropolis in which authorities meticulously control both the internal atmosphere and public places, "replacing the empty spaces of time with a consumption of syndicated entertainment" (cf. Wagenfeld 2011, 157; Lanz 2013).

The Park of Freedom may just seem "purpose-free" at first. But it offers a range of "freedoms for" too. Instead of an infrastructure of outbound travel in search of peace and quiet elsewhere, Tempelhof now is an escape space itself. The field has become a near destination for Berliners who crave both the sense of freedom *from* cluttered urban space and freedom *for* leisurely types of expression and activity, like kite- and skateboarding. The airport's former runways are ready-made playgrounds as they uniquely afford long skateboard rides—a built environment that can hardly be rivaled by any other, even intentionally created, skate park. The sudden explosion of the kite-boarders' scene in Berlin neatly overlaps with the opening of the Tempelhof Park, indicating the key role of physical space in shaping social possibilities. As one of the regular fans of the sport, Florian Giehl, explains, "the field regulates itself" in the capacity of a perfect and sole urban ground in Berlin for this still license-free hobby (cited in Schwarzbeck 2013, 26).

The aspect of experimentation and self-regulation is not to be underestimated in the self-consciously experimental Berlin. As Berlin's Senat discontinued the airport, it removed a surveillance-heavy heterotopia in Foucault's sense. Instead, the citizens gained a chance to actualize a quasi-utopian space of "organic" social visibility without excessive supervision and mediated overexposure. At the very least, they could enjoy the atmosphere that is relatively free from the intrusiveness of the urban policing apparatus and thus good for relaxation and gatherings. Keeping in mind that numerous Berlin-based movements and agencies fighting for freedom of spaces like Tempelhof have their roots in former squats and left-leaning countercultural projects (Lanz 2013, 1311, 1313), one is not surprised to see regular park users and supporters champion the park as a space of hope for freedom. It is a counter-site. Its monumentality helps it to work as a monument to the disappearing free urban spaces. Its horizontality unavoidably hints at nonhierarchical spaces of experience. In this sense Tempelhof affords an emergence of highly evocative liminal topography. It is both a metaphorical and literal space for navigating new urban sociotechnological situations, constituting an irreplaceable opportunity to experience nongoverned public activities within the city and imagine alternative futures.[1] While the space is fenced off from the rest of the city and it closes its gates for the night, what it offers inside its physical and symbolic borders makes it live up to its name. Even if the trope of freedom is not always *articulated* by the regular users of Tempelhof (reportedly thirty thousand on a nice day), it is apparent to any witness that it is perceived, felt, and enjoyed by them. They "get the point" without necessarily reflecting on it in exactly those terms. After all, for some the point is precisely to reflect less and rejoice more, suspending judgment and experiencing immersion, something to savor and behold rather than couch in words. That's the "language of things" Adorno thematized in his seminal essay "Functionalism Today," an observation that led him to write that there is a factor of expression in every object, including obsolete and disused ones, which eventually lends itself to symbolic roles" (1965, 7).

Free Place in Urban Space

The atmosphere exuded by the openness and vastness of Tempelhof field contrasts with the dense modern urbanity of Berlin and this contrast crucially amplifies the affordances of the site. The aforementioned connotations of steppe, or fallow meadow, were evaluated by many local communities as "wonderful" precisely because the place sits "in the middle of a hectic metropolis" (Die Initiative 100% Tempelhofer Feld). It is this binary of the serene clear openness and the maze of busy streets around it that constitutes the greater interpretive field in which the actual field is distinguished as an abode of calm and regeneration rather than a wasteland. *Die Zeit* writer Hans Korfmann lauded this aspect with literary panache, calling it the "magic of emptiness" (*die Magie der Leere*), a rather unexpected feature in the middle of a European metropolis. He reflects on the uniqueness of seeing "people entering this landscape, widely spread across greenery, resembling the animals of Serengeti" (Korfmann 2012, 59). These various geographical tropes were quite explicitly echoed and given a distinctly American spin in May 2011 when the Scottish firm Gross Max won a contract to redesign the park. Its plan prioritized maintaining Tempelhof's flatness to create a "contemporary prairie for the urban cowboy." The park is unusual also because its flatness and very few trees open up an urban perspective otherwise rarely available in dense cities. Kept unchanged and undeveloped, Tempelhof can offer an urban horizon of city icons—church and mosque towers, the TV Tower, etc.—and thus rearticulate the city's character as a visual synthesis, offering a more holistic perception of the cityscape (Figure 10.1). From a phenomenological point of view, this widened perspective simply frees one's perception and offers a vantage point hard to find elsewhere in the city, and unavailable in other dense European capital cities like London or Paris. The panorama is free in a double sense: it's free of charge and visually unobstructed.

The prevalence of such positive, somewhat enchanted interpretations of Tempelhof as a space of free perception and action illustrates a related fact, namely that perceptions of constitutive features of things are filtered by experiential, background assumptions about the feeling they provide, and by "semiotic ideologies" which are concerned "not just with signs but with kinds of objects found in the world more generally" (Keane 2005, 190–91). The open greenery inside the dense and tightly ordered urban fabric: that is special. Thus, not only the sheer vastness and flatness of the territory but also Tempelhof's specific situatedness and the involved material relations produce the field's key meanings. The field is a vastness tightly enclosed by the concrete labyrinth of the massive capital city. It is a meadow within a concrete jungle. The unusually enormous, mostly treeless park is quite literally framed by the dense cityscape and its busy infrastructure, parts of which can be observed and heard in the distance; for example, the city's railway ring and a highway to the south.

This circumstance makes Tempelhof at once *a space* and *an image* of freedom because it effectively relies on the experience of binary values, such as bounded/unbounded, structured/unstructured, regulated/unregulated, ordered/spontaneous, complex/plain, organized/wild, concrete/green, hard/soft, and so forth. Some of them could perhaps be seen as variants of the Lévi-Straussian binary of the cooked versus the raw. The principle of iconic resemblance is visibly operative here and the place receives more symbolic weight as smaller but similar open spaces keep disappearing in former East Berlin, especially along Spree River. An event of special meaning in this respect was the partial commercial redevelopment of the bank of the river next to the iconic fragment of the Wall called East Side Gallery, which underwent radical changes that fragmented the public space, discontinued free movement along the

Figure 10.1. The north side of Tempelhof Airfield. In the background, a church tower in Kreuzberg, the TV Tower at Alexanderplatz, built in 1969 in then-communist East Berlin, and the minarets of a mosque in Neukoelln. *Source*: Author

river, and forced the displacement or destruction of iconic graffiti on the remainder of the Wall for which Berlin is famous. The intense commercialization of the entire area continues today.

Importantly, because the Tempelhof Park felt needed and has been experienced as being about inclusion, freedom, fitness, ecology, and such liberal values, it stood a chance of overriding some of its previous, anti-civil meanings. It became a giant playground astonishingly fast given the fact that part of the airfield had once been a concentration camp. However, many are unaware of this part of the past. "As Berliners transformed 950 acres of open space into a sprawling playground/stage/urban laboratory where joggers and gardeners cross paths with runway models and techno DJs, few realise that below their bicycles, rollerblades and high heels lie some of Berlin's darkest secrets—remnants of around 20 barracks of Berlin's own Nazi slave labor camp" (Borden 2012). However, this is not an extraordinary but a rather common situation in Berlin. The architectural style of the airport's building seemed not untainted either, and it was pointed out that before Tempelhof became a historical icon of freedom thanks to its role in the 1948–49 Berlin Airlift, "it was a symbol of Nazi megalomania, brutality and repression" (Borden 2012). According to one author, Tempelhof's "blocky, undecorated forms" and "pure and indestructible rows of limestone columns" could be likened to the overall German Nazi attitude (Borden 2012). However, Reinhard Mohr (2008) offers a different perspective: "The fact that the airport facilities did not go down in history as a Nazi creation is due in part to its unquestionable aesthetic quality and in part to American influences." Indeed, Americans completed the terminal in the late 1950s and reequipped it after it was gutted by the Soviet soldiers. In 1948–49 iconic American "candy bombers" were landing there and the U.S. troops remained present until 1993.

Aesthetically, both the exterior and interior of the airport building is complex enough to afford alternative interpretations and impressions. For those uninitiated in historical aesthetic discourses, the building's features may not seem very different from those of other modern eras and styles, especially monumental architecture of the municipal and governmental buildings in Berlin or American cities such as New York and Chicago. The industrial feel of several big halls (Figure 10.2) and the central airport gates reminds one of huge factory buildings more than anything else. Like other postindustrial infrastructures today, they have been seen as contrastively austere homes and brutalist backdrops for refined workings of cultural industry, for example music shows or fashion events. Among other things, an electronic music studio named Non Standard Studios is located there and underscores the iconic currency of its location by announcing on its website that it is "based in former CIA offices in Berlin's historical Tempelhof Airport."

The issue of the labor camp mentioned above is more troubling because it is subject not just to aesthetic or current political but also to moral and historical judgment. Excavations led by scientists from Berlin's Free University began when the landscape redesigning plans were announced in 2011. The story they unveiled and brought to Berlin's public attention laid bare yet another integument of the city's widely tainted topography and consequently inspired a discourse tellingly entitled "Tempelhofer Unfreiheit"—Tempelhof Unfreedom (Lackmann 2012). However, the site occupies only a fragment of Tempelhof's field and does

Figure 10.2. A massive disused hall in the interior of the former main airport building, as of 2015 inaccessible to the public. *Source*: Author

not visually dominate it. The symbolic pollution it represents is indelible but it remained an archaeological rather than commemorative site during the park's formative years. To adapt the conception cited before, an emerging discourse did not manage to "exhaust the reality" of the park in the city, where much of the urban area bears traces of the tragic past. Similarly, although the field was once imagined by Hitler as a giant rally space and the roof of the crescent building was being specially reinforced to host one hundred thousand spectators, thus becoming a kind of giant amphitheater, it remains a historical discourse untranslated to current experiences of the field. As those plans never fully materialized and layers of other meanings accrued to the space and its objects, the polluted Nazi connotations of the architecture have not overpowered the general public knowledge.

What we observe here is an effect of the accretion of various emblematic meanings, some sacred, others profane or of liminal quality, each of which adds to the layered sedimentation of references of the place. New discursive accretions build on the extant ones, some are rediscovered or reframed, others recede to the background as the discursive surround evolves. As Tempelhof's semiotic spiral expands, the present uses outshine the past ones, indicating that visually constituted objects that make up our environment "are not simply a reflection of something happening else-where" (Pinney 2005, 266). In fact, one of the criteria of urban iconicity is the ability of an object to "break loose from its checkered history in the local context" (Akbar 2006, 76). What seems crucial in Tempelhof's case, however, is the fact that its history is long and varied enough to withstand the discursive pressure of a single period. Its current connections to the city and its social life are likewise multiple. At the same time, the main phenomenological affordances I described earlier remain unchanged, or even underscored by the disappearance of similar places elsewhere in the city under pressure of developers. Importantly, there is not only post-Nazi American reference but also the pre-Nazi history of the "Roaring Twen-ties" in which Tempelhof has its own lighter role too.[2] The iconicity of Tempelhof's architecture is nowadays confirmed by its status of a legally protected, listed landmark and by its widespread reputation as an "icon of an airport," as architect Axel Schultes once referred to it (Mohr 2008).

All those aspects of material infrastructure and architectural mean-ings endow Tempelhof's building with temporal complexity, heritage nar-ratives, and logistical potential that resist clear-cut historical reduction. The architectural substance may in fact play a role of an iconic bridge out of troubled history, pointing to the more inclusive future. In fact, follow-ing the refugee crisis of 2015, a part of the place was once more turned into a ground for temporary solution to pressing social demands despite legal obstacles. The controversial overturning of the 2014 plebiscite that excluded other uses of the park turned a fraction of Tempelhof field adja-cent to the main terminal and some hangars themselves into Germany's biggest refugee camp, designed to house up to seven thousand people (Dassler 2015; Deutsche Welle 2016b). This decision is contested on orga-nizational, legal, and humanitarian grounds. Now, when only less than two thousand refugees live at the temporary facility, the spokeswoman for the 100% Tempelhofer Feld organization, Esther Witt, points out deficient planning on the city's part (Deutsche Welle 2016a). In this new context Tempelhof has again assumed a historical and politically charged role. As a result, some original descriptions of the struggle over how to define its second life may again ring familiar, as they recognized its "drama" as a "microcosm of contemporary life" (Goldmann 2011).

CONCLUSION

Concluding the feature on Tempelhof at the time of its closure, Jess Smee (2008) wrote, "In true Berlin style, plans are yet to be drawn up—but Tempelhof Park in its current form is something to be savoured." The explicit emphasis on "Berlin style" regarding Tempelhof's liminal character corresponded with the manifesto-like description of the city in the Taschen book entitled *Berlin Style* and published in the *Icons Series* before Tempelhof's fate was decided: "Berlin doesn't stipulate any style and sets no limits. It offers an endless amount of space and makes everything possible" (Reiter 2004, 7). To the extent that this common narrative is still an adequate approximation of Berlin's character, Tempelhof could be invoked as the city's privileged icon; not just as "Berlin's biggest playground" (Korfmann 2012, 59) but as a more general "metaphor for contemporary Berlin" (Goldmann 2011).

At a time when other iconic sites in Berlin are tending to disappear due to direct or indirect pressure from developers and politicians, the contemporary meanings of the park gain additional social traction. The park initially consolidated the connotations of open, free, environmentally conscious space, whose social rather than economic value defines its right to existence. It was the well-being of birds that nested there rather than the well-being of investors that carried the day.[3] If it's accurate to claim that "urban commons have radical potential" because "it's not just about community gardens" (McGuirk 2015), then the story of Tempelhof's transformation offers an insightful lesson. It has become a symbolic place of leisurely metropolitan life and inclusiveness in a world that remains as divided and unequal as ever. For all its unique characteristics, this iconic airport-turned-park quite literally stages and brings to sharp focus a series of experiential, often politically loaded oppositions: public/private, leisure/work, organic/industrial, horizontal/vertical, green/concrete, inclusion/exclusion, and so on. If the story of Tempelhof's transformation strikes a powerful chord inside and outside its famous host city, it is because it is capable of crystallizing such binaries, giving them form and substance that can be felt and seen, not just narrated and discussed. Tempelhof's transformation practically iconizes the meanings of civil society. The park's relational materiality exemplifies how civil social commitments can be catalyzed by site-specific affordances and their connectedness to critical social values. These values tend to gain additional traction in deeply unsettled times of crisis. When international political leaders continually fail their constituencies, returning to simple collective principles and grounded practices may offer a modicum of hope, at least for the time being, sometimes acting as transformative, liminal antistructure.

As the story continues to unfold, perhaps the park will also become an exemplification of how liminal sites tend to get at least partially "routinized," thus setting a template for consensual civil deconstruction of disused spaces beyond the temporary use paradigm. Social scientists argue that liminal places are unstable, or that their stabilization may deprive them of their unique aura and enchantment. Even if eventually normalized and "domesticated" as yet another central urban park, Tempelhof will have become a historical icon of one civil battle won. Yet to lose this battle could deprive other civil hopes of a great deal of emotional energy, and it would certainly void Berlin of the free open urban surface that touches the souls and bodies of so many of its inhabitants. Ultimately, as Georg Simmel once suggested, it is mundane practical liberties that often undergird our sacred social hopes.

NOTES

1. It is fitting in this context that one of Europe's biggest tech fests occurred in Tempelhof buildings and ran under the slogan "changing Europe's operating system," with an ostensible goal of making the city and the region more democratic and a better place to live. At the same time, it is not surprising either that the relatively scant attention paid to it in Germany was linked to the partly commercial character of the fest sponsored by big telecommunication companies like O2 (Horchert 2012). This meaning shares some similarity with the parallel resignification of the TV Tower, which is claimed to have semiotically shifted from the political *party* watchtower to an icon of a disco ball suspended over Berlin's *partying* crowds (see Berger, Siewert, and Müller 2003).

2. It was one of the first modern airports in the world when opened in 1923. Shortly before Hitler came to power, the Tempelhof field witnessed the first scheduled flight of Lufthansa, Germany's flagship airline which had also been housed for decades in one of the building's wings. The integration with the subway system in 1927 included Tempelhof in the chain of material signifiers of accelerated progress and mobility. The meaning of German modernity gained another valence as the air seemed to be conquered by industrial technology.

3. It's worth remembering that it was partly the plans to endanger the civil/ecological meanings of the Gezi Park in Istanbul which triggered the sweeping antigovernmental upheavals in Turkey in 2013.

References

Abu El-Haj, Nadia. 1998. "Translating Truths: Nationalism, the Practice of Archaeology and the Remaking of Past and Present in Contemporary Jerusalem." *American Ethnologist* 25(2): 166–188.

———. 2001. *Facts on the Ground: Archaeological Practice and Territorial Self-fashioning in Israeli Society.* Chicago: University of Chicago Press.

Adams, Julia. 2005. *The Familial State: Ruling Families and Merchant Capitalism in Early Modern Europe.* Ithaca: Cornell University Press.

———. 2007. "The Rule of the Father: Patriarchy and Patrimonialism in Early Modern Europe." *Working paper*, Russell Sage Foundation.

Adorno, Theodor. 1965. "Functionalism Today." http://isites.harvard.edu/fs/docs/icb.topic1412058.files/Week%201/AdornoFT.pdf

Agulhon, Maurice. 1981. *Marianne into Battle: Republican Imagery and Symbolism in France, 1789–1880.* Cambridge: Cambridge University Press.

Akashi, Nobuko. 2007. *Serebu na Osahō: Wa no Shikitari to Otona no Manaa. Tokyo:* Bijinesusha.

Akbar, Omar. 2006. "Preface." In Walter Prigge (ed.), *Icon of Modernism: The Bauhaus Building Dessau.* Berlin: Jovis, 76–77.

Alabarces, Pablo. 2000. *"'Aguante' y represión: Fútbol, violencia y política en la Argentina."* In Pablo Alabarces (ed.), *Peligro de Gol.* Buenos Aires: Buenos Aires University Press, 211–232.

Alexander, Jeffrey C. 2003. *The Meanings of Social Life: A Cultural Sociology.* Oxford: Oxford University Press.

———. 2008a. "Iconic Experience in Art and Life Surface/Depth Beginning with Giacometti's Standing Woman." *Theory, Culture and Society* 25(5): 1–19.

———. 2008b. "Iconic Consciousness: The Material Feeling of Meaning." *Environment and Planning* 26: 782–794.

———. 2012. "Iconic Power and Performance: The Role of the Critic." In J. C. Alexander, D. Bartmański, and B. Giesen (eds.), *Iconic Power: Materiality and Meaning in Social Life.* London: Palgrave, 25–38.

American Jewish Yearbook. 1992, 1995, 2002, 2003, 2004, 2007. New York: American Jewish Committee.

Anderson, Benedict. (1983) 1991. *Imagined Communities: Reflections on the Origins and Spread of Nationalism*. New York: Verso.

Anderson, Perry. 1974. *Lineages of the Absolutist State*. London: N.L.B.

Apostolidès, Jean-Marie. 1981. *Le roi-machine: Spectacle et politique au temps de Louis XIV*. Paris: Editions de Minuit.

Appadurai, Arjun (ed.). 1986. *The Social Life of Things: Commodities in Cultural Perspective*. Cambridge: Cambridge University Press.

Apter, Andrew. 1999. "The Subvention of Tradition: A Genealogy of the Nigerian Durbar." In George Steinmetz (ed.), *State/Culture: State Formation after the Cultural Turn*. Ithaca: Cornell University Press, 213–252.

Archetti, Eduardo. 1999. *Masculinities: Football, Polo and the Tango in Argentina*. London: Bloomsbury Academic.

———. 2001. *El potrero, la pista y el ring: Las patrias del deporte argentino*. Buenos Aires: Fondo de Cultura Económica.

Auslander, Leora. 2009. *Cultural Revolutions: Everyday Life and Politics in Britain, North America, and France*. Los Angeles: University of California Press.

Bajc, Vida. 2006. "Collective Memory and Tourism: Globalizing Transmission through Localized Experience." *Journeys: The International Journal of Travel and Travel Writing* 7(1): 1–14.

Balle, Catherine. 1997. "La ville et son patrimoine: l'exemple d'Avignon." In D. Poulot and Grange (eds.), *L'esprit des lieux*. Presses Universitaires de Grenoble.

Bandelj, Nina, and Frederick Wherry. 2011. *The Cultural Wealth of Nations*. Stanford: Stanford University Press.

Barney, Darin. 2017. "Who We Are and What We Do: Canada as a Pipeline Nation." In S. Wilson, A. Carlson, and I. Szeman (eds.), *Petrocultures: Oil, Energy, and Culture*. Montreal: McGill-Queen's University Press.

Barthes, Roland. (1957) 2009. *Mythologies*. London: Vintage.

Bartmański, Dominik. 2011. "Successful Icons of Failed Time: Rethinking Post-communist Nostalgia." *Acta Sociologica* 54(3): 213–232.

———. 2012. "The Word/Image Dualism Revisited: Toward an Iconic Conception of Visual Culture." *Journal of Sociology* 50(2): 1–18.

Bartmański, Dominik, and Jeffrey C. Alexander. 2012. "Introduction." In Jeffrey Alexander, Dominik Bartmański, and Bernard Giesen (eds.), *Iconic Power: Materiality and Meaning in Social Life*. New York: Palgrave.

Bartmański, Dominik, and Werner Binder. 2015. "Being and Knowledge: On Some Liabilities of Reed's Interpretivism." *Czech Sociological Review* 3: 499–511.

Bartmański, Dominik, and Ian Woodward. 2015. *Vinyl: The Analogue Record in the Digital Age*. London: Bloomsbury Academic.

BCC (Boston Cultural Council). 2014. "The Boston Cultural Council Awardees." http://bostonculturalcouncil.com/2014/03/18/the-boston-cultural-council-awardees/ (accessed 18 March 2016).

Beauregard, Robert A. 2015. *Planning Matter: Acting with Things*. Chicago: University of Chicago Press.

Beck, Ulrich, and Edgar Grande. 2007. *Cosmopolitan Europe.* Cambridge: Polity.

Becker, Howard Saul. 1963. *Outsiders: Studies in the Sociology of Deviance.* London: Free Press of Glencoe.

———. 1982. *Artworlds.* Berkeley and Los Angeles: University of California Press,

Becker, Howard, Robert Faulkner, and Barbara Kirshenblatt-Gimblett. 2006. *Art from Start to Finish: Jazz, Painting, Writing and Other Improvisations.* Chicago: University of Chicago Press.

Beik, Paul Harold. 1944. *A Judgment of the Old Régime: Being a Survey of the Parlement of Provence of French Economic and Fiscal Policies at the Close of the Seven Years War.* New York: Columbia University Press.

Beik, William. 1985. *Absolutism and Society in Seventeenth-century France.* Cambridge: Cambridge University Press.

———. 1997. *Urban Protest in Seventeenth-century France: The Culture of Retribution.* Cambridge: Cambridge University Press.

Benjamin, Walter. 1986. *Illuminations.* New York: Schocken Books.

Bennet, Jane. 2010. *Vibrant Matter: A Political Ecology of Things.* Durham: Duke University Press.

Bennett, Andy. 2011. "The Post-subcultural Turn: Some Reflections 10 Years On." *Journal of Youth Studies* 14: 493–506.

Bennett, Tony. 1995. *The Birth of the Museum: History, Theory, Politics.* Culture: Policies and Politics. London: Routledge.

Benzecry, Claudio E. 2011. *The Opera Fanatic: Ethnography of an Obsession.* Chicago: University of Chicago Press.

Berezin, Mabel. 1994. "Cultural Form and Political Meaning: State-subsidized Theater, Ideology, and the Language of Style in Fascist Italy." *American Journal of Sociology* 99(5): 1237–1286.

Berger, Carl. 1976. *The Writing of Canadian History: Aspects of English-Canadian Historical Writing: 1900–1970.* Toronto: Oxford University Press.

Berger, Dirk, Sandra Siewert, and Ingo Müller. 2003. *Von der Partei zur Party: Der Berliner Fernsehturm als grafisches Symbol, 1969–2003.* Berlin: s-wert design.

Bernard, Auguste. 1966. *Histoire de l'Imprimerie royale du Louvre.* Amsterdam: P. Schippers.

Bernt, Matthias, Britta Grell, and Andrej Holm (eds.). 2013. *The Berlin Reader: A Compendium on Urban Change and Activism.* Bielefeld: Transcript.

Berton, Pierre. (1970) 2001a. *The National Dream: The Great Railway, 1871–1881.* Toronto: Anchor Canada.

———. (1971) 2001b. *The Last Spike: The Great Railway, 1881–1885.* Toronto: Anchor Canada.

Biddle, Ian, and Vanessa Knights (eds.). 2007. *Music, National Identity and the Politics of Location: Between the Global and the Local.* London: Ashgate.

Billig, Michael. 1995. *Banal Nationalism.* London: Sage.

———. 2009. "Reflecting on a Critical Engagement with Banal Nationalism—Reply to Skey." *Sociological Review* 57(2): 347–352.

Birch, Samuel. (1857) 1873. *History of Ancient Pottery, Egyptian, Assyrian, Greek, Etruscan, and Roman.* London: John Murray.

Blunt, Anthony. 1980. *Art and Architecture in France, 1500 to 1700.* Harmondsworth: Penguin Books.

Bodenschatz, Harald. 2010. "Preface." In Richter, Jana (ed.) *The Tourist City Berlin: Tourism and Architecture.* Braun: Berlin.

Bonnell, Victoria. 1997. *Iconography of Power: Soviet Political Posters under Lenin and Stalin.* Berkeley: University of California Press.

Borden, D. 2012. "Save Berlin: Tempelhof's Buried Demons." *Exberliner.* www.exberliner.com/features/lifestyle/save-berlin-tempelhofs-buried-demons/ (accessed 27 June 2013).

Bordier, Cyril. 1998. *Louis Le Vau: Architecte.* Paris: L. Laget.

Bostwick Davis, Elliot. 2009. "Communicating through Design and Display: The New American Wing at the Museum of Fine Arts, Boston." In Selma Holo and Mari-Tere Alvarez (eds.), *Beyond the Turnstile: Making the Case for Museums and Sustainable Values.* Lanham, MD: AltaMira Press, 182–185.

Bourdieu, Pierre. 1984. *Distinction: A Social Critique of the Judgment of Taste.* Cambridge: Harvard University Press.

———. 1991. *Language and Symbolic Power.* Cambridge: Harvard University Press.

Bouzarovski, Stefan, and Mark Bassin. 2011. "Energy and Identity: Imagining Russia as a Hydrocarbon Superpower." *Annals of the Association of American Geographers* 101(4): 783–794.

Bowen, Sarah, and Marie Sarita Gaytán. 2012. "The Paradox of Protection: National Identity, Global Commodity Chains, and the Tequila Industry." *Social Problems* 59(1): 70–93.

Brewer, John. 1989. *The Sinews of Power: War, Money, and the English State, 1688–1783.* New York: Knopf.

Brown, Ann Cynthia. 1968. *Catalogue of Italian Terra-Sigillata in the Ashmolean Museum.* Oxford: Clarendon Press.

Brubaker, Rogers. 1992. *Citizenship and Nationhood in France and Germany.* Cambridge: Harvard University Press.

———. 1996. *Reframing Nationalism: Nationhood and the National Question in the New Europe.* Cambridge: Cambridge University Press.

Brubaker, Rogers, and Frederick Cooper. 2000. "Beyond 'Identity.'" *Theory and Society* 29(1): 1–47.

Brubaker, Rogers, Margit Feischmidt, Jon E. Fox, and Liana Grancea. 2006. *Nationalist Politics and Everyday Ethnicity in a Transylvanian Town.* Princeton: Princeton University Press.

Burke, Peter. 1992. *The Fabrication of Louis XIV.* New Haven: Yale University Press.

Butler, Judith. 2010. "Performative Agency." *Journal of Cultural Economy* 3(2): 147–161.

Cafiero, Antonio. 1998. "A Transpirar la Camiseta." *Clarín* [Buenos Aires], 24 March.

Caldwell, Melissa L. 2002. "The Taste of Nationalism: Food Politics in Postsocialist Moscow." *Ethnos* 67: 295–319.

Calhoun, Craig J. 2008. "Cosmopolitanism in the Modern Social Imaginary." *Daedalus* 137(3): 105–114.

Calhoun, Craig J., and Richard Sennett. 2007. *Practicing Culture*. Milton Park, Abingdon: Routledge, 2007.

Callon, Michel. 2007. "What Does It Mean to Say That Economics Is Performative?" In D. Mackenzie, F. Muniesa, and L. Siu (eds.), *Do Economists Make Markets? On the Performativity of Economics*. Princeton: Princeton University Press, 311–357.

Canadian Pacific Railway Company. 1881. "Land Grant Bonds—Indenture of Mortgage." https://archive.org/details/cihm_00415 (accessed 15 July 2014).

Carroll-Burke, Patrick. 2002. "Material Designs: Engineering Cultures and Engineering States—Ireland 1650–1900." *Theory and Society* 31(1): 75–114.

Cerulo, Karen A. 1995. *Identity Designs: The Sights and Sounds of a Nation*. New Brunswick: Rutgers University Press.

Ceserani, Giovanna. 2012. *Italy's Lost Greece: Magna Graecia and the Making of Modern Archaeology*. Oxford: Oxford University Press.

CFM (Center for the Future of Museums). 2008. *Museums and Society 2034: Trends and Potential Futures*. Washington, DC: American Association of Museums. www.aam-us.org/docs/center-for-the-future-of-museums/museumssociety2034.pdf?sfvrsn=0

Chapman, John. 2000. *Fragmentation in Archaeology: Peoples, Places and Broken Objects in the Prehistory of South Eastern Europe*. London: Routledge.

Chapman, John, and Bisserka Gaydarska. 2007. *Parts and Wholes. Fragmentation in Prehistoric Context*. Oxford: Oxbow Books.

Charland, Maurice. 1986. "Technological Nationalism." *Canadian Journal of Political and Social Theory* 10(1–2): 196–220.

Chatterjee, Partha. 1993. *The Nation and Its Fragments: Colonial and Postcolonial Histories*. Princeton: Princeton University Press.

Choay, Françoise. 2001. *The Invention of the Historic Monument*. New York: Cambridge University Press.

Chomątowska, Beata. 2012. *Stacja Muranów*. Sękowa: Wyd. Czarne.

Cole, Charles Woolsey. 1964. *Colbert and a Century of French Mercantilism*. Hamden, CT: Archon Books.

Colla, Elliott. 2007. *Conflicted Antiquities: Egyptology, Egyptomania, Egyptian Modernity*. Durham: Duke University Press.

Collins, Randall. 2004. *Interaction Ritual Chains*. Princeton: Princeton University Press.

Comaroff, John L., and Jean Comaroff. 2009. *Ethnicity, Inc.* Chicago: University of Chicago Press.

Connor, Walker. 1994. *Ethno-nationalism: The Quest for Understanding.* Princeton: Princeton University Press.

Creighton, Donald. 1937. *The Commercial Empire of the St. Lawrence, 1760–1850.* Toronto: Ryerson Press.

Cupers, Kenny, and Markus Miessen. 2002. *Spaces of Uncertainty.* Wuppertal: Müller + Busmann Verlag.

Cushing, Lincoln, and Ann Tompkins. 2007. *Chinese Posters: Art from the Great Proletarian Cultural Revolution.* San Francisco: Chronicle Books.

Da Vinha, Mathieu. 2004. *Les valets de chambre de Louis XIV.* Paris: Perrin.

Daragahi, Borzou. 2010. Nazi Airport Becomes Berlin's Tempelhof Park. *Los Angeles Times,* 19 July. http://articles.latimes.com/2010/jul/19/world/la-fg-germany-tempelhof-20100719 (accessed 27 February 2013).

Dassler, Sandra. 2015. "Notunterkunft in Berlin: Flughafen Tempelhof." *Tagespiegel Mobil, Berlin,* 25 October. www.tagesspiegel.de/berlin/notunterkunft-in-berlin-flughafen-tempelhof-erste-fluechtlinge-sind-angekommen/12492564.html (accessed 8 July 2016).

Daugbjerg, Mads. 2009. "Pacifying War Heritage: Patterns of Cosmopolitan Nationalism at a Danish Battlefield Site." *International Journal of Heritage Studies* 15(5): 431–446.

———. 2013. *Borders of Belonging: Experiencing History, War, and Nation at a Danish Heritage Site.* New York: Berghahn Books.

Davidson, Debra, and Mike Gismondi. 2011. *Challenging Legitimacy at the Precipice of Energy Calamity.* New York: Springer.

Defcon, Robert, and Max Dax. 2014. "An Alternative History of the Fall of the Wall: Squats, Techno and the Police." *Electronic Beats Magazine: Conversations on Essential Issues* (39): 68–81.

DeHaye, Pierre. 1970. *Les médailles au temps de Louis XIV.* Paris: Imprimerie Nationale.

Delestre, Maurice, and Jules Bouillon. 1894. *Catalogue d'estampes anciennes et modernes, partie de l'oeuvre d'Israel Silvestre.* Paris: D. Dumoulin et Cie.

Dennis, George. 1848. *Cities and Cemeteries of Etruria.* Vols. 1 and 2. London: J.M. Dent & Co.

DeNora, Tia. 2000. *Music in Everyday Life.* Cambridge: Cambridge University Press.

DeSoucey, Michaela. 2010. "Gastronationalism Food Traditions and Authenticity Politics in the European Union." *American Sociological Review* 75: 432–455.

Deutsche Welle. 2016a. "Berlin to Build on Tempelhof despite Drop in Refugees." 25 March. www.dw.com/en/berlin-to-build-on-tempelhof-despite-drop-in-refugees/a-19143212 (accessed 8 July 2016).

———. 2016b. "Berlin to Extend Tempelhof Airport Refugee Camp." 28 January. www.dw.com/en/

berlin-to-extend-tempelhof-airport-refugee-camp/a-19010260 (accessed 8 July 2016).

Domínguez Rubio, Fernando. 2014. "Preserving the Unpreservable: Docile and Unruly Objects at MoMA." *Theory and Society* 43(6): 617–645.

———. 2015. "Semiosis beyond Culture: An Ecological Approach." *American Sociological Association's Culture Section Newsletter* 27(2).

———. Forthcoming. *MoMA and the Relentlessness of Things.* Chicago: University of Chicago Press.

Douglas, Mary. 1966. *Purity and Danger.* London: Routledge.

Douglas, Mary, and Baron Isherwood. 1979. *The World of Goods: Toward an Anthropology of Consumption.* New York: Basic Books.

Duara, Prasenjit. 1995. *Rescuing History from the Nation.* Chicago: University of Chicago Press.

Duncan, Carol, and Alan Wallach. 2004. "The Universal Survey Museum." In Bettina Messias Carbonell (ed.), *Museum Studies: An Anthology of Contexts.* New York: Wiley-Blackwell, 51–80.

Durkheim, Émile. (1912) 1995. *The Elementary Forms of Religious Life.* New York: Free Press.

———. 2010. "Value Judgements and Judgements of Reality." In D. F. Pocock (trans.), *Sociology and Philosophy.* New York: Routledge.

Edensor, Tim. 2002. *National Identity, Popular Culture and Everyday Life.* Oxford: Berg.

Elias, Norbert. 1983. *The Court Society.* New York: Pantheon Books.

European: Das Debatten-Magazin, The. 2012. No. 4.

Farrell, Betty, and Maria Medvedeva. 2010. *Demographic Transformation and the Future of Museums.* Washington, DC: American Association of Museums.

Favell, Adrian. 2008. *Eurostars and Eurocities: Free Movement and Mobility in an Integrating Europe.* Oxford: Wiley-Blackwell.

Fehérváry, Krisztina. 2009. "Goods and States: The Political Logic of State-Socialist Material Culture." *Comparative Studies in Society and History* 51(2): 426–459.

———. 2013. *Politics in Color and Concrete: Socialist Materialities and the Middle Class in Hungary.* Bloomington: Indiana University Press.

Feischmidt, Margit, Rita Glózer, Zoltán Ilyés, Veronika K. Kasznár, and Ildikó Zakariás. 2014. *Nemzet a mindennapokban: Az újnacionalizmus populáris kultúrája.* Budapest: L'Harmattan.

Feldman, Marian H. 2014. *Communities of Style: Portable Luxury Arts, Identity, and Collective Memory in the Iron Age Levant.* Chicago: University of Chicago Press.

Fischer, Joachim. 2004. *Der Potsdamer Platz aus der Perspektive der Philosophischen Antropologie.* Munich: Fink Verlag.

Flierl, Thomas (ed.). 2008. *List und Schicksal der Ost-Moderne.* Berlin: form+zweck Verlag.

Flügge, Matthias. 2002. "Zeichen der Stadt." In Ulrich Wüst (ed.), *Hauptstadt: Berlinbilder*. Berlin: Berlin Edition in der Quintessenz Verlag.

Foster, Robert. 2002. *Materializing the Nation: Commodities, Consumption, and Media in Papua New Guinea*. Bloomington: Indiana University Press.

Foucault, Michel. (1975) 1991. *Discipline and Punish: The Birth of the Prison*. London: Penguin Books.

Fox, Jon E., and Cynthia Miller-Idriss. 2008. "Everyday Nationhood." *Ethnicities* 8(4): 536–563.

Francis, Daniel. 1997. *National Dreams: Myth, Memory, and Canadian History*. Vancouver: Arsenal Pulp Press.

Freedberg, David. 1991. *The Power of Images: Studies in the History and Theory of Response*. Chicago: University of Chicago Press.

Frydenberg, Julio. 2011. *Historia social del fútbol*. Buenos Aires: Siglo XXI.

Fujiwara, Masahiko. 2006. *Kokka no Hinkaku*. Tokyo: Shinchocha.

Garriga, José. 2007. *Haciendo amigos a las piñas*. Buenos Aires: Prometeo.

Gell, Alfred. 1998. *Art and Agency*. London: Oxford.

Gentile, Emilio. 2009. *La Grande Italia. The Myth of the Nation in the 20th Century*. Madison: University of Wisconsin Press.

Gerstenblith, Patty. 2008. *Art, Cultural Heritage, and the Law*. 2nd ed. Durham: Carolina Academic Press.

Gibbon, James. 1937. *Steel of Empire: The Romantic History of the Canadian Pacific*. New York: Tudor Publishing.

Glaeser, Andreas. 1999. *Divided in Unity: Identity, Germany and the Berlin Police*. Chicago: University of Chicago Press.

Glendinning, Miles. 2013. *The Conservation Movement: A History of Architectural Preservation: Antiquity to Modernity*. New York: Routledge.

Główny urząd statystyczny. 2015. *Struktura narodowo-etniczna, językowa ludności Polski: Narodowy Spis Powszechny Ludności i Mieszkań 2011*. Warsaw: Główny urząd statystyczny.

Goff, Patricia M. 2005. "It's Got to Be Sheep's Milk or Nothing! Geography, Identity, and Economic Nationalism." In Helleiner and Pickel, *Economic Nationalism in a Globalizing World*, 183–201.

Goffman, Erving. 1974. *Frame Analysis: An Essay on the Organization of Experience*. Cambridge: Harvard University Press.

Goldmann, A. J. 2011. "Repurposing Tempelhof." *Wall Street Journal*. http://online.wsj.com/article/SB10001424052702303823104576391572709176418.html (accessed 24 June 2013).

Goldstein, Claire. 2008. *Vaux and Versailles: The Appropriations, Erasures, and Accidents That Made Modern France*. Philadelphia: University of Pennsylvania Press.

Goody, Jack. 2006. *The Theft of History*. Cambridge: Cambridge University Press.

Goubert, Pierre. 1974. *The Ancien Régime: French Society, 1600–1750*. New York: Harper & Row.

Graham, Brian, Greg J. Ashworth, and John E. Tunbridge. 2000. *A Geography of Heritage: Power, Culture and Economy.* London: Arnold.

Grant, George. 1873. *Ocean to Ocean: Sandford Fleming's Expedition through Canada in 1872.* Toronto: James Campbell & Son; London: Sampson Low, Marston, Low, & Searle.

Griswold, Wendy. 1987. "A Methodological Framework for the Sociology of Culture." *Sociological Methodology* 17: 1–35.

Griswold, Wendy, Mangione, Gemma, and Terence McDonnell. 2013. "Objects, Words and Bodies in Space: Bringing Materiality into Cultural Analysis." *Qualitative Sociology* 36(4): 343–364.

Grubbauer, Monika, and Joanna Kusiak (eds.). 2012. *Chasing Warsaw: Socio-material Dynamics of Urban Change since 1990.* Frankfurt: Campus.

Guibernau, Monserrat. 2007. *The Identity of Nations.* Cambridge: Polity Press.

Guldi, Jo. 2012. *Roads to Power: Britain Invents the Infrastructure State.* Cambridge: Harvard University Press.

Hagen, Joshua. 2004. "The Most German of Towns: Creating an Ideal Nazi Community in Rothenburg ob der Tauber." *Annals of the Association of American Geographers* 94: 207–227.

Hall, John R., Blake Stimson, and Lisa Tamiris Becker (eds.). 2006. *Visual Worlds.* New York: Routledge.

Hamilakis, Yannis. 2007. *The Nation and Its Ruins: Antiquity, Archaeology, and National Imagination in Greece.* New York: Oxford University Press.

Handler, Richard. 1997. *The New History in an Old Museum: Creating the Past at Colonial Williamsburg.* Durham: Duke University Press.

Harré, Rom. 2002. "Material Objects in Social Worlds." *Theory, Culture and Society* 19(5–6): 23–33.

Hart, E. J. 1983. *The Selling of Canada: The CPR and the Beginnings of Canadian Tourism.* Banff: Altitude.

Harvey, David. 2012. *Rebel Cities. From the Right to the City to the Urban Revolution.* London: Verso.

Hebdige, Dick. 1979. *Subculture: The Meaning of Style.* London: Methuen.

Hegenbart, Sarah, and Sven Mündner. 2012. *Mythos Berlin: A London Perspective.* London: White Review.

Heidegger, Martin. 1962. *Being in Time.* New York: Harper & Row.

Helleiner, Eric. 2002. "Economic Nationalism as a Challenge to Economic Liberalism? Lessons from the 19th Century." *International Studies Quarterly* 46: 307–329.

Helleiner, Eric, and Andreas Pickel (eds.). 2005. *Economic Nationalism in a Globalizing World.* Ithaca: Cornell University Press.

Hennion, Antoine. 1993. *La passion musicale: Une sociologie de la médiation.* Paris: Métailié: Diffusion Seuil.

Hennion, Antoine, Sophie Maisonneuve, and Emilie Gomart. 2000. "Figures de l'amateur: formes, objets, pratiques de l'amour de la musique aujourd'hui." Paris: La Documentation française: Ministère de la culture et de la communication, Direction de l'administration générale, Département des études et de la prospective.

Hewison, Robert. 1987. *The Heritage Industry: Britain in a Climate of Decline.* London: Methuen.

Heyden, Mathias. 2011. "Evolving Participatory Design: A Report from Berlin, Reaching Beyond." In Hinkel, *Urban Interior*, 63–78.

Hicks, Dan, and Mary C. Beaudry. 2010. *The Oxford Handbook of Material Culture Studies.* Oxford: Oxford University Press.

Hinsley, Curtis. 1981. *Savages and Scientists: The Smithsonian Institution and the Development of American Anthropology, 1846–1910.* Washington, DC: Smithsonian Institution Press.

Hirsh, Dafna. 2013. "Hummus: The Making of an Israeli Culinary Cult." *Journal of Consumer Culture* 13(1): 25–45.

Hirshler, Erica E. 2009. *Sargent's Daughters: The Biography of a Painting.* Boston: MFA Publications.

Hoberg, George. 2014. "Canada: The Overachieving Petro-State." Green Policy Prof. http://greenpolicyprof.org/wordpress/?p=952 (accessed 1 June 2015).

Hobsbawm, Eric, and Terrence Ranger (eds.). 1983. *The Invention of Tradition.* Cambridge: Cambridge University Press.

Hodder, Ian. 2012. *Entangled: An Archaeology of the Relationships between Humans and Things.* Oxford: Wiley-Blackwell.

Holland, Dorothy C., William Lachicotte, Debra Skinner, and Carole Cain. 1998. *Identity and Agency in Cultural Worlds.* Cambridge: Harvard University Press.

Hooper-Greenhill, Eileen. 2000. *Museums and the Interpretation of Visual Culture.* London: Routledge.

Horchert, Judith. 2012. "Campus Party Europe: World's Largest Tech Fest Begins in Berlin." *Spiegel Online.* www.spiegel.de/international/business/largest-technology-and-computer-festival-under-way-in-berlin-a-851457.html (accessed 29 June 2013).

Hunt, John Dixon, Michel Conan, and Claire Goldstein. 2002. *Tradition and Innovation in French Garden Art: Chapters of a New History.* Philadelphia: University of Pennsylvania Press.

Hunt, Lynn. 1986. *Politics, Culture and Class in the French Revolution.* Berkeley: University of California Press.

Ichijo, Atsuko, and Ronald Ranta. 2015. *Food, National Identity and Nationalism: From Everyday to Global Politics.* London: Palgrave Macmillan.

Ignatieff, Michael. 1995. *Blood and Belonging: Journeys into the New Nationalism.* New York: Farrar, Straus and Giroux.

——— (ed.). 2005. *American Exceptionalism and Human Rights.* Princeton: Princeton University Press.

Ingold, Tim. 2007. "Materiality against Materials." *Archaeological Dialogues* 14(1): 1–16.

———. 2012. "Toward an Ecology of Materials." *Annual Review of Anthropology* 41: 427–442.

Innis, Harold. (1930) 1962. *The Fur Trade in Canada*. New Haven: Yale University Press.

Izzet, Vedia. 2007. "Greeks Make It; Etruscans Fecit: The Stigma of Plagiarism in the Reception of Etruscan Art." *Etruscan Studies* 10(1): 223–237.

Jackel, David. 1979. "Ocean to Ocean: G. M. Grant's 'Round Unvarnish'd Tale.'" *Canadian Literature* 81: 7–23.

Janicka, Elżbieta. 2012. *Festung Warschau*. Warsaw: Wyd. *Krytyki Politycznej*.

Junge-Reyer, Ingeborg. 2007. "Preface." In *Urban Pioneers: Temporary Use and Urban Development in Berlin*. Berlin: Berlin Senate & Jovis, 17–18.

Kabisch, Nadja, Dagmar Haase, and Annegret Haase. 2012. "Urban Population Development in Europe, 1991–2008: The Examples of Poland and the UK." *International Journal of Urban and Regional Research* 36(6): 1326–1348."

Kania-Lundholm, Magdalena. 2014. "Nation in Market Times: Connecting the National and the Commercial: A Research Overview." *Sociology Compass* 8(6): 603–613.

Kaplan, Flora (ed.). 1994. *Museums and the Making of "Ourselves": The Role of Objects in National Identity*. Leicester: Leicester University Press.

Karl, Terry Lynn. 1997. *The Paradox of Plenty: Oil Booms and Petro-States*. Berkeley: University of California Press.

Keane, Webb. 2003. "Semiotics and the Social Analysis of Material Things." *Language and Communication* 23: 403–425.

———. 2005. "Signs Are Not the Garb of Meaning: On the Social Analysis of Material Things." In Daniel Miller (ed.), *Materiality*. Durham: Duke University Press, 182–205.

———. 2006. "Subjects and Objects." In Chris Tilley, Webb Keane, Susanne Küchler, Mike Rowlands, and Patricia Spyer (eds.), *Handbook of Material Culture*. London: Sage, 197–202.

Kettering, Sharon. 1986. *Patrons, Brokers, and Clients in Seventeenth-century France*. New York: Oxford University Press.

Kliems, Alfrun, and Marina Dmitrieva (eds.). 2010. *The Post-Socialist City: Continuity and Change in Urban Space and Imagery*. Berlin: Jovis.

Koch, Natalie, and Anssi Paasi. 2016. "Banal Nationalism 20 Years On: Rethinking, Re-formulating and Re-contextualizing the Concept." *Political Geography*. doi:10.1016/j.polgeo.2016.06.002

Kokoro no Nooto. 2002. Tokyo: Ministry of Education, Culture, Sports, Science, and Technology.

Korfmann, Hans W. 2012. "Berlins Grösster Spielplatz." *Die Zeit* 39: 59.

Körner, Axel. 2009. *The Politics of Culture in Liberal Italy: From Unification to Fascism*. London: Routledge.

Kowalski, Alexandra. 2011. "When Cultural Capitalization Became Global

Practice." In N. Bandelj and F. Wherry (eds.), *The Cultural Wealth of Nations*. Stanford: Stanford University Press, 73–89.

———. 2012. "The Nation, Rescaled: Theorizing the Decentralization of Memory in Contemporary France." *Comparative Studies in Society and History* 54(2): 308.

Kugelmass, Jack, and Anna-Maria Orla-Bukowska. 1998. "If You Build It They Will Come: Recreating a Jewish District in Post-Communist Kraków." *City and Society Annual Review* 10(1): 315–353.

Kymlicka, Will, and Wayne Norman (eds.). 2000. *Citizenship in Diverse Societies*. London: Oxford University Press.

La Gorce, Jérôme de, Pierre Jugie, and Archives nationales. 2010. *Dans l'atelier des Menus-Plaisirs du roi. Spectacles, fêtes et cérémonies aux XVIIe et XVIIIe siècles [exposition, Paris, Archives nationales, 19 janvier-24 avril 2011]*. Paris.

Lacan, Jacques. 2007. *Ecrits: The First Complete Edition in English*. New York: Norton.

Lachièze-Rey, Marc, and Jean-Pierre Luminet. 2001. In Joe Laredo (trans.), *Celestial Treasury*. Cambridge: Cambridge University Press.

Lackmann, Thomas. 2012. "Tempelhofer Unfreiheit." *Der Tagesspiegel*. www.tagesspiegel.de/berlin/tempelhofer-unfreiheit/6940642.html (accessed 27 June 2013).

Ladd, Bryan. 1997. *The Ghosts of Berlin*. Chicago: University of Chicago Press.

Lakoff, George, and Mark Johnson. 2003. *Metaphors We Live By*. Chicago: University of Chicago Press.

Lanz, Stephan. 2013. "Be Berlin! Governing the City through Freedom." *International Journal of Urban and Regional Research* 37(4): 1305–1324.

Lash, Scott, and Celia Lury. 2007. *Global Cultural Industry: The Mediation of Things*. London: Polity.

Latour, Bruno. 2002. "What Is Iconoclash? Or Is There a World beyond the Image Wars?" In Bruno Latour and Peter Wiebel (eds.), *Iconoclash: Beyond the Image Wars in Science, Religion and Art*. Boston: MIT Press, 16–40.

———. 2004. "Whose Cosmos, Which Cosmopolitics?" *Common Knowledge* 10(3): 450–462.

———. 2007a. "Can We Get Our Materialism Back, Please?" *Isis* 98(1): 138–142.

———. 2007b. *Reassembling the Social: An Introduction to Actor-Network-Theory*. Oxford: Oxford University Press.

Laurent, Xavier. 2003. *Grandeur et misère du patrimoine, d'André Malraux À Jacques Duhamel, 1959-1973*. Paris: Comité d'histoire du ministère de la culture.

Le Roy Ladurie, Emmanuel. 1996. *The Ancien Régime: A History of France, 1610-1774*. Oxford: Blackwell.

Lebovics, Herman. 2004. *Bringing Empire Back Home*. Ithaca: Cornell University Press.

Lee, Benjamin, and Edward LiPuma. 2002. "Cultures of Circulation: The Imaginations of Modernity." *Public Culture* 14(1): 191–213.

Lee, Dong Ok. 1992. "Commodification of Ethnicity: The Sociospatial Reproduction of Immigrant Entrepreneurs." *Urban Affairs Review* 28: 258–275.

Lehrer, Erica. 2013. *Jewish Poland Revisited: Heritage Tourism in Unquiet Places*. Bloomington: Indiana University Press.

Leoussi, Athena. 1998. *Nationalism and Classicism: The Classical Body as National Symbol in Nineteenth-century England and France*. Basingstoke: Macmillan.

———. 2001. "Myths of Ancestry." *Nations and Nationalism* 7(4): 467–486.

Leoussi, Athena, and Steven Grosby (eds.). 2007. *Nationalism and Ethnosymbolism: History, Culture and Ethnicity in the Formation of Nations*. Edinburgh: Edinburgh University Press.

Levi, Donata. 2008. "The Administration of Historical Heritage: The Italian Case." In Stefan Fisch (ed.), *National Approaches to the Governance of Historical Heritage over Time: A Comparative Report*. Amsterdam: IOS Press, 103–126.

Levitt, Peggy. 2015. *Artifacts and Allegiances: How Museums Put the Nation and the World on Display*. Oakland: University of California Press.

Levitt, Peggy, and Pal Nyiri (eds.). 2014. "Books, Bodies, and Bronzes: Comparing Sites of Global Citizenship Creation." *Ethnic and Racial Studies* 37(12): 2149–2157.

Levy, Daniel, Jeffrey K. Olick, and Vered Vinitzky-Seroussi. 2011. *The Collective Memory Reader*. Oxford: Oxford University Press.

Levy, Daniel, and Natan Sznaider. 2006. *The Holocaust and Memory in the Global Age*. English ed. Philadelphia: Temple University Press.

Lin, Jan. 1998. *Reconstructing Chinatown: Ethnic Enclaves and Global Change*, Vol. 2. Minneapolis: University of Minnesota Press.

Linnitt, Carol. 2013. "Letter Reveals Harper Government Granted Oil and Gas Industry Requests." *Desmogblog*. www.desmogblog.com/2013/01/10/letter-reveals-harper-government-grants-oil-and-gas-industry-requests (accessed 18 January 2015).

List, Friedrich. 1904. *The National System of Political Economy*, translated by Sampson S. Lloyd M.P. New York: Longmans, Green.

Löfgren, Orvar. 1989. "The Nationalization of Culture." *Ethnologia Europaea* 19: 5–24.

Löw, Martina. 2008a. "The Constitution of Space: The Structuration of Spaces through the Simultaneity of Effect and Perception." *European Journal of Social Theory* 11(25): 25–49.

———. 2008b. "A City's Own Logic: The Perspective of Spatial Sociology on Urban Theory." In Jolanta Bielanska et al. (eds.), *Urban Potentials: Ideas and Practice*. Berlin: Jovis, 280–285.

———. 2013. "The City as Experiential Space: The Production of Shared Meaning." *International Journal of Urban and Regional Research* 37(3): 894–908.

Lowenthal, David. 1985. *The Past Is a Foreign Country*. Cambridge: Cambridge University Press.

Lumley, Robert (ed.). 1988. *The Museum Time-Machine: Putting Cultures on Display*. London: Routledge.

Lury, Celia. 2004. *Brands: The Logos of the Global Economy*. London: Routledge.

Luvaas, Brent. 2013. "Material Interventions: Indonesian DIY Fashion and the Regime of the Global Brand." *Cultural Anthropology* 28(1): 127–143.

Lynn, John A. 1997. *Giant of the Grand Siècle: The French Army, 1610–1715*. Cambridge: Cambridge University Press.

Macdonald, Sharon (ed.). 2011. *A Companion to Museum Studies*. Chichester: Wiley-Blackwell.

———. 2013. *Memorylands: Heritage and Identity in Europe Today*. London: Routledge.

Machiavelli, Niccolò, and D. Donno. 1966. *The Prince*. New York: Bantam.

Mannheim, Karl. 1964. *Essays on the Sociology of Knowledge*. London: Routledge.

Marchand, Suzanne. 1996. *Down from Olympus: Archaeology and Philhellenism in Germany, 1750–1970*. Princeton: Princeton University Press.

Marin, Louis. 1981. *Le portrait du roi*. Paris: Editions de Minuit.

Marks, Lawrence E. 1978. *The Unity of the Senses: Interrelation among the Modalities*. New York: Academic Press.

Mazzarella, William. 2003. *Shoveling Smoke*. Durham: Duke University Press.

McClellan, Andrew. 2003. *Art and Its Publics: Museum Studies at the Millennium*. New York: Wiley.

McCrone, David, Angela Morris, and Richard Kiely. 1995. *Scotland—The Brand: The Making of Scottish Heritage*. Edinburgh: Edinburgh University Press.

McDannell, Colleen. 1995. *Material Christianity: Religion and Popular Culture in America*. New Haven: Yale University Press.

McDonnell, Terence. 2010. "Cultural Objects as Objects: Materiality, Urban Space, and the Interpretation of AIDS Campaigns in Accra, Ghana." *American Journal of Sociology* 115(6): 1800–1852.

———. 2016. *Best Laid Plans: Cultural Entropy and the Unraveling of AIDS Media Campaigns*. Chicago: University of Chicago Press.

McGuirk, Justin. 2015. "Urban Commons Have Radical Potential." *The Guardian*, 15 June. www.theguardian.com/cities/2015/jun/15/urban-common-radical-community-gardens (accessed 8 July 2016).

McKay, George A., and Michael N. Goddard. 2009. "Introduction: (Post-) subculture Theory, and Practice in East-Central Europe." In G. McKay, C. Williams, and M. Goddard (eds.), *Cultural Identity Studies: Subcultures and New Religious Movements in Russia and East-Central Europe*. Oxford: Peter Lang, 3–14.

McKenna, Frank. 2012. "Let's Build a Canadian Oil Pipeline from Coast to Coast." *The Globe and Mail,* 18 June.

McKillop, Brian. 2011. *Pierre Berton: A Biography.* Toronto: McClelland and Stewart.

Mead, George Herbert. 1964. *On Social Psychology: Selected Papers.* Chicago: University of Chicago Press.

Mead, George Herbert, and Charles William Morris. 1962. *Mind, Self, and Society from the Standpoint of a Social Behaviorist.* Chicago: University of Chicago Press.

Meng, Michael. 2011. *Shattered Spaces: Encountering Jewish Ruins in Postwar Germany and Poland.* Cambridge: Harvard University Press.

Merleau-Ponty, Maurice. 2012. *Phenomenology of Perception.* London: Routledge.

Meskell, Lynn. 2015. "Globalizing Heritage." In Meskell, Lynn (ed.), *Global Heritage: A Reader.* Oxford: Wiley Blackwell, 1–21.

Mettam, Roger. 1988. *Power and Faction in Louis XIV's France.* Oxford: Blackwell.

Miller, Daniel (ed.). 2005. *Materiality.* Durham: Duke University Press.

Miller, Daniel, and Lynn Meskell. 2005. *Materiality: Politics, History, and Culture.* Oxford: Oxford University Press.

Miller-Idriss, Cynthia. 2014. "Marketing National Pride: Commercialization and the Extreme Right in Germany." In Gavin Brent Sullivan (ed.), *Understanding Collective Pride and Group Identity: New Directions in Emotion Theory, Research and Practice.* New York: Routledge, 149–161.

Mitchell, Timothy. 2011. *Carbon Democracy: Political Power in the Age of Oil.* London: Verso.

Mitchell, W.J.T. 1986. *Iconology: Image, Text, Ideology.* Chicago: University of Chicago Press.

———. 1998. "Showing Seeing: A Critique of Visual Culture." In Nicholas Mirzoeff (ed.), *The Visual Culture Reader.* 2nd ed. New York: Routledge, 86–101.

———. 2005. *What Do Pictures Want? The Lives and Loves of Images.* Chicago: University of Chicago Press.

Mohr, Reinhard. 2008. "The Mother of All Airports: The Myth of Berlin's Tempelhof." *Spiegel Online.* www.spiegel.de/international/germany/the-myth-of-berlin-stempelhof-the-mother-of-all-airports-a-549685.html (accessed 23 June 2013).

Molnár, Virág. 2016. "Civil Society, Radicalism, and the Rediscovery of Mythic Nationalism." *Nations and Nationalism* 22(1): 165–185.

Momigliano, Arnaldo. 1966. "Ancient History and the Antiquarian." *Terzo Contributo alla storia degli studi classici e del mondo antico.* Rome: Ed. di Storia e Letteratura, 1–39.

Monocle Magazine. 2009. "The Most Liveable Cities Index." *Monocle* 25(3): 16–30.

Morgan, David. 1999. *Visual Piety: A History and Theory of Popular Religious Images*. Berkeley: University of California Press.

———. 2005. *The Sacred Gaze: Religious Visual Culture in Theory and Practice*. Berkeley: University of California Press.

Mosse, George L. 1975. *The Nationalization of the Masses: Political Symbolism and Mass Movements in Germany from the Napoleonic Wars through the Third Reich*. Ithaca: Cornell University Press.

———. 1996. *Nationalism and Sexuality: Respectability and Abnormal Sexuality in Modern Europe*. London: Howard Fertig.

Mukerji, Chandra. 1994. "Toward a Sociology of Material Culture: Science Studies, Cultural Studies and the Meanings of Things." In Diana Crane (ed.), *The Sociology of Culture: Emerging Theoretical Perspectives*. New York: Wiley, 143–162.

———. 1997. *Territorial Ambitions and the Gardens of Versailles*. Cambridge: Cambridge University Press.

———. 2009. *Impossible Engineering: Technology and Territoriality on the Canal du Midi*. Princeton: Princeton University Press.

———. 2010. "The Territorial State as a Figured World of Power: Strategics, Logistics and Impersonal Rule." *Sociological Theory* 28(4): 402–425.

———. 2012. "Space and Political Pedagogy at the Gardens of Versailles." *Public Culture* 24(368): 515–540.

Murzyn, Monika. 2006. *Kazimierz: The Central European Experience of Urban Regeneration*. Kraków: International Cultural Centre.

Nakano, Takeshi. 2004. "Theorising Economic Nationalism." *Nations and Nationalism* 10(3): 211–229.

Nakassis, Constantine. 2013. "Brands and Their Surfeits." *Cultural Anthropology* 28(1): 111–126.

Neilson, Leighann. 2011. "John Murray Gibbon (1875–1952): The Branding of a Northern Nation." *Conference on Historical Analysis and Research in Marketing Proceedings* 15: 127–144. http://faculty.quinnipiac.edu/charm/CHARM%20proceedings/Proceedings%20Vol.%2015.htm (accessed 15 July 2014).

Néraudau, Jean-Pierre. 1986. *L'Olympe du Roi-Soleil: Mythologie et idéologie royale au grand Siècle*. Paris: Les Belles Lettres.

Newell, Eric. 1994. "Canada's Oil Sands: It's Time to Awaken the Sleeping Giant." *Empire Club of Canada Addresses*, 8 December, 525–538. http://speeches.empireclub.org/61089/data?n=31 (accessed 1 July 2014).

Newsome, W. Brian. 2009. *French Urban Planning, 1940–1968: The Construction and Deconstruction of an Authoritarian System*. Oxford: Peter Lang.

Nora, Pierre (ed.). 1984. *Realms of Memory: The Construction of the French Past*. New York: Columbia University Press.

——— (ed.). 1997. *Les lieux de mémoire*, Vol. 1: *La république, la nation*. Paris: Gallimard (Quarto).

Novy, Johannes. 2010. "What's New about New Urban Tourism? What Do

Recent Changes in Travel Imply for the Tourist City Berlin." In Richter, *Tourist City Berlin.*

Novy, Johannes, and Claire Colomb. 2012. "Struggling for the Right to the (Creative) City in Berlin and Hamburg: New Urban Social Movements, New 'Spaces of Hope.'" *International Journal of Urban and Regional Research* 37(5): 1816–1838.

Oberschall, Anthony. 2000. "The Manipulation of Ethnicity: From Ethnic Cooperation to Violence and War in Yugoslavia." *Ethnic and Racial Studies* 23(6): 982–1001.

Ogasawara, Keishōsai. 1999. *Utsukushii Furumai.* Text edition. Kyoto: Tankōsha.

Oldfather, William Abbott. 1920. "A Note on the Etymology of the Word 'Ceramic.'" *Journal of the American Ceramic Society* 3(7): 537–542.

Olick, Jeffrey K. 2007. *The Politics of Regret: On Collective Memory and Historical Responsibility.* London: Routledge.

Olick, Jeffrey K., Vered Vinitzky-Seroussi, and Daniel Levy. 2011. *The Collective Memory Reader.* New York: Oxford University Press.

Ortner, Sherry B. 2006. *Anthropology and Social Theory: Culture, Power, and the Acting Subject.* Durham: Duke University Press.

Oushakine, Serguei Alex. 2010. "Somatic Nationalism: Theorizing Post-Soviet Ethnicity in Russia." In C. Bradatan and S. A. Oushakine (eds.), *In Marx's Shadow: Knowledge, Power, and Intellectuals in Eastern Europe and Russia.* New York: Lexington Books, 155–174.

Ozouf, Mona. 1988. *Festivals and the French Revolution.* Cambridge: Harvard University Press.

Patriarca, Silvana. 2010. *Italian Vices: Nation and Character from the Risorgimento to the Republic.* Cambridge: Cambridge University Press.

Peel's Prairie Provinces, University of Alberta Libraries. n.d. http://peel.library.ualberta.ca/index.html (accessed 1 June 2015).

Perkins, Phil. 2009. "DNA and Etruscan Identity." In Phil Perkins and J. Swaddling (eds.), *Etruscan by Definition.* London: British Museum Press, 95–111.

———. 2016. "Bucchero in Context." In Sinclair Bell and Alexandra Carpino (eds.), *A Companion to the Etruscans.* Malden, MA: Wiley-Blackwell, 224–236.

Perrault, Charles, and Jacques Bailly. 1629. *Le Labyrinthe de Versailles.* Paris: Graçay.

Peterson, Richard. 1997. *Creating Country Music: Fabricating Authenticity.* Chicago: University of Chicago Press.

Pickel, Andreas. 2005. "Introduction: False Oppositions: Reconceptualizing Economic Nationalism in a Globalizing World." In Helleiner and Pickel, *Economic Nationalism in a Globalizing World,* 1–20.

Pilkington, Hilary. 2012. "'Vorkuta Is the Capital of the World': People, Place and the Everyday Production of the Local." *Sociological Review* 60(2): 267–291.

Pilkington, Hilary, and Gary Pollock (eds.). 2015. *Radical Futures? Youth, Politics and Activism in Contemporary Europe*. Sociological Review Monograph Series. Oxford: Wiley-Blackwell.

Pinna, Giovanni. 2001. "Heritage and 'Cultural Assets.'" *Museum International* 53(2): 62–42.

Pinney, Christopher. 2005. "Things Happen: Or, From Which Moment Does That Object Come?" In Miller, *Materiality*.

Plomb, Reinier. 1999. "A Longitude Timekeeper by Isaac Thuret with the Balance Spring Invented by Christiaan Huygens." *Annals of Science* 1: 379–394.

Pomian, Krzysztof. 1990. *Collectors and Curiosities: Paris and Venice, 1500–1800*. Oxford: Polity.

Prentice, Jim. 2011. "Nation-building Infrastructure: A Road Map to Economic Growth." *Address to the Edmonton Chamber of Commerce*, 21 November. www.cibc.com/ca/pdf/investor/prentice-edmonton-november-11.pdf (accessed 30 July 2014).

Promey, Sally (ed.). 2014. *Sensational Religion: Sensory Cultures in Material Practice*. New Haven: Yale University Press.

Quilley, Geoff. 2011. *Empire to Nation: Art, History and the Visualization of Maritime Britain*. New Haven: Yale University Press.

Quintinie, Jean de la. 1692. *Instructions pour les jardins fruitiers et potagers*. Amsterdam: Henri Desbordes.

Ramond, Pierre. 2011. *André-Charles Boulle ébéniste, ciseleur & marqueteur ordinaire du Roy*. Dourdan: Vial.

Rasmussen, Tom. 1979. *Bucchero Pottery from Southern Etruria*. Cambridge: Cambridge University Press.

Reed, Isaac A. 2011. *Interpretation and Social Knowledge: On the Use of Theory in the Human Sciences*. Chicago: University of Chicago Press.

Reiter, Christiane. 2004. "Time for Berlin." In Angelika Taschen (ed.), *Berlin Style: Scenes, Interiors, Details*. Cologne: Taschen.

Renfrew, Colin. 2001. "Symbol before Concept: Material Engagement and the Early Development of Society." In Ian Hodder (ed.), *Archaeological Theory Today*. Cambridge: Polity Press, 122–140.

Rennella, Mark. 2008. *The Boston Cosmopolitans: International Travel and American Arts and Letters*. New York: Palgrave Macmillan.

Richter, Jana (ed.). 2010. *The Tourist City Berlin: Tourism and Architecture*. Berlin: Braun.

Rivera, Lauren A. 2008. "Managing 'Spoiled' National Identity: War, Tourism, and Memory in Croatia." *American Sociological Review* 73(4): 613–634.

Rogers, Thomas 2015. "Authoritarian Outfitters." *New Republic*. https://newrepublic.com/article/121199/germanys-thor-steinar-neo-nazis-favorite-clothing-brand (accessed 30 June 2015).

Rogoff, Irit. 1998. "Studying Visual Culture." In Nicholas Mirzoeff (ed.), *The Visual Culture Reader*. 2nd ed. New York: Routledge, 24–36.

Ronfort, Jean Nérée, and Museum für angewandte Kunst. 2009. *André Charles

Boulle, 1642–1732 un nouveau style pour l'Europe [exposition, Francfort-sur-le-Main, Museum für angewandte Kunst, 30 octobre 2009–31 janvier 2010] préface de monsieur Nicolas Sarkozy. Paris: Somogy.

Rose-Greenland, Fiona. 2013a. "The Parthenon Marbles as Icons of Nationalism in 19th Century Britain: From Pre-national to Supra-national." *Nations and Nationalism* 19(4): 654–673.

———. 2013b. "Seeing the Unseen: Prospective Loading and Knowledge Forms in Archaeological Discovery." *Qualitative Sociology* 36(3): 251–277.

———. 2016. "Color Perception in Sociology: Materiality and Authenticity at the *Gods in Color* Show." *Sociological Theory* 34(2): 81–105.

Ruggie, John Gerard. 2005. "American Exceptionalism, Exemptionalism, and Global Governance." In Ignatieff, *American Exceptionalism and Human Rights*, 304–339.

Saito, Hiro. 2011. "An Actor-Network Theory of Cosmopolitanism." *Sociological Theory* 29(2): 124–149. doi:10.1111/j.1467-9558.2011.01390.x

Scheppele, Kim Lane. 2012. "Constitutional Awe: Hungary's Holy Crown of St. Stephen's." Unpublished manuscript.

Schlögel, Karl. 2008. *Die Mitte Liegt Ostwärts: Europa im Übergang.* Frankfurt: Fischer.

Schwarzbeck, Martin. 2013. "Wir Sind das Feld." *Zitty Magazine* (21): 22–27.

Scott, James C. 1998. *Seeing like a State: How Certain Schemes to Improve the Human Condition Have Failed.* New Haven: Yale University Press.

Searle, John. 1995. *The Construction of Social Reality.* London: Penguin.

Seel, Martin. 2007. *Die Macht des Erscheinens.* Frankfurt: Suhrkamp.

Sewell, William H., Jr. 1996. "Historical Events as Transformations of Structures: Inventing Revolution at the Bastille." *Theory and Society* 25(6): 841–881.

———. 1999. "The Concept(s) of Culture." In V. E. Bonnell and L. Hunt (eds.), *Beyond the Cultural Turn.* Berkeley: University of California Press, 35–61.

———. 2005. *Logics of History: Social Theory and Social Transformation.* Chicago: University of Chicago Press.

Shakai Keizai Seisansei Honbu. 2006. *Rejaa Hakusho.* Tokyo: Buneisha.

Shea, Andrea. 2010. "High Stakes for MFA's $504M Americas Wing." *WBUR*, 12 November. www.wbur.org/2010/11/12/mfa-opening.

Sherman, Daniel J. 2008. *Museums and Difference.* Bloomington: Indiana University Press.

Shiotsuki, Yaeko. 2005. *Suteki na Josei no tame no Jōkyū Manaa Resson.* Tokyo: Shōgakkan.

Shirane, Haruo. 2012. *Japan and the Culture of the Four Seasons: Nature, Literature, and the Arts.* New York: Columbia University Press.

Siegert, Hubertus. 2001. *Berlin Babylon.* German Documentary, Philip-Gröning Filmproduktion.

Silberman, Neil Asher. 2015. "Is Every Sherd Sacred? Moving beyond the Cult of Object-Centered Authenticity." *Journal of Eastern Mediterranean Archaeology and Heritage Studies* 3(1): 61–63.

Silver, Dan. 2011. "Moodiness of Action." *Sociological Theory* 29(3): 199–222.

Simmel, Georg. 2008. *Englischsprachige Veröffentlichungen: 1893–1919*. Frankfurt: Suhrkamp.

Simmen, Jeannot, and Thorsten Heinze. 2010. *Berlin-2010.eu: Vom Narrenhaus West Berlin zur Kunst-Metropole Europas*. Berlin: Edition Club Bel Etage.

Sims, Lowery Stokes (ed.). 2015. *Common Wealth: Art by African Americans in the Museum of Fine Arts, Boston*. Boston: MFA Publications.

Skey, Michael. 2009. "The National in Everyday Life: A Critical Engagement with Michael Billig's Thesis of Banal Nationalism." *Sociological Review* 57(2): 331–46. doi:10.1111/j.1467–954X.2009.01832.x

Slavtcheva-Petkova, Vera. 2014. "Rethinking Banal Nationalism: Banal Americanism, Europeanism, and the Missing Link between Media Representations and Identities." *International Journal of Communication* 8: 43–61.

Smee, Jess. 2008. "Last Call for Berlin's Tempelhof Airport: Sadness as Nazi-built Hub That Became a Lifeline for Starving Germans Closes." *The Guardian*. www.guardian.co.uk/world/2008/oct/31/germany-architecture (accessed 28 June 2013).

Smilde, David, and Geneviève Zubrzycki. 2016. "The Sources of Cultural Power: Beyond the Cultural Arbitrary." *Qualitative Sociology* 39(2): 195–198.

Smith, Anthony D. 1987. *The Ethnic Origins of Nations*. New York: Blackwell.

———. 1999. *Myths and Memories of the Nation*. New York: Oxford University Press.

———. 2004. *The Antiquity of Nations*. Cambridge: Polity Press.

———. 2013. *The Nation Made Real: Art and National Identity in Western Europe, 1600–1850*. Oxford: Oxford University Press.

Smith, Philip. 1999. "The Elementary Forms of Place and Their Transformations: A Durkheimian Model." *Qualitative Sociology* 22(1): 13–36.

Soll, Jacob. 2009. *The Information Master: Jean-Baptiste Colbert's Secret State Intelligence System*. Ann Arbor: University of Michigan Press.

Sonnino, Paul. 1990. *The Reign of Louis XIV*. London: Humanities Press.

Steets, Silke. 2015. "Taking Berger and Luckmann to the Realm of Materiality: Architecture as a Social Construction." *Cultural Sociology* 10(1): 93–108.

Strohmaier, Brenda. 2014. *Wie man lernt, Berliner zu sein: Die deutsche Hauptstadt als konjunktiver Erfahrungsraum*. Frankfurt: Campus Verlag.

Suny, Ronald G. 2006. "Why We Hate You: The Passions of National Identity and Ethnic Violence." Lecture delivered at Oxford University, 24 April.

———. 2009. "Affective Communities: The Contradictions of National and Soviet Identity in the USSR." Unpublished manuscript, Collegiate Professorial Lecture, University of Michigan, 8 December.

Surak, Kristin. 2010. "The Business of Belonging." *New Left Review*, 151–159.

———. 2011. "From Selling Tea to Selling Japaneseness: Symbolic Power and the Nationalization of Cultural Practices." *European Journal of Sociology* 52(2): 175–208.

———. 2012a. "Die Ethnizitäsindustrie." *Lettre International*, 114–118.

———. 2012b. "Nation-Work: A Praxeology of Making and Maintaining Nations." *European Journal of Sociology* 53(2): 171–204.

———. 2013. *Making Tea, Making Japan: Cultural Nationalism in Practice.* Stanford: Stanford University Press.

———. Forthcoming. "Tea Flows: A Praxeological Perspective on Rituals." In Paul Heike, Kay Kirchmann, and Markus Gottwald (eds.), *(Extra-)Ordinary Presence: Social Configurations and Cultural Repertoires.* Bielefeld: Transcript-Verlag.

Swidler, Ann. 1986. "Culture in Action: Symbols and Strategies." *American Sociological Review* 51: 273–286.

Szporluk, Roman. 1988. *Communism and Nationalism: Karl Marx versus Friedrich List.* Oxford: Oxford University Press.

Sztompka, Piotr. 1993. *The Sociology of Social Change.* Cambridge: Blackwell.

Tavory, Iddo, and Stefan Timmermans. 2013. "A Pragmatist Approach to Causality in Ethnography." *American Journal of Sociology* 119(3): 682–714.

Taylor, Martin Brook. 1989. *Promoters, Patriots, and Partisans: Historiography in Nineteenth-century English Canada.* Toronto: University of Toronto Press.

Tei, Munetetsu. 2009. *Seiza to Nihonjin.* Tokyo: Kōdansha.

Therborn, Goran. 2011. "End of Paradigm: The Current Crisis and the Idea of Stateless Cities." *Environment and Planning A* 43: 272–285.

Tichar, Sian, and Nils Peters. 2004. *Style City: Berlin.* London: Thames & Hudson.

Tilley, Chris, Webb Keane, Susanne Küchler, Mike Rowlands, and Patricia Spyer (eds.). 2006. *Handbook of Material Culture.* London: Sage.

Tilly, Charles. 1975. *The Formation of National States in Western Europe*, Vol. 8. Princeton: Princeton University Press.

Tokio Narejji. 2013. *Otona no Manaa Joshiki.* Tokyo: Takarajimasha.

Tornatore, Jean-Louis. 2010. "L'esprit de patrimoine." *Terrain: Revue d'ethnologie de l'Europe* no. 55 (September): 106–127. doi:10.4000/terrain.14084

Trevelyan, George Macaulay. 1908. *Garibaldi's Defence of the Roman Republic.* London: Longmans, Green.

Trigger, Bruce. 2006. *A History of Archaeological Thought.* 2nd ed. Cambridge: Cambridge University Press.

Tuck, Andrew. 2013. "Boring Is Banished." *Monocle (Special Report on Germany)* 61(7): 32–33.

Turner, Victor. 1967. *The Forest of Symbols: Aspects of Ndembu Ritual.* Ithaca: Cornell University Press.

Turner-Graham, Emily. 2015. "Subcultural Style: Fashion and Britain's Extreme Right." In N. Copsey and J. E. Richardson (eds.), *Culture of Post-War British Fascism.* Abingdon: Routledge, 128–141.

Udy, Daniel. 2012. "Creative Stasis in a Post-industrial Utopia." In Hegenbart and Mündner, *Mythos Berlin,* 69–72.

United Nations Information Service. 2014. "232 Million International Migrants Living Abroad Worldwide—New UN Global Migration Statistics Reveal." 9 September. www.unis.unvienna.org/unis/en/pressrels/2013/unisinf488.html

Urry, John. 1990. *The Tourist Gaze: Leisure and Travel in Contemporary Societies*. Theory, Culture and Society. London: Sage.

van Wijngaarden, Gert Jan. 1999. "The Complex Past of Pottery: An Introduction." In J. P. Crielaard, V. Stissi, and G. J. van Wijngaarden (eds.), *The Complex Past of Pottery: Production, Circulation and Consumption of Mycenaean and Greek Pottery*. Proceedings of the ARCHON International Conference, Amsterdam, 8–9 November 1996. Amsterdam: J.C. Gieben, 1–19.

Ventsel, Aimar. 2014. "'That Old School Lonsdale': Authenticity and Clothes in German Skinhead Culture." In R. Cobb (ed.), *The Paradox of Authenticity in a Globalized World*. London: Palgrave, 261–276.

Verdery, Katherine. 1991. *National Ideology under Socialism: Identity and Cultural Politics in Ceausescu's Romania*. Berkeley: University of California Press.

Vergo, Paul. 1989. *The New Museology*. London: Reaktion Books.

Vincentelli, Moira. 2000. *Women and Ceramics: Gendered Vessels*. New York: Manchester University Press.

Visscher, Jochen. 2008. "Timeless Modernism or Modernism of the Times." In Jochen Visscher (ed.), *Berlin Modernism*. Berlin: Jovis.

Wagenfeld, Malte. 2011. "The Porous-City: Atmospheric Conversations of the Urban | Interior." In Hinkel, *Urban Interior*.

Wagner-Pacifici, Robin. 2005. *The Art of Surrender: Decomposing Sovereignty at Conflict's End*. Chicago: University of Chicago Press.

———. 2010. "The Cultural Sociological Experience of Cultural Objects." In John R. Hall, Laura Grindstaff, and Ming-Cheng Lo (eds.), *Handbook of Cultural Sociology*. London: Routledge, 110–118.

Wagner-Pacifici, Robin, and Barry Schwartz. 1991. "The Vietnam Veterans Memorial: Commemorating a Difficult Past." *American Journal of Sociology* 97(2): 376–420.

Waldinger, Roger David. 1986. *Through the Eye of the Needle: Immigrants and Enterprise in New York's Garment Trades*. New York: New York University Press.

———. 1993. "The Ethnic Enclave Debate Revisited." *International Journal of Urban and Regional Research* 17: 444–452.

Waligórska, Magdalena. 2008. "Fiddler as a Fig Leaf: The Politicization of Klezmer in Poland." In Manfred Sapper (ed.), *Impulses for Europe: Tradition and Modernity in East European Jewry*. Berlin: Osteuropa, 227–238.

———. 2013. *Klezmer's Afterlife: An Ethnography of the Jewish Music Revival in Poland and Germany*. New York: Oxford University Press.

Wallerstein, Immanuel Maurice. 1974. *The Modern World-system*. New York: Academic Press.

Walters, Henry Beauchamp. 1905. *History of Ancient Pottery: Greek, Etruscan, and Roman*, Vols. 1 and 2. London: John Murray.

Weber, Eugen. 1976. *Peasants into Frenchmen: The Modernization of Rural France, 1870–1914*. Stanford: Stanford University Press.

Weber, Max. 1968. *Economy and Society: An Outline of Interpretive Sociology*. New York: Bedminster Press.

Weber, Max, Guenther Roth, and Claus Wittich. 1978. *Economy and Society: An Outline of Interpretive Sociology*. Berkeley and Los Angeles: University of California Press.

Weiner, Mark. 1996. "Consumer Culture and Participatory Democracy: The Story of Coca-Cola During World War II." *Food and Foodways* 6: 109–129.

Welling, Dominic. 2011. "Berlin Airlift Veterans Opposed Tempelhof Plans." *Airport World Magazine*. www.airport-world.com/home/item/646-berlin-airlift-veterans-oppose-tempelhof-plans (accessed 28 June 2013).

Weszkalnys, Gisa. 2010. *Berlin, Alexanderplatz: Transforming Place in a Unified Germany*. New York: Berghahn Books.

Wherry, Frederick F. 2008. *Global Markets and Local Crafts: Thailand and Costa Rica Compared*. Baltimore: Johns Hopkins University Press.

Wilson, Kenneth L., and Alejandro Portes. 1980. "Immigrant Enclaves: An Analysis of the Labor Market Experiences of Cubans in Miami." *American Journal of Sociology* 86: 295–319.

Wimmer, Andreas. 2013. *Waves of War: Nationalism, State Formation, and Ethnic Exclusion in the Modern World*. Cambridge: Cambridge University Press.

Winthrop, John. 1838. "A Modell of Christian Charity (1630)." *Collections of the Massachusetts Historical Society* 3(7): 33–48.

Wittmann-Englert, Kerstin. 2008. "Modern Architecture in Berlin: An Introduction." In Jochen Visscher (ed.), *Berlin Modernism*. Berlin: Jovis.

Woodward, Ian. 2007. *Understanding Material Culture*. London: Sage.

Yatabe, Hidemasa. 2007. *Utsukushii Nihon no Shintai*. Tokyo: Chikuma Shinsho.

Yoshino, Kosaku. 1992. *Cultural Nationalism in Contemporary Japan: A Sociological Inquiry*. New York: Routledge.

Zannoni, Antonio. 1871. *Sugli scavi della certosa: Relazione letta all'inaugurazione del Museo Civico di Bologna*. Bologna: Regia tipografia.

Zelizer, Viviana A. 2010. *Economic Lives: How Culture Shapes the Economy*. Princeton: Princeton University Press.

Zhou, Min. 1992. *Chinatown: The Socioeconomic Potential of an Urban Enclave*. Philadelphia: Temple University Press.

———. 2004. "Revisiting Ethnic Entrepreneurship: Convergencies, Controversies, and Conceptual Advancements." *International Migration Review* 38: 1040–1074.

Zubrzycki, Geneviève. 2001. "'We, the Polish Nation': Ethnic and Civic Visions of Nationhood in Post-Communist Constitutional Debates." *Theory and Society* 30(5): 629–669.

———. 2006. *The Crosses of Auschwitz: Nationalism and Religion in Post-Communist Poland*. Chicago: University of Chicago Press.

———. 2010. "What Is Pluralism in a 'Monocultural' Society? Considerations from Post-Communist Poland." In Courtney Bender and Pamela Klassen (eds.), *After Pluralism: Re-imagining Models of Interreligious Engagement*. New York: Columbia University Press, 277–295.

———. 2011. "History and the National Sensorium: Making Sense of Polish Mythology." *Qualitative Sociology* 34(1): 21–57.

———. 2013a. "Aesthetic Revolt and the Remaking of National Identity in Québec, 1960–1969." *Theory and Society* 42(5): 423–475.

———. 2013b. "Narrative Shock and (Re)Making Polish Memory in the Twenty-first Century." In Florence Vatan and Marc Silberman (eds.), *Memory and Postwar Memorials: Confronting the Violence of the Past*. New York: Palgrave, 95–115.

———. 2016a. "Nationalism, 'Philosemitism' and Symbolic Boundary-making in Contemporary Poland." *Comparative Studies in Society and History* 58(1): 66–98.

———. 2016b. *Beheading the Saint: Nationalism, Religion, and Secularism in Quebec*. Chicago: University of Chicago Press.

Acknowledgments

This volume emerged out of the close collaboration between the authors. Our exchange began in a series of panels held at the American Sociological Association in 2014 and at the Social Science History Association in the same year. My thanks to all the participants and interlocutors at these meetings for their many incisive questions and comments. Many other friends and colleagues have substantially contributed along the way. My conversations with Kriszti Ferhérváry and Webb Keane at the University of Michigan, as well as with the members of the ASA's material culture research network, have been tremendously influential in my thinking about the role materiality plays in national identity and nationalism, and the importance for cultural sociology to fully embrace the material turn. The ideas presented in the introduction are the fruit of all of these conversations.

Special thanks to Jenny Gavacs for her support of this project since its inception, and to Kate Wahl at Stanford University Press for bringing it to fruition. Thanks also to Drew Foster, whose level-headed attention to detail kept me sane during the final preparations of the manuscript, and to Jeff Wyneken for his careful copyediting.

I'm especially grateful to Paul Christopher Johnson, who patiently read and commented on several versions of the introduction and of my own chapter, and to the two anonymous reviewers, whose critical comments guided our revisions, strengthening every individual contribution as well as the book's theoretical architecture.

Contributors

Melissa Aronczyk is Associate Professor in the School of Communication and Information at Rutgers University. Her research addresses critical issues in promotional culture, nationalism and national consciousness, and political and cultural interpretations of globalization. She is the author of *Branding the Nation: The Global Business of National Identity* (2013), and coeditor of *Blowing Up the Brand: Critical Perspectives on Promotional Culture* (2010).

Dominik Bartmański works at the Technical University of Berlin. He is interested in material culture, cultural icons, the sociology of music, and social theory. He is coeditor and contributor to *Iconic Power: Materiality and Meaning in Social Life* (2012), and coauthor of *Vinyl: The Analogue Record in the Digital Age* (2015). He is the recipient of the International Studies Association Junior Theorist Prize for his article "How to Become an Iconic Social Thinker: The Intellectual Pursuits of Malinowski and Foucault" published in the *European Journal of Social Theory* (2012).

Claudio E. Benzecry is Associate Professor of Communications Studies at Northwestern University. His current research examines the everyday work of producing globalization by following the imagination, production, and circulation of a shoe from design pattern to urban markets. He is the author of *The Opera Fanatic: Ethnography of an Obsession* (2011), which won the 2012 Mary Douglas Award from the Sociology of Culture Section of the American Sociological Association, which in 2014 received the Honorable Mention for the ASA Distinguished Scholarly Book Award.

Fiona Greenland is a postdoctoral fellow at the University of Chicago. With funding from the Social Science Research Council (USA), her current research examines the policing of national culture in Italy, and especially the links between statecraft and nationhood as consecrated through specific aesthetic modalities. Her article "The Parthenon Marbles as Icons of Nationalism in 19th Century Britain," which appeared in *Nations and Nationalism*, won the 2013 Jacquin-Berdal Best Paper Prize from the Association for the Study of Ethnicity and Nationalism at the London School of Economics. Her book, *Ruling Culture: Art Police, Tomb Robbers, and the Rise of Cultural Power in Italy*, is forthcoming with the University of Chicago Press.

Alexandra Kowalski is Assistant Professor of Sociology at the Central European University. Her research deals with the modern history of cultural institutions, especially "heritage." Her work has been published in *Comparative Studies in Society and History*, the *Sociological Review*, and *Social Anthropology*, and she is currently completing a book entitled *The Birth of Heritage: History and the Politics of Space in Postwar France*.

Peggy Levitt is Chair of Sociology and the Luella LaMer Slaner Professor in Latin American Studies at Wellesley College, and co-Director of Harvard University's Transnational Studies Initiative. Her books include *Artifacts and Allegiances: How Museums Put the Nation and the World on Display* (2015), *Religion on the Edge* (2012), *God Needs No Passport* (2007), *The Transnational Studies Reader* (2007), *The Changing Face of Home* (2002), and *The Transnational Villagers* (2001). In 2014, she received an Honorary Doctoral Degree from Maastricht University. A film based on her work, *Art Across Borders,* came out in 2009.

Virág Molnár is Associate Professor of Sociology at the New School for Social Research. Her research explores the intersections of culture, politics, social change, and expert knowledge with special focus on urban and political subcultures and the symbolic politics of the built environment. Her first book, *Building the State: Architecture, Politics and State Formation in Postwar Central Europe* (2013), received the 2014 Mary Douglas Prize for Best Book in the Sociology of Culture from the American Sociological Association.

Chandra Mukerji is Distinguished Professor Emeritus at the University of California, San Diego. Her scholarship analyzes how changes in the built environment are furthered by science, and how materiality shapes social life. Her groundbreaking work in *Territorial Ambitions and the Gardens of Versailles* (1997), and *Impossible Engineering: Technology* *and Territoriality on the Canal du Midi* (2009), has earned her multiple awards from the American Sociological Association.

Kristin Surak is an Associate Professor of Politics at SOAS, University of London. She specializes in nationalism, culture, ethnicity, and international migration. Her book *Making Tea, Making Japan: Cultural Nationalism in Practice* (2013) received the Outstanding Book Award from the American Sociological Association's Section on Asia and Asian America in 2014. She received awards and fellowships from the American Academy of Political and Social Science, Japan Foundation, Fulbright-Hays Foundation, and Leverhulme Foundation, among others.

Geneviève Zubrzycki is Associate Professor of Sociology and Director of the Weiser Center for Europe and Eurasia at the University of Michigan. Her work examines politics and religion, nationalism, as well as national mythology and the politics of commemorations. Her book *The Crosses of Auschwitz: Nationalism and Religion in Post-Communist Poland* (2006) received awards from the American Sociological Association and the Association for Slavic, East European and Eurasian Studies. She is also the author of *Beheading the Saint: Nationalism, Religion and Secularism in Quebec* (2016).

Index

The authorized representative in the EU for product safety and compliance is:
Mare Nostrum Group
B.V Doelen 72
4831 GR Breda
The Netherlands

www.ingramcontent.com/pod-product-compliance
Lightning Source LLC
Chambersburg PA
CBHW030343270326
41926CB00009B/938